CONVERSATIONS ON ETHICS

ABOUT THE AUTHOR

ALEX VOORHOEVE is Senior Lecturer in Philosophy at the London School of Economics. He writes on moral and political philosophy and on the theory of rational choice. His articles have been published in *Philosophy and Public Affairs*, *Economics and Philosophy*, and *The Journal of Political Philosophy*, among other places. You can read more about the author on http://personal.lse.ac.uk/voorhoev.

ABOUT THE PHOTOGRAPHER

Throughout his career, STEVE PYKE has developed, funded, and then published a number of personal projects. Best known are those on the world's leading thinkers—*Philosophers* (London: Zelda Cheatle Press, 1995)—and on youth identity as expressed through *Uniforms*. More recently he completed his series *Astronauts*. He has had eight books published. In 2004 he received the MBE in the Queen's New Years Honours list for his services to the Arts. In 2006 he was made a Friend of the Royal Photographic Society. Steve Pyke has been a staff photographer at *The New Yorker* since 2004 and a contributor since 1998. He lives in New York City. For more information, see http://www.pyke-eye.com

CONVERSATIONS ON ETHICS

ALEX VOORHOEVE

OXFORD
UNIVERSITY PRESS

OXFORD
UNIVERSITY PRESS

Great Clarendon Street, Oxford OX2 6DP

Oxford University Press is a department of the University of Oxford.
It furthers the University's objective of excellence in research, scholarship,
and education by publishing worldwide in

Oxford New York

Auckland Cape Town Dar es Salaam Hong Kong Karachi
Kuala Lumpur Madrid Melbourne Mexico City Nairobi
New Delhi Shanghai Taipei Toronto

With offices in

Argentina Austria Brazil Chile Czech Republic France Greece
Guatemala Hungary Italy Japan Poland Portugal Singapore
South Korea Switzerland Thailand Turkey Ukraine Vietnam

Oxford is a registered trade mark of Oxford University Press
in the UK and in certain other countries

Published in the United States
by Oxford University Press Inc., New York

British Library Cataloguing in Publication Data

Data available

Library of Congress Cataloging in Publication Data

Conversations on ethics / [compiled by] Alex Voorhoeve.
p. cm.
Includes bibliographical references and index.
ISBN 978 – 0 – 19 – 921537 – 9 (alk. paper)
I. Voorhoeve, Alex.
BJ1012.C663 2009
170 — dc22
2009023410

Typeset by Laserwords Private Limited, Chennai, India
Printed in Great Britain
on acid-free paper by
CPI Antony Rowe, Chippenham, Wiltshire

ISBN 978 – 0 – 19 – 921537 – 9

1 3 5 7 9 10 8 6 4 2

For my parents

ACKNOWLEDGEMENTS

Many people contributed to this book. My first debts of gratitude are to all those who agreed to be interviewed for it. Without exception, they approached these interviews as an opportunity to have a frank discussion of some of the strengths and weaknesses of their ideas in terms accessible to a non-specialist audience. Contributors were also generous with their time after the initial interviews, improving my drafts to be sure we got things right.

My second debt is to Steve Pyke for contributing his arresting, powerful portraits. I am also grateful to my encouraging and patient editor, Peter Momtchiloff; to Catherine Berry, Nir Eyal, Annabelle Lever, and Clara Perez-Adamson, who helped in the design of the cover; to Mark Fisher, who transcribed the interviews with Daniel Kahneman and Alasdair MacIntyre; to T. W. Bartel, Ben Ferguson, Judy Jaffe, and Jean McVeigh, who proofread the manuscript and saved me from many errors; and to Joe Mazor and Elaine Scarry, whose suggestions improved the Introduction. A Fellowship from the Safra Center for Ethics at Harvard in 2008/9 gave me time to finish the manuscript.

Several chapters are based on previously published material:

Chapter 1 is a revised version of 'In Search of the Deep Structure of Morality: Frances Kamm Interviewed', *Imprints* 9 (2006): 93–117.

Chapter 4 is a revised version of 'The Grammar of Goodness: An Interview with Philippa Foot', *Harvard Review of Philosophy* 11 (2003): 32–44.

Chapter 6 is a very substantially revised and expanded version of 'The Good, the Right, and the Seemly: Ken Binmore Interviewed', *Philosophers' Magazine* 21 (2002): 48–51.

Chapter 8 is a revised and expanded version of 'T. M. Scanlon: Kant on the Cheap', *Philosophers' Magazine* 16 (2001): 29–30.

Chapter 9 is a revised version of 'A Mistrustful Animal: Bernard Williams Interviewed', *Harvard Review of Philosophy* 12 (2004): 81–92.

Chapter 10 is a revised version of 'Harry Frankfurt on the Necessity of Love', *Philosophical Writings* 23 (2003): 55–70.

Many thanks to the original publishers for permission to make use of this material.

For many years, Luc Bovens and Michael Otsuka have been great mentors, wonderful colleagues, and loyal friends; both also offered incisive comments on the manuscript. Clara Perez-Adamson has been a support and an inspiration. This book is dedicated to my parents, for all our lively discussions of moral and political issues.

TABLE OF CONTENTS

INTRODUCTION

SOCRATES: You know, Phaedrus, writing shares a strange feature with painting. The offsprings of painting stand there as if they are alive, but if anyone asks them anything, they remain most solemnly silent. The same is true of written words . . . . [A]nd when [writing] is faulted or attacked unfairly, it always needs its father's support; alone, it can neither defend itself nor come to its own support.

PHAEDRUS: You are absolutely right about that, too.

SOCRATES: Now tell me, can we discern another kind of discourse, a legitimate brother of this one? Can we say how it comes about, and how it is by nature better and more capable? . . .

PHAEDRUS: You mean the living, breathing discourse of the man who knows, of which the written one can be fairly called an image?

SOCRATES: Absolutely right.

The *Phaedrus* recounts a discussion between Phaedrus and Socrates that takes place while they are relaxing in the shade of a plane tree by the banks of the Ilissus. Towards the end of the dialogue, Socrates raises the question of the best way to do philosophy. He argues that philosophical texts do not produce true understanding, because they do not fully engage with their audience. A text, he points out, cannot pick up on a reader's misinterpretations or emotional resistance to its message, and so cannot respond to them. Nor can it respond to requests for clarification, or defend its theses against unforeseen objections. Finally, a text makes for a passive audience because it doesn't prompt a reader to examine its arguments critically by, say, challenging their premises or showing that they have unwelcome implications. As a result, readers do not necessarily struggle with the arguments in a way required to master them. Socrates goes on to claim that, pursued in the right way, discussion is superior to writing in these respects. He concludes that those who wish to impart knowledge should eschew writing and take on the role of a dialectician, who 'chooses a proper soul and plants and sows within it discourse accompanied by knowledge — discourse . . . which is not barren, but produces a seed from which more discourse grows in the character of others'. 'Such discourse,' Socrates promises, 'makes the seed forever immortal and renders the man who has it happy as any human being can be.'

As a soul in which the knowledgeable women and men interviewed here have sown their discourse, I hope that Socrates is right. But I am doubtful — and not just because I have not yet become supremely happy. For Socrates neglects some of the obvious advantages that writing has over discourse: it allows for the expression of more complex, detailed arguments, gives us the chance to reflect without the pressure to respond quickly, and allows us better to articulate our thoughts — to find the right turn of phrase, the striking illustration, or the killer counterexample that often eludes us in discussion. Most importantly, we do not have the opportunity to spend a summer's day by the riverside talking with Socrates; books are the only access we have to most great minds.

Nonetheless, Socrates' arguments draw attention to the advantages that a dialogue between a philosopher and an interlocutor might have over other forms of writing. After all, if the question on the reader's lips is posed in the dialogue, then the text will not 'remain solemnly silent'. Moreover, the 'father' (or mother) is on hand to prevent his or her ideas being misunderstood and to defend them against objections. Finally, a dialogue allows the interlocutor to express common feelings of resistance to the ideas advanced, and gives their author a chance to overcome them. Of course, these objectives may also be achieved in an ordinary piece of writing, where an author can raise and answer questions and objections, and anticipate and attempt to allay fears. But, at their best, dialogues are lively and revealing precisely because the author of the ideas under discussion is deprived of control over these matters and is forced to respond to an independent questioner.

A dialogue will possess these advantages only if the interlocutor's concerns match those of the reader. It seems appropriate, therefore, to sketch briefly the three main puzzles that motivated me to engage in conversation with some of the leading thinkers on ethics. These puzzles will, I think, be familiar, since they arise in the course of reflection on our everyday experience of morality and figure in ethical discussions from Plato's dialogues onwards. Nonetheless, they have been articulated in different ways, and it may be useful to explain how I understand them.

The first puzzle concerns our 'everyday moral sense'—our capacity to arrive at moral judgements by making use of intuitive responses to particular cases along with some inchoate general rules. Its verdicts frequently carry strong conviction; moreover, they are often powerfully motivating. For instance, we are typically averse to performing an act we think is wrong, and transgressions arouse some of our harshest emotions—including indignation, resentment, and guilt—while righteous acts inspire emulation, admiration, and pride. Nonetheless, it can be difficult to articulate their rationale. Consider, for example, the case of the California transplant surgeon Dr Roozrokh, who, in 2008, was prosecuted (and acquitted) for attempting to hasten the death of a moribund patient in order to harvest his organs for transplant before they deteriorated. (The patient was registered as a post-mortem donor, but no consent had been given to interventions with the intended effect of hastening his death.) Many of us would judge such an action to be wrong, even if we were certain it could be done secretly and successfully. But, on reflection, this response is not easy to justify. After all, the benefit to those who needed the organs would be far greater than the loss suffered by the patient (who, in any case, did not have long to live); and it is not easy to see what, if anything, trumps that consideration in this case. Still, many of us will retain our initial conviction that killing the patient is wrong, despite realizing that we are not yet able to formulate a justification for this opinion. This phenomenon raises several questions. What are the hidden determinants of such everyday judgements? To what extent are they implicitly sensitive to morally significant considerations (and therefore trustworthy), and to what extent are they determined by irrelevant factors (and therefore unreliable)?

The second puzzle is this. Many of our moral judgements seem objective—we think that others would be in error if they did not share them. To defend the objectivity of our judgements, we must provide impersonal criteria for good moral judgement and for carrying out moral enquiry in the right way; we must also argue that those whose views are wrong have not met these criteria. But it seems that serious enquirers who have the characteristics of good moral judges (such as impartiality, empathy, and the ability to articulate moral principles and their implications) may arrive at different ethical conclusions, even after considering the same information and range of relevant positions, simply because they 'see' certain basic normative issues differently. Let us suppose that in the case of the moribund patient, we conclude after careful enquiry that hastening his death would be wrong because killing someone without his consent in order to use him as a means for others' ends is a particularly important wrong-making property of an action. Suppose further that others, after no less careful enquiry, believe that only the well-being of those involved is morally relevant, and therefore that it would be right to kill the patient. What are the implications of such disagreements?

Of course, no enquirer is perfect—reflection on a wider range of cases and views is always possible, and we may assume that such reflection would vindicate one or another of the views in question, or would show both to be mistaken. Nonetheless, we must decide how to respond to disagreements between good, though imperfect, enquirers. There appear to be three alternatives, each of which has its drawbacks. First, if we stand by our judgement that those who have arrived at an opposing view are, like us, good judges who have enquired well, it would seem that consistency requires us to accord their view some weight. After all, who are *we* to claim special insight? Such disagreement, then, would require us to be more amenable to our opponents' view than we were prior to learning that they disagreed with us. But this is difficult to accept—could we really be rationally compelled to move towards accepting views we find abhorrent simply because these views are endorsed by people who appear to be good judges? To avoid this consequence, we might revise our standards for a good judge so that those people who are insensitive to the considerations we find compelling are excluded. (This is our second option.) But this seems like cheating—it is all too easy to dismiss others simply because they disagree with us. And so we come to the third option: we can give up our belief in the objectivity of judgements in such cases and accept that, in reality, there is nothing here to be mistaken about. In sum, this kind of disagreement presses upon us the following questions: Are these three options the only ways to respond to this kind of disagreement? If so, which one should we choose?

The third puzzle arises from the fact that morality appears to give us reasons of great importance—for example, that an act is morally wrong seems to be a reason for not doing it that typically trumps competing considerations; and that an act is morally admirable seems to be reason enough to perform it. But it is unclear what these reasons are. This lacuna in our knowledge is critical, because we may be called upon to sacrifice our happiness, our projects, or the interests of our loved ones for morality's sake. Before we do so, we should know it is 'worth it'—that some important interest of ours or some important value is at stake. Consider, for example, the following twist on our case: imagine that your daughter will die unless she receives one of the donor's organs, and you are in a position to kill him secretly by entering his room (where he is unconscious and alone) and increasing his dose of sedatives. Let us suppose you feel, correctly, that it would be morally wrong to do so. What reasons do you have to listen to the voice of your conscience? And do they outweigh the reason you have to save your child's life?

This book aims to provide insight into contrasting answers to these three puzzles—about the reliability of our everyday moral judgements, the objectivity of ethics, and the reasons we have to be moral—by asking eleven eminent thinkers to explain and defend their views on these and related topics. The choice of the interviewees was based on personal criteria: I invited experts whose opinions I found perceptive and provocative, and whose views contrasted with the views of other interviewees in an interesting way. Although most are professional philosophers, some have done their principal work in the sciences, insights from which, it seems to me, are relevant to answering these questions. To take just one example: the psychology of intuitive judgement can help us understand what we are responding to when we make visceral moral judgements, and so can play an important part in deciding whether these judgements are reliable.

Almost every thinker interviewed has something to say on each of the three main puzzles. The book is therefore organized not into parts that address each question separately, but into parts that bring together interviews that are most directly relevant to each other. In Part I, 'Ethics and Intuitions', I interview two philosophers and a psychologist, all with strongly contrasting attitudes towards our intuitive moral judgements. Frances Kamm takes our everyday moral sense seriously and tries to uncover the principles and values that underlie and justify these judgements. Peter Singer, by contrast, argues that these judgements are typically determined by unreliable factors, including simple rules of thumb, ways of thinking formed by religious outlooks that we no longer regard as authoritative, and prejudice. He argues for strongly revisionary ethical views, which he grounds in certain basic values. The third discussion is with Daniel Kahneman, a Nobel Prize winner for his work on the determinants of intuitive judgements. Kahneman outlines ways in which our intuitive moral judgements may be unreliable, and discusses the extent to which they are revisable on reflection. While some of our apparently erroneous intuitions are malleable, he argues, others seem immune to reflection. He concludes that our inability to shake off some unfounded judgements and the accompanying, powerfully motivating moral emotions condemns us, to a certain extent, to be driven by emotions we do not endorse.

Part II, 'Virtue and Flourishing', consists of conversations with two philosophers who approach moral questions from the perspective of virtue ethics. Philippa Foot points to a particular kind of evaluation of living things, which involves assessing them as defective or sound members of their species. (For example, a deer should be swift, and if it is not, it is defective.) The attribution of virtues and vices, Foot argues, is just one instance of this kind of evaluation, involving cases in which a human's will is either defective or as it should be. For example, humans have need of the virtue of temperance, and if they lack it, this is a defect, just as not being fleet is a defect in a deer. She concludes that norms for attributing virtues and vices are objective, because they are norms for good functioning *qua* member of our species.

Alasdair MacIntyre is well known for his excoriating criticism of contemporary moral discourse, which, he has claimed, traps us in rationally interminable disputes. He has also argued, however, that a reformulated version of Aristotle's idea of a human *telos*, or aim in life, can provide a standpoint from which we *can* rationally evaluate moral judgements. Our conversation focuses on his ideas about the ends of human life and the account of the virtues that he derives from them.

Part III, 'Ethics and Evolution', discusses the origin and current function of some of our moral sentiments and convictions. Ken Binmore, a leading contributor to the evolutionary theory of strategic interaction, outlines the ways in which our sense of fairness helps us coordinate with others in mutually advantageous ways by suggesting how to divide the benefits of coordinated action. He also argues that generally this is *all* that our sense of fairness can motivate us to do; with limited exceptions, it moves us to act only in ways that are in our interests. (For example, under normal circumstances, it won't prompt us to direct aid or resources towards someone in need when it is not in our interest to do so.) Fairness, he concludes, should be stripped of its veneer of nobility.

Allan Gibbard agrees that morality has its origin in our need to coordinate our behaviour advantageously with others, but draws less revisionary conclusions from this fact. He argues that this understanding of the origins and current function of morality vindicates two elements of our moral life: our search for agreement in ethics, and the punitive moral emotions of indignation, resentment, and guilt. We must engage in normative discussion with others, he explains, because such discussion is essential for settling on the terms of social life. And once we enter into such discussion, consistency in according authority to ourselves and others as normative judges moves us towards accepting shared norms. Gibbard also argues that moral anger and guilt are relatively cost-effective ways of policing these norms, so that we have reason to be glad that we experience these emotions.

Part IV, 'Unity and Dissent', contrasts T. M. Scanlon's attempt to give a unified account of morality with Bernard Williams's suspicion of such accounts. Scanlon argues that the morality of 'what we owe to each other' encompasses those principles to which everyone would agree if they were motivated to find practical principles that others, similarly motivated, could not reasonably reject. To act rightly, on this view, is to act in ways that people could not reasonably reject; to act wrongly is to act in ways they could so reject. Scanlon argues that this conception of morality reveals to us a reason to be moral: acting rightly places us in an attractive relationship to others — we can justify our actions to them — while acting wrongly ruptures the relationship. This relationship, he claims, is attractive to humans in all times and places. Moreover, he argues, it is a precondition for many other valuable relationships, such as friendship and love. As a consequence, it rightly has special importance in our lives.

Williams explains why he is sceptical of Scanlon's and other attempts to offer a systematic account of morality and a single motive for accepting its verdicts. He also comments on the historical and genealogical methods of enquiry that he thinks can help us, as he puts it, 'make *some* sense of the ethical' even though we cannot have an idealized, unified version of it.

The final part, 'Love and Morality', addresses the relationship between moral reasons and the reasons of love. Harry Frankfurt argues that the answer to the question 'How should one live?' should not be sought in moral requirements. Rather, he believes, it must be sought in the structure of our will, by uncovering the desires we have and want most fervently to maintain and act on. (The desire to be moral, he adds, may not figure prominently among them.) Among the things we are so committed to desiring and pursuing, Frankfurt singles out the things we love. We love something, Frankfurt says, when we *cannot help* wanting to desire and pursue it. (Our children's well-being is typically such a thing.) When we realize that we love something, Frankfurt argues, we realize that we have found something we are unshakeably committed to wanting. When we know what we love, he concludes, we know how we want to live.

David Velleman argues that this is a misguided view of love. Rather than seeing love as a particular structure of unwavering desires, he regards it as an arresting awareness of an individual's value *qua* person that disarms our emotional defences. Stripped of these tendencies to close ourselves off from her, we become vulnerable to emotions like sympathy and disappointment. Nevertheless, we need not have any desire to be or do anything for the object of our love; we may, in Velleman's words, 'care *about* this person without caring *for* her or wanting to take care *of* her'.

Velleman also draws attention to the ways in which love and moral sentiments are kindred attitudes. For according to his view, both love and morality are a response to the value of each person, *qua* person, taken separately. He concludes that our love of some people does not threaten our attachment to morality. Instead, he argues, love provides us with a moral education by making us vividly aware of the value of each person.

At the beginning, I mentioned my doubts about Socrates' claim that the knowledge gained through philosophical discourse will make us 'happy as any human being can be'. It is an interesting question, though, what we can reasonably hope to gain from discourse on ethics. In the first place, I think we can expect to correct some of the errors to which we are prone. Many of the convictions that have been central, over the centuries, to people's common-sense morality seem clearly wrong, including the justifiability of slavery; the inferiority of foreigners, of people of different races, of women, of atheists, and of people of other religions; the wrongness of homosexuality; and the legitimacy of wars of conquest. It would therefore be naive to suppose that our common-sense morality is not mistaken on some counts. Where our everyday moral judgements *are* correct, however, we may hope to find a deeper justification for these judgements, so that we can act on them with greater confidence.

We also have reason to hope that our moral sentiments will match the judgements we endorse on reflection. This is not something we can take for granted: experience teaches that there are acts we believe are wrong but that we do not shrink from performing; it also shows that we may continue to have aversive responses to certain acts long after we have concluded that these responses are unwarranted. Insofar as our sentiments are at odds with our considered judgements, we are alienated from these sentiments; in serious cases, this threatens our sense of self-control. The better the fit between our judgements and emotional responses, the more we will be at one with and in control of ourselves.

With regard to the objectivity of ethics, I hope we can conclude that it makes sense to engage in joint enquiry into ethics, even with people who have strikingly different views. We must settle on some rules for living together; and it is a more attractive prospect to be able to reason with others about what these rules should be than to relate to them only as people whom we can pressure, cajole, or seduce into adopting our way of seeing things.

Finally, I think we have reason to hope that our enquiries will vindicate our sense of morality's importance. Of course, morality can feel unduly constraining — sometimes we want to be unhampered by moral scruples and free from the sting of guilt that accompanies our transgressions. Nonetheless, I do not believe it would be liberating to conclude that we have no important reason to be moral. Rather, I imagine it would be a profoundly disorienting experience, and difficult to recognize ourselves in the people who would emerge from it. More positively, the discovery of a rationale for being moral would eliminate some of our misgivings about acting on moral motives when doing so comes at a cost. When we act on these motives after reflectively endorsing them, we may act more wholeheartedly, and with greater conviction, than before.

My experience in writing this book has left me optimistic about the prospect of finding at least partial solutions to some of our ethical puzzles. Some of the answers proposed here strike me as true, at least in part; all of them yield unexpected insights. I remain uncertain, however, whether my hopes for ethical enquiry will be realized. Still, for those of us gripped by ethical questions, it matters little whether the answers will prove heartening; we must simply follow the arguments where they lead.

References

The quotations from Plato's *Phaedrus* are from the translation by Alexander Nehamas and Paul Woodruff (Indianapolis: Hackett, 1995), 275d–276a and 276e–277a. The case of Dr Roozrokh is reported in Jesse McKinley, 'Surgeon Accused of Speeding a Death to Get Organs', *New York Times*, 27 February 2008.

I

ETHICS AND INTUITIONS

1
FRANCES KAMM

IN SEARCH OF THE DEEP STRUCTURE
OF MORALITY

In *The Gay Science*, Friedrich Nietzsche argued that only a form of philosophizing that sprung from a deep commitment to the subject could ever hope for success. 'All great problems,' he wrote, 'demand *great love*.' He continued:

> It makes the most telling difference whether a thinker has a personal relationship to his problems and finds in them his destiny, his distress, and his greatest happiness, or an 'impersonal' one, meaning he is only able to touch them with the antennae of cold, curious thought. In the latter case nothing will come of it, that much can be promised; for even if great problems should let themselves be *grasped* by them, they would not allow frogs and weaklings to *hold on* to them.

Nietzsche went on to complain that, to his knowledge, no one had yet approached moral philosophy in this way:

> Why, then, have I never yet encountered anyone, not even in books, who approached morality in this personal way and who knew morality as a problem, and this problem as his own personal distress, torment, voluptuousness, and passion?

No one familiar with Frances Kamm's work in moral philosophy could share Nietzsche's complaint. In her two-volume book *Morality, Mortality* and in her other work in moral theory and applied ethics, Kamm meticulously and imaginatively analyses moral cases in order to gain insight into our fundamental moral concepts and principles. The tenacity with which she pursues this aim springs from her personal engagement with the issues she investigates — an engagement reflected in her dedication of the second volume of *Morality, Mortality* to 'the love of morality'.

At the centre of Kamm's work lies her development and defence of a nonconsequentialist ethical theory. Consequentialism holds that the rightness or wrongness of our conduct is determined solely by the expected goodness or badness of the consequences of our acts or of the rules to which these acts conform. According to consequentialism, to act rightly is to act in ways that bring about the best possible expected consequences. To act wrongly is to fail to act in such ways.

Nonconsequentialists deny this. In support of this denial, many nonconsequentialists argue that our intuitive judgements of moral cases are inconsistent with consequentialism. The 'Bridge Case' is a standard example. Imagine that you are standing beside a large stranger on a bridge over a trolley track. You see a runaway, driverless trolley heading down the track towards five trapped individuals, whom it would certainly kill upon impact. Before it reaches the five, it must pass under the bridge you are standing on. You realize that you will save the five if and only if you push the large stranger off the bridge and onto the tracks, where the trolley would hit him, kill him, and grind to a halt before it reaches the five. According to consequentialism, since pushing the stranger into the path of the trolley would ensure the fewest number of deaths, you should push him. Many, however, judge intuitively that it would be impermissible to do so. Of course, intuitive judgements of this kind stand in need of justification. Those who pursue this line of criticism of consequentialism must, therefore, find principles that explain these nonconsequentialist case judgements; they must also show that these principles reflect important moral values.

These are difficult tasks. Consider, for example, the following attempt at formulating a principle that explains why it is impermissible to push the large man: killing someone is worse than letting him die, and indeed so much worse that it is impermissible to kill one person (who would otherwise be all right) in the course of saving five others from death. The 'Side-track Case' shows, however, that this principle is problematic. Imagine you see a runaway trolley heading down a main track where it will hit and kill five people. You can divert the trolley onto a dead-end side-track, where it will instead hit and kill a different person. In this case, most people judge it permissible to divert the trolley onto the side-track, even though, like the Bridge Case, it involves killing one and saving five. We therefore need to appeal to something other than the distinction between killing and letting die to explain the contrasting judgements in the Bridge and Side-track cases.

Frances Kamm, professor of philosophy at Harvard University, has been at the forefront of the attempts to formulate principles that explain and justify our judgements in these and myriad other moral cases. We met in London in January 2003 to discuss her case-based method, her conclusions about the morality of harming people and saving people from harm, and the view of the moral status of human beings that she believes grounds these conclusions.

℘

ALEX VOORHOEVE: *What first drew you to philosophy?*

FRANCES KAMM: I went to a high school for music and art. People there were interested in existentialism, Sartre in particular, so I started reading some philosophy of the Continental variety. I found that I liked thinking about these issues. Then, at Barnard College (the women's college of Columbia University) I took an introductory philosophy course with Robert Wolff. Of course, it had nothing to do with Continental philosophy — it was on Descartes' *Meditations*. What was wonderful about it was that you could read just a page or two and think about it for weeks. I was interested in history and in literature too — I took a wonderful course devoted to Tolstoy and

Dostoevsky. But it involved so much reading! 'Read *The Brothers Karamazov* in three days,' they told us. The trouble was that I wanted to read just a few pages and think about it.

I wanted to go to medical school, but these ambitions were dashed because, although I enjoyed the theory, I was a complete disaster in the lab. They would bring people over to watch me do experiments so they could have a laugh. So I wasn't going to be a lab person. I considered becoming a psychiatrist, but during a summer internship in psychiatric social work I realized that I simply didn't have enough patience with the patients. So I decided on philosophy.

I went to graduate school at MIT because I thought I would do philosophy of psychology, and its graduate programme connected philosophy, psychology, and linguistics. But when I got there, I didn't feel strongly motivated in that area. Then I took an ethics course with Bob Nozick at Harvard—and that's what did it, because I found what he was doing *really* interesting. You know, about one-and-a-half years before he died, Nozick gave a talk in my ethics colloquium at NYU, where I was teaching at the time. And when I introduced him, I said that for the last twenty years I had been finishing the term paper for his class. Most of the topics I have worked on were there: the distinction between harming and not aiding, the distinction between intentionally harming someone and harming them as a foreseen but unintended side-effect of one's actions, the question of abortion, and others.

ALEX VOORHOEVE: *What in that class captured your imagination?*

FRANCES KAMM: First of all, I should say that we were all captured by Judith Thomson's imagination. She was a professor at MIT, but at that time she wasn't teaching what she was writing on, which was on the topics in moral theory we discussed in Nozick's class. In her class, we spent about half a semester on three or four pages of G. E. Moore's *Principia Ethica*. I was going out of my mind! At the time, this was not for me. Still, it was an eye-opening experience to see the level of care, detail, and rigour with which she approached Moore's writing. I wasn't used to that. Nozick, however, *was* dealing with topics that interested me, and his classes introduced me to this case-based method of moral analysis. So what captured my imagination was the combination of my discovery of these new standards of rigour, of imaginativeness, and the use of cases or thought-experiments in ethics. I seemed to be able to do this, and after finding that I wasn't capable of doing other things, I thought, 'Well, I might not be a Renaissance woman, but I have one little ability, I enjoy doing it, and it seems to be something that the world would like to see done. So why don't I do this?'

ALEX VOORHOEVE: *'It seems to be something the world would like to see done'—what did you mean by that?*

FRANCES KAMM: I meant I thought I could get a Ph.D. by doing it! You must realize that I wasn't the person voted most likely to succeed in philosophy by a long shot. I was hopeless for a while. It took me a long time to find my way. I went back to New York, hung around Columbia.... My supervisor, Barbara Herman, was very patient; she saved my life.

I do think, though, that moral philosophy is very important, even when it doesn't relate to public policy issues, though that is probably what the world is interested in. I think that, nowadays, people realize that philosophy is not just the explication of erudite texts or incomprehensible discourses, but that it emphasizes rigour and clarity—well, at least Anglo-American philosophy does. So people come to philosophy for practical guidance, certainly in bioethics. We now even have philosophers on medical wards, wearing beepers, who get asked by doctors, 'Come advise me whether I should pull the plug on this person's ventilator.' I have never done that. I tried teaching at the medical school at NYU, but they were more interested in answers to specific real-life cases and I was more interested in theoretical issues that related to questions of practical import.

ALEX VOORHOEVE: *Why do philosophers have authority in these matters?*

FRANCES KAMM: Well, philosophers are different from religious thinkers in that they obviously are not referring to sacred texts; nor are they claiming that they have answers that have been revealed to them by a higher power. I mean, they are simply trying to provide universally accessible reasons for certain judgements. (Of course, there are individuals within religious traditions that do the same. Aquinas, for example, says that natural reason can give us answers to many things.) I think that philosophers very often do it better than others. When I look at arguments on war, abortion, or stem-cell cloning that are put out by people who have some interest in ethics, but who are not philosophers, but rather, say, literature professors, or even scholars who are well-known in the Catholic or Jewish traditions for doing this kind of work, I find that people who are trained in philosophy generally present better papers and are much better able to judge the validity of positions other than their own. I think people with analytic training simply have better argumentative skills.

ALEX VOORHOEVE: *Is part of what sets philosophers apart a willingness to explore a very wide range of possible judgements, to imagine and consider cases or arguments that others might find too wacky to consider?*

FRANCES KAMM: It is interesting that I would agree with that, since Peter Unger, who was a colleague of mine when I taught at NYU, calls me a 'preservationist' in philosophy because I very rarely reach conclusions that differ radically from our everyday morality. Consequentialists are the ones who are prepared to accept anything if it will maximize good consequences, no matter how much it is at odds with our everyday moral thinking—like chopping up one healthy person to get organs to save five people who are in need of a life-saving transplant. My approach is generally to stick with our common moral judgements, which I share and take seriously.

I also think that some of the consequentialist philosophers who argue that we have very demanding duties to aid and that not aiding is morally equivalent to harming, but who don't live up to these demands, do not really believe their own arguments. You can't seriously believe that you have a duty to give almost all your money away to help others who would die without your aid and that refusing to do so is just as bad as killing them, and then, when we ask why you don't live up to that, say, 'Well, I'm weak.' Because if you found yourself killing someone on the street to save $1000, you wouldn't just say, 'Well, I'm weak!' You would realize that you had done something terribly wrong. You would go to great lengths to avoid becoming a person who would do that. Now *that* is a sign that you believe you have a moral obligation not to kill someone. But when somebody says, 'My theory implies that you should be giving $1000 to save someone's life and that failing to do so is just as bad as killing someone' and he also says, 'I don't give the $1000 because I'm weak!,' then I can't believe he really thinks he has that obligation to aid and that his not aiding is equivalent to killing. Imagine him saying, 'I just killed someone for $1000 because I'm weak.' Give me a break! This is ridiculous. Either there is something wrong with that theory, or there is something wrong with its proponents.

But I admit that when you put together some intuitive judgements, sometimes you get surprising conclusions. For example, it may be that many people are opposed to euthanasia or physician-assisted suicide and assume that only philosophers would regard it as permissible. But in my article 'A Right to Choose Death?' I take ideas that people would ordinarily accept and show that they have surprising implications.[1]

So sometimes you can shock yourself. Sometimes you are amazed, you know. You think, 'Look at that!' Even *I* come up with unusual conclusions, starting off in perfectly ordinary places, just by trying

---

[1] The article argues that when a patient wants to die and when his death is a lesser evil and the relief of his pain a greater good, it is sometimes permissible to intend the patient's death for the sake of relieving his pain.

to think carefully. In a way, it is like what an artist does, creating something surprising from ordinary colours and shapes.

ALEX VOORHOEVE: *Is there an analogy between what an art critic does when discussing an image and what an ethicist does when discussing a moral case? Faced with an observer who does not find a masterpiece beautiful, an art critic might direct the observer's attention to aspects of the image in order to explain to him why it is beautiful; she might do the same for an observer who finds the painting beautiful while being incapable of articulating his reasons for this judgement. Analogously, in a moral case about which the observer's initial judgement may be uncertain, or about which he may have a strongly held intuitive judgement that he is unable to support with reasons, an ethicist's role may be to draw attention to various aspects of the case that provide reasons for coming to a moral judgement about it.*

FRANCES KAMM: Yes. This may be just an autobiographical fact, but I don't really have a considered judgement about a case until I have a visual experience of it. I have to deeply imagine myself in a certain situation, with an open mind. It is almost as if you are looking at something with no preconceptions. You have to attend to it, and then things will pop out at you. First you may get the intuitive judgement of what you really should do in the circumstance you are imagining. Then you wonder, 'Why am I reaching this conclusion?' And your inner eye focuses on one factor as driving this judgement. I suppose that it is the same sort of thing when you look at a painting. Make sure you are attending to it and aren't having stray thoughts. You start to focus on what is so fascinating about it. And it can take a while. You can develop a whole theory about what is causing you to have an aesthetic judgement, and the same can be said about judgements in moral cases.

ALEX VOORHOEVE: *The idea that we just 'see' or 'intuit' the right response to a moral case suggests that such judgements are simply personal emotional responses or that we use a mysterious faculty in order to make them. You distance yourself from this interpretation of our case judgements. Why do you do so and what alternative view do you have of them?*

FRANCES KAMM: The term 'intuition' has a long history, and when you use it people tend to think that you are talking about immediate access to atomic entities of some sort. I am not talking about intuitive judgements about the atomic structure of some substance—I am just talking about a judgement about a case. These judgements may be wrong, and we need to be able to give reasons for them, reasons which are not simply our emotional responses. What I am saying is that, in order to have a judgement about a case, you really have to situate yourself in the case. For example, imagine a case in which a runaway trolley will kill five people if a bystander does not divert it onto another track where she foresees that it will kill one different person. You have to imagine this case in detail. For example, you have to ask yourself, 'Which way is the side-track going? Is there a loop in the side-track, so that if you diverted the trolley away from the five, it would rush around and run into the five from the other side were it not that the trolley will hit the one person (thereby killing him) and grind to a halt?' You have to sink into these details, not just say immediately, 'Oh, it is one versus five, so of course you have to sacrifice the one', or, 'Oh, the track is going around, so . . .' Just *situate* yourself in the case.

I think this is what Judith Thomson is trying to get us to do in her famous discussion of the case where there is a loop in the track. In this Loop Case, some would immediately draw on a general principle like, 'Don't treat someone as a mere means!'[2] People who would

---

[2]   This principle is attractive because it is consistent with the common judgements in the cases mentioned above. In the Bridge Case, it would prohibit pushing the man in front of the trolley because this would involve using him harmfully as a means to the greater good. By contrast, in the Side-track Case, the killing of the one, though a foreseen (and unintended) consequence of diverting the trolley away from the five, would not be a means to saving them. The principle would, therefore, not rule out switching the trolley onto the side-track in this case.

immediately invoke this principle would say, 'In the Loop Case, the hitting of the one is causally necessary to save the five, so if we turned the trolley onto the one, we would be using him as a mere means to the greater good. So it is impermissible.' But I take Judith Thomson to be saying: 'Forget about the principle! What do you think when you really have in place all the facts?' And, surprisingly, people often say, 'Well, I *do* think it is impermissible to use people as mere means, but I also think it is all right to turn the trolley in this case.' You can be very surprised about your own responses to a case like this one.

ALEX VOORHOEVE: *But the principle that one should not treat someone as a mere means for other people's ends is an important one that appears to capture an idea of moral significance, since it prohibits involuntary harmful exploitation. Why should we abandon it merely because of our — possibly tentative — response to an imaginary Loop Case of which we have had no experience?*

FRANCES KAMM: Well, the Loop Case may show not that you should abandon the principle, but rather that turning the trolley away from the five in this case does not actually violate it. Instead, the Loop Case may indicate that there is a moral difference between acting to turn the trolley away from the five *only because* you will hit someone and treating someone as a mere means. In the Loop Case, you are turning the trolley away from the five for some goal (final or intermediate) other than hitting the one, since your intermediate goal is to stop the threat the five are facing now — being hit from the front. This is not true in the Bridge Case, where your intermediate goal is to push the man onto the tracks.[3]

---

[3] Of course, in the Loop Case, once you turn the trolley away from the five, thereby eliminating the first threat to the five, they face another threat — being hit after the trolley loops around — which is averted only by the presence of the one on the side-track. And you turn the trolley away from the five only because you know that this second threat will be nullified by the trolley ploughing into and killing the one. Nonetheless, your initial aim does not involve the death of the one, and this might make a moral difference, Kamm believes.

So, I think we don't really understand what believing in a principle amounts to until we consider various cases to which it might apply. But I also think that our responses to other cases may undermine the validity of the mere-means principle. In the first volume of *Morality, Mortality*, I consider a case in which we have to choose between saving either a doctor's or a janitor's life with an organ transplant. Assume that the doctor could do a great deal more good than the janitor: he would, let's imagine, go on to save another five people. In this case, I actually thought, 'Well, no, we shouldn't give the doctor priority, even if he will go on to save five lives.' This appears to support the principle 'Don't treat people only as a means!' But then I thought about a case where I have several organs to distribute. One of these organs can help either person A or person B, both of whom are on my side of a river that I am too weak to cross. The rest of these organs can help five people on the other side of the river. Suppose that if I give the first transplant organ to person B, then she will be strong enough to cross the river; suppose also that A does not have this ability. Now, in this case, I thought, 'Ah, now that's interesting. I think it *is* permissible to give a transplant organ to B in this case even though I think it is *not* permissible to give it to the doctor rather than to the janitor — if A's ability is *connected to* distributing the resource I have, then it *is* okay. An instrumental difference between A and B is then a permissible ground for distribution. By contrast, the doctor is useful to people who need *him*, but not useful to the people who need what *I* have to distribute.' Right away, this showed me that it wasn't just the purely instrumental use of people that was the issue.

The lesson I draw from such cases is that these variations save you from overgeneralization, from an immediate attachment to a moral principle. There is so much variation, there are so many delicate distinctions to be drawn, that I don't think these very general principles we immediately jump to can possibly be correct.

ALEX VOORHOEVE: *I don't understand what these cases have to do with the injunction not to use people merely as a means. For when we give B priority, we do not treat her merely as a means — we are also counting the* *fact that the transplant would save B's life as a reason for giving her the transplant. Moreover, B would presumably consent to being 'used' in this way. So the preference for saving B would not violate the injunction. The same would apply to the doctor, should we decide to give him priority over the janitor.*

FRANCES KAMM: You have to consider it from the perspective of the person who is being *denied* the transplant because he is *not* useful. Take A: he is being treated as a mere means because we consider whether he could serve our goal and then refuse him the transplant because he will not. So I think the judgement that we should give the transplant to B violates the injunction. But it is true that, in saying this, I am relying on my sense that one can treat someone as a mere means even when he is not being made into something causally useful.

ALEX VOORHOEVE: *What do you think about the following explanation for your judgements about these cases that, if correct, would undermine their purported authority? In actual cases our limited knowledge and limited ability to think through all the consequences of our acts, together with the advantages of specialization, lead to a moral division of labour and a concomitant division of responsibility. This division of responsibility is, roughly, one in which you are required to think only about your resource, about how you could put it to best use. So when what someone could go on to do with his life is relevant to the use of your resource, you take that into account. But you don't think in general about everything that the people who you are helping will do with their lives. The moral intuitions you have in these cases are a product of being educated into practices that embody this division of responsibility. But since the grounds for this division of responsibility are absent in your imaginary cases (where we know and can take into account everything that people will do with their lives) these moral intuitions may not be trustworthy.*

FRANCES KAMM: Your explanation seems to be this: 'Well, ordinarily, we don't know what doctors will do with the life we give them, so we just tend to ignore this question — we'll make it an irrelevant good. Whereas here we *do* know.' But I don't think this explanation is sensitive enough to what is going on. In this case, I *can* suppose that I know that the doctor is going straight from his treatment to his surgery to treat five people only he can save. When I imagine this, I still see a difference between these cases. But then you might say: 'You have these ingrained tendencies from ordinary life; you are reasoning in a habitual mode. I know you think you've convinced yourself that the doctor is going to do this, but your habitual mode of thinking is: "Who knows what's going to happen? I am going to block out what the doctor is going to do."' I simply don't believe our capacity to reason about cases is so limited by habitual responses.

Nonetheless, I must admit that I was worried when my colleague Marc Hauser, a psychologist, reported to me in a research seminar that the moral distinctions people make in the various trolley cases are respected cross-culturally, in the sense that people from different cultures would turn the trolley onto the one to save the five in the Side-track Case, but would not throw an innocent bystander in front of the trolley to save the five in the Bridge Case. I was also worried when a famous developmental psychologist told me that children had the same response. Because even though I have taken the view that many intuitive judgements reflect some deep structure not completely accessible to the person who has it and that this structure may be universal, I thought: 'That's terrible! I am just reporting some ingrained response! If even babies share this view . . .'

ALEX VOORHOEVE: Babies?

FRANCES KAMM: Well, you know, young children.

ALEX VOORHOEVE: *Why does that worry you?*

FRANCES KAMM: It doesn't *really* worry me. I just meant that it doesn't necessarily help us with the principles we are trying to explain and justify. That a lot of people agree doesn't show that something is correct. It doesn't help to support the normative authority of the judgement. Now, Marc Hauser himself recognizes that. But there was a colleague of his at the research seminar who said upon hearing the empirical data, 'Well, that's great. What more do you need?' Now, what worries me about that view is, of course, that *everyone could be wrong*. For example, the research by Daniel Kahneman and Amos Tversky on the psychology of decision-making under risk reveals that everyone makes certain mistakes when making decisions based on the probabilities of things happening. That everyone in fact decides as though they have a certain theory of probability ingrained in them doesn't mean that the theory they are using is correct!

In addition, I was worried that if even very young children have these responses, then what is at work here is some remnant of the primitive part of the organism rather than a rational capacity — although I suppose someone might dismiss my worries, saying, 'That's a good thing! Maybe morality is more widespread than we thought. Even *reptiles* would have this morality; they would flick their tails to turn the trolley onto one lizard rather than five, but they wouldn't push another lizard in front of the trolley.'

ALEX VOORHOEVE: *I don't see why you should be worried simply because a particular response is ingrained. For example, vampire bats tend to rest next to the same neighbours day after day, and a bat who returns from his hunt to the bats' resting place well-fed will often regurgitate blood into a hungry neighbour's mouth. This pattern of interaction is repeated over time, and a bat who has fed his neighbour will, on other occasions, be fed by his neighbour in return. If a bat's future access to such feeding is dependent on him feeding his neighbour when the occasion calls for it, then a disposition to engage in this kind of reciprocal altruism can be favoured by evolutionary pressures. Suppose that we have a similarly deep-rooted disposition to engage in acts of reciprocal altruism. That would not show that this tendency would be something that we would disapprove of on reflection.*

FRANCES KAMM: I guess you could give an explanation of this ingrained tendency that is consistent with morality being something that you would have reason to follow. But we want to know if morality is something that rational beings could choose to develop; we don't just want to know that they did develop it. The point is that the mere fact that we have a certain response to various trolley cases doesn't indicate to us that there is a good reason to act on that response. It doesn't solve the problem of normativity.

ALEX VOORHOEVE: *You claim that this problem of normativity would be solved if we managed to find principles that explain our case judgements and that express morally significant ideas. But what if the principles that best explain our case judgements fail to embody morally significant ideas?*

FRANCES KAMM: Well, I guess that ultimately, you *could* reject all our moral judgements once you find out what is driving them. But I must admit that when I find a principle that appears to explain my judgement in a particular case and my reaction to it is, 'How could *that* be of any importance?,' then my next response is that I should think more deeply about it because I must be missing something. It *could* be the case that when I see everything that is there, I will think, 'This can't be right.' But I am much less willing to give up my intuitions in particular cases than some proponents of the method of reflective equilibrium.[4]

Nonetheless, for me, these intuitions don't provide sufficient justification. I am interested in figuring out our everyday moral consciousness, but I am prepared to accept as a possibility that once

---

[4] This method consists in working back and forth among our judgements about particular cases, the principles we believe to govern them, and the considerations we believe to bear on accepting these judgements or principles, revising any of these elements wherever necessary in order to achieve an acceptable coherence among them. We achieve reflective equilibrium when we arrive at an acceptable coherence among these beliefs.

we see what the fundamental principles are, we will conclude that the intuitive judgements in particular cases are not worth adhering to.

ALEX VOORHOEVE: *Can you give an example of this process of examining the moral significance of a principle that captures some of our intuitions?*

FRANCES KAMM: Suppose that in order to explain my judgements in various cases I come up with a principle that says that the greater good itself can cause lesser evil, but the means that lead up to the greater good cannot.[5] Then I need to ask, 'Why should that be true? The person is going to die as a result of the greater good happening in both cases, so why should it make a difference whether the means that bring it about involve harming someone rather than that the harm is produced by the greater good itself?' I also need to ask, 'What might this constraint express about what it means to be a person?' In the second volume of *Morality, Mortality*, I propose an answer based on the idea that it is a different matter when the fate of a person, who is of worth as an end-in-himself, is confronted *directly* with the good of other ends-in-themselves than when he is confronted with a chain of events which in themselves have no worth but which are means to a good end. Now, when I look back on that stuff I ask myself, 'What does this amount to?' But my point is that if you can't find something of this sort, then there is something very unsatisfying about the whole thing.

I also want to say that when I look at these cases, maybe I can come up with something entirely new, something that may have nothing to do with treating people as ends or with the worth of a person. I might

---

[5] This is a rough version of Kamm's proposed Principle of Permissible Harm. At a first approximation, this principle states that it is permissible to harm some people when it is necessary to save a greater number of other people just in case the harm is an effect or aspect of the greater good that one produces. One may do greater good for some even though lesser harm to others may come of it. One may not, however, do harm to some in order that good to others will come of it. It is easy to verify that this principle fits our intuitions in the Side-track and Bridge cases.

be awakened to some new aspect of the universe never before seen. When you read Kant, there is something that happens to students (it certainly happened to me!) — it is like a whole new dimension of the moral universe is opening up to you, but it comes to be known *a priori* as opposed to via empirical methods. That is why it is so difficult to understand Kant. Sometimes I think I am such a primitive form of humanity compared to the kind of being that he is on about. As Kant says, 'We have reason not for the purpose of producing happiness, for instinct would have been better at that' — now whether that is true I don't know — 'but for the purpose of producing a will that is good in itself'. You know, a will that is good in itself? *That* is the point of my life? That is a standard I had never thought of measuring my life against! I taught a course on Kant once, and I thought, 'What is going on here?' But you feel there is gold to be mined. It involves a completely different conception of what your life is about. We should always be open to the idea that life has dimensions that we haven't recognized yet.

Now, not everyone agrees with me on this. Baruch Brody [a professor of philosophy at Rice University] once said to me:

> 'I'll go along with your intuitive analysis, but why are you always searching for deeper principles? It is important that we realize that our judgements don't display the superficial irrationalities that consequentialists claim they display when we don't believe it is permissible to chop up one (who would otherwise live) in order to get transplant organs with which we can save five, or to push the large bystander under the trolley, but we do believe it is permissible to turn the trolley, even though it will hit a single person on a dead-end side-track. But all you have to do is show, as you do, that in the latter case the greater good leads to the lesser evil and in the former cases the lesser evil leads to the greater good. These intuitions wear it on their face that they are correct. Why do you have less confidence in them and more confidence in some deeper underlying theory of the person, or of interpersonal relations, or something like that? I

am less confident about the correctness of the latter than I am that these intuitive judgements are correct.'

I don't see it this way, even though I admit that we might never have the confidence in the theory that we have in our intuitions.

◈

The reason we can't simply stop at the considered case judgements in which we have greatest confidence, or at the relatively superficial principles that explain them is that there is a further question to ask: Why should we act as our moral judgement tells us we should? After all, adhering to moral requirements may be costly — we may have to sacrifice our aims, our lives, or the lives of others in order to respect moral requirements. A critical understanding of morality therefore requires that we understand which values are expressed in the moral principles that explain our case judgements and that we can judge whether these values are worth respecting or promoting.

The need to uncover a deeper rationale for our everyday judgements is particularly apparent in the case of nonconsequentialist rights against being harmed. (These rights constrain others' permissible actions towards a person and are therefore often referred to as 'constraints'.) These rights are notoriously hard to justify, because it appears irrational that one is prohibited from violating a right when such a violation will prevent more of the same type of right from being violated. By way of illustration, imagine a murderous twist on the Bridge Case. Someone has maliciously sent a trolley hurtling towards five people with the intention of killing them. It is impermissible, nonconsequentialists hold, to kill an innocent bystander by pushing him in front of the trolley, even when this is the only way to prevent the murder of the five. But if it is so important that rights are not violated, how can the violation of the *single* bystander's right outweigh *five* equally harmful violations of the very same right?

In response to this question, Kamm attempts to formulate an idea of human status that such rights express and to show that this status would be undermined by the permissibility of acting to minimize the number of rights violations.

∽

ALEX VOORHOEVE: *Could you explain your idea of status and how it relates to constraints on harming?*

FRANCES KAMM: When I developed this idea, I was grappling with the so-called 'paradox of deontology': if you care about rights, about people not being harmed in certain ways, then if you can stop five from being harmed in a certain way by harming one (who would otherwise be all right) in the same way, why wouldn't you do that? This would be a kind of consequentialism of rights-violations. Now, most people working in this area, like Bernard Williams and Thomas Nagel, attempted to resolve this paradox by bringing in an agent-centred perspective—they said, 'Well if *I* violated the rights of the one in order to stop the five from having their rights violated by *someone else* it would be *me* doing it, whereas if *I* did nothing it would be *someone else* violating their rights.' Then I thought, 'If I had produced the threat, if *I* had, for example, set a bomb that would kill five, and the only way that *I* could now prevent this bomb from going off would be to kill a single, different person, would it then be permissible for *me* to kill this person in order to minimize the number of rights that *I* was violating?' And I realized that the answer was 'No'.

So I decided to look in a different direction: not to focus on the *agent* who would violate the constraint, but instead to consider the potential *victims* of violations of the constraint. Because I thought, 'Suppose it *was* the case that I could kill the one to stop five from being killed? That would imply something about *all of us*. It would imply that *all of us* were useable in a certain way.' You see, there is a kind of status that is defined in terms of what it is permissible to do to people. One measure of people's worth is what we consider permissible to do to them. It is true that the five will be mistreated if I don't harm the one in order to stop their mistreatment. But they will still be the kind of beings *who should not be treated in that way*—who are *inviolable* insofar as it is *wrong* to harm them in a certain way, even in order to realize the greater good of minimizing that type of harm. If it were permissible to kill the one to save the others, then *no one* — neither the one nor the five nor anyone else — would have the status of a highly inviolable being. So it is this value that is being expressed by this constraint. True, the constraint stands in the way of saving more lives and preventing more wrongs. But it expresses the fact that the nature of the individual is such that we are required to treat her in certain ways and are barred from treating her in other ways.

ALEX VOORHOEVE: *What is it about our nature that gives rise to these requirements?*

FRANCES KAMM: I don't know, although I suspect it has something to do with the fact that we are rational beings. But that was not what I was trying to establish. What I cared about was this paradox of deontology. And I realized that the answer lies in the fact that a moral system expresses the worth of a person, and that the worth of a person increases when people are less violable — as there are fewer constraints that it is permissible to violate. It is not only *what happens* to people that matters, but also *how their nature requires us to treat them*. The latter determines their worth.

ALEX VOORHOEVE: *What about the following, different response to the paradox of deontology? The question, 'If you care about rights, why not aim to minimize rights violations?' might derive its force from the idea that caring about something (e.g. that people's rights be respected) always involves taking oneself to have reason to promote its occurrence, other things being equal. But it is not true of every valuable thing that if I care about it, I should promote its occurrence. Caring about friendship, for example, doesn't commit me to 'promote its occurrence' by maximizing the number or quality of friendships I have. Breaking off one relatively time-consuming friendship so I can have two new friends would not show* *that I cared deeply about friendship. Perhaps what is true of friendship is true of rights.*

FRANCES KAMM: Though this may be right about friendship, it doesn't work in the case of rights. Take a case where a single person and five different people are having their rights violated. Suppose we have to decide whether to save the single person or the five from this rights violation (we cannot save all six). In this case, we should save the five from having their rights violated. So it is clear to me that when I don't have to mistreat a person, I should maximize the number of people whose rights are respected. So maximizing the number of people whose rights are respected *is* important.

ALEX VOORHOEVE: *That's very interesting . . .*

FRANCES KAMM: [*laughs*] I've just said something interesting! I can't believe it!

I mean, the other response is to say that one life is as precious as any number of lives — that faced with a choice between saving one life and a million other lives, you should flip a coin. But I think the view that I am proposing — the view about the importance of constraints in determining the status of a human being — has nothing to do with a refusal to count numbers.

You know, I am glad you are looking like you are interested, because that is what this stuff is all about. I mean, we are trying to do something important here. I am always surprised when people say, 'Oh, that was a nice discussion. That was fun.' I think, 'Fun? *Fun?* This is a serious matter!' You try and try to get the right account of the moral phenomena in moral cases, and getting it right is just as important as when you are doing an experiment in natural science or any other difficult intellectual undertaking. If we had worked on a NASA rocket and it launched well, we wouldn't say, 'Well, that was fun!' It was awe-inspiring — that would be the right way of putting it!

ALEX VOORHOEVE: *What about Shelly Kagan's challenge to your argument for the status-enhancing role of constraints? Kagan pointed out that as we increase our inviolability, thereby increasing our moral status because less may be done to us for the sake of maximizing the balance of good over evil, we also decrease 'saveability', or what may or must be done in order to save us. And saveability, too, is a mark of moral status . . .*

FRANCES KAMM: I don't always dwell on the objections that critics raise, because . . . well, because I don't always know how to answer them, but also because it is important for someone who believes they are on the right track to keep going. But let me say something about it. Shelly is deriving a person's degree of saveability from facts about how much has to be done to save him when he is a member of a *group* of people who can be saved. But saveability seems to be a mark of someone's status only if it is a mark of how much you should do to save him *as an individual*. The status of a person *qua* individual is a function of what is true of any individual person. So Shelly's case isn't an indication of the status of a person as an individual. I guess the test for saveability is more like: if someone were drowning, how much of a loss would you impose on someone else, less than death, to save this person? That would be a way to argue that a degree of saveability shows someone's value. That is different from the question, 'How many would you kill to save a thousand people?' For the answer to *that* question is a function of the total size of the group. Look, you might have a very valuable jug in your house, and a lot of *tshatshkes* [knick-knacks]. And given a lot of them, you might be willing to sacrifice the jug for them. But that wouldn't be a mark of their high status as individual items.

ALEX VOORHOEVE: *Still, how many of the tshatshkes it would take before you sacrifice the jug might reveal something about the value of each tshatshke. Likewise, it seems that I am more inviolable when my right not to be killed can be overridden only in order to save the lives of more than twenty others than I am when it can be overridden to save just two.*

FRANCES KAMM: It isn't straightforward that the number of people whose lives must hang in the balance before we can consider harming you in order to save these others bears on the determination of your inviolability. For example, Judith Thomson thinks that when it is a question of the violation of rights in order to help others, you have to engage in pairwise comparison of the loss that the right-holder would sustain if we violated his right and the harm that would thereby be prevented for *each* of the other people. You have to ask about each of these people how much worse off he or she would be if the right-holder's right were respected. The degree of violability of a person's rights is then determined by how bad the fate of *one* other person would have to be before you transgress the right. The analogous idea in the saveability case would be that you have to think about it *one person at a time*; it would be to see, for example, how much I could take from one person to save another person.

ALEX VOORHOEVE: *If inviolability is a mark of status, why shouldn't we make ourselves more inviolable—thereby giving ourselves higher status—by making it impermissible to turn the trolley away from the five and onto the one in the Side-track Case?*

FRANCES KAMM: I don't believe that this idea of our 'making' something is correct. I don't believe that we construct morality—that we can make it the case that we have a certain status. Given what we are, we either have it or we don't. I believe that given a certain conception of the person, the rest of it follows.

ALEX VOORHOEVE: *Even though you don't have this conception of the person?*

FRANCES KAMM: I don't know what it is yet. I have it. I have it. There is no doubt about that, because I must have it, since I have the intuitions that express it.

ALEX VOORHOEVE: *But you don't have it articulated . . .*

FRANCES KAMM: I don't have it articulated. It is there, but I don't know what it is. If I ever manage to articulate it, it might be like one of those revelations when you read Kant. The thing is, I have beliefs that don't fit into a consequentialist model. I believe that I shouldn't throw a fat bystander in front of the trolley when that is the only way to stop it from hitting the five if that will paralyse him, but that I can turn the trolley away from the five and onto the one and kill him when the one is on a dead-end side-track. There are certain ways in which you can bring about a result — it can't just be legislated. You might ask, 'Why don't we just eliminate that restriction and introduce another?' It isn't like that. It's a package deal. It's like a theory of grammar. Once you have the core, everything else follows. About a million billion sentences. And you can't say, 'Let's take five sentences and make the adverb work differently here.' You can't. The structure is hard, rigid. It is not something we put together, or can fool around with. And you have to figure out why it is rigid in exactly this way.

ALEX VOORHOEVE: *Why did you dedicate the second volume of* Morality, Mortality *to the love of morality?*

FRANCES KAMM: When I was writing that book, I was so immersed in it. Going over it again and again, you become completely detached from other people. And there is this structure that looms in your presence. At certain points, I just had to sit in my bedroom — the most secure place I could find — with a big bag of potato chips and a big bag of popcorn, and try to read the whole thing in one go. I had to encompass the whole thing in my mind all at once to see whether it would all fit together. Remember that when I think of these examples I have to think, to feel myself into them. And when I was doing this with the whole structure, I was trying to think as deeply as I possibly could — and I am no Saul Kripke! — and I just felt there wasn't anything else. This morality structure that I thought I had uncovered just seemed to me to be life. And it seemed to me to be so completely different to care about these things — most people I know didn't seem to grasp these principles. It was like a new world that I was having insight into and that other people weren't aware of. And I dedicated my book to it, because I felt like I had been granted admission into this new world.

References and further reading

Much of Frances Kamm's work is collected in her two-volume *Morality, Mortality* (Oxford: Oxford University Press, 1993, 1996) and *Intricate Ethics* (Oxford: Oxford University Press, 2006). She is also the author of *Creation and Abortion* (Oxford: Oxford University Press, 1992). The article on euthanasia referred to is F. M. Kamm, 'A Right to Choose Death?', *Boston Review*, Summer 1997 (available online). Michael Otsuka, 'Kamm on the Morality of Killing', *Ethics* 108 (1997): 197–207 provides an accessible critical summary of Kamm's central ideas. Peter Unger vigorously criticizes what he calls Kamm's 'preservationist' approach to our moral intuitions in his *Living High and Letting Die* (Oxford: Oxford University Press, 1996). Kamm replies in *Intricate Ethics*.

The quotations from Nietzsche are from *The Gay Science*, ed. Bernard Williams, trans. Josefine Nauckhoff (Cambridge: Cambridge University Press, 2001), remark 345. Philippa Foot first formulated various trolley cases in her 'The Problem of Abortion and the Doctrine of the Double Effect', collected in *Virtues and Vices* (Oxford: Oxford University Press, 1978): 19–33, and Judith Thomson developed other versions in her 'Killing, Letting Die, and the Trolley Problem', *The Monist* 59 (1976): 204–17, 'The Trolley Problem', *Yale Law Journal* 94 (1985): 1395–415, and 'Turning the Trolley', *Philosophy and Public Affairs* 36 (2008): 359–74. Thomson discusses rights in her *The Realm of Rights* (Cambridge: Cambridge University Press, 1990). How people respond to trolley cases is reported in Marc Hauser, *Moral Minds* (New York: HarperCollins, 2006) and in Joshua Greene, 'The Secret Joke of

Kant's Soul' (with discussion by John Mikhail and Mark Timmons), in *Moral Psychology. Volume 3: The Neuroscience of Morality: Emotion, Disease, and Development*, ed. Walter Sinnott-Armstrong (Cambridge, Mass.: MIT Press, 2007). Kazuo Ishiguro's novel *Never Let Me Go* (New York: Knopf, 2005) imagines a world in which healthy people are routinely killed to harvest organs for transplantation and therefore offers a look at a world in which it is common practice to treat people merely as means to others' ends.

Some of the research on the psychology of decision-making under risk to which Kamm refers is collected in *Judgement Under Uncertainty: Heuristics and Biases*, ed. Daniel Kahneman, Paul Slovic, and Amos Tversky (Cambridge: Cambridge University Press, 1982). Reciprocity among vampire bats is discussed in G. S. Wilkinson, 'Food Sharing in Vampire Bats', *Scientific American* 262 (1991): 64–70.

The method of reflective equilibrium in moral theory was first proposed by John Rawls in *A Theory of Justice* (Oxford: Oxford University Press, 2nd edn 1999): ch. 1, sect. 4. See also Norman Daniels, 'Reflective Equilibrium', in *The Stanford Encyclopaedia of Philosophy Online* (2003).

The passage about Kant and the good will to which Kamm refers can be found in *Grounding for the Metaphysics of Morals*, trans. J. W. Ellington (Indianapolis: Hackett, 1994), Akademie page nos 395–6.

Robert Nozick first drew attention to the paradox of deontology in *Anarchy, State, and Utopia* (New York: Basic Books, 1974): 30. Kamm refers to Bernard Williams's contribution to J. J. C. Smart and Bernard Williams, *Utilitarianism: For and Against* (Cambridge: Cambridge University Press, 1973): 93–100 and to Thomas Nagel, *The View from Nowhere* (New York: Oxford University Press, 1986): 175–80. Shelly Kagan discusses the trade-off between inviolability and saveability in 'Replies to My Critics', *Philosophy and Phenomenological Research* 51 (1991): 919–20.

2
PETER SINGER

EACH OF US IS JUST ONE AMONG OTHERS

impson's-in-the-Strand is a London institution famous for its roasts, which are carved at guests' tables on antique, silver-domed trolleys. Early on a spring morning in 2006, British politicians and business leaders have gathered in one of its wood-panelled rooms to attend a breakfast forum on global poverty. One of the speakers is Princeton University professor Peter Singer, a leading utilitarian moral philosopher. Utilitarianism holds that the well-being (or 'utility') of every sentient being counts equally, and that, insofar as we are considering a given population of such beings, there is only one supreme moral requirement: to maximize the sum of the utility of the members of that population. Applied to the question of global poverty, this principle yields the conclusion that each person should devote his resources towards preventing others' deprivation up to the point at which he can do more good by spending them on himself. It also follows that those who purchase luxuries with money that could have saved the lives of others (who would not otherwise be saved) have these people's deaths on their conscience. As I listen to Singer present this argument, I glance at the breakfast menu. The top item is 'The Ten Deadly Sins', which includes servings of Cumberland sausage, streaky and back bacon, liver, lamb's kidneys, fried bread, and eggs any style. It comes to £20.95 (around $37 at the time), equivalent to the cost of providing three insecticide-treated bed nets to an African family, which would significantly reduce their chance of dying from malaria. Singer would think the breakfast aptly named.

Apart from his defence of an uncommonly demanding conception of our duties to aid others, Singer is best known for his attempts to change common ethical views on two topics: the status of animals and questions at the margins of life. In *Animal Liberation*, a book that has become a classic of the animal rights movement, Singer argues forcefully that we must give the interests of non-human animals the same moral weight as comparable human interests, and that we should therefore put an end to many of our current methods of raising and using animals. In *Practical Ethics* and *Rethinking Life and Death*, Singer argues that abortion and voluntary euthanasia are permissible; that infanticide, if it is bad at all, is not nearly as bad as killing a young adult; and that if an infant is born with severe disabilities, its parents should have the right to have it painlessly killed shortly after its birth if this would be for the good of the newborn (in case its disabilities are so severe that its life would not be worth living) or if they decide it is in the interest of their family as a whole (because caring for a child with severe disabilities would place great burdens on them or on other family members).

Singer is a talented writer: he knows how to make complex arguments transparent without oversimplifying them, and he derives arresting conclusions from premises that often seem reasonable, even to non-utilitarians. The clarity, accessibility, and provocativeness of his writing, coupled with the fact that it deals with pressing moral issues, have made Singer perhaps the most widely read contemporary ethicist. Many of his conclusions, though, have generated ardent opposition. In particular, his views on the permissibility of killing infants born with severe disabilities appear to some not merely misguided, but also dangerous, because (so these critics claim) they undermine the standing of people with disabilities. As a consequence, some universities have come under pressure not to give Singer a platform, and he has faced aggressive protests at his lectures. Between 1989 and 1999, for example, several of Singer's speaking engagements at German universities were cancelled due to planned demonstrations, while others were violently disrupted.

(Opposition in Germany to Singer's views now appears to have died down; during the last decade, he has spoken in Germany on several occasions without anyone attempting to stop him speaking.) Singer's appointment at Princeton in 1999 also occasioned strong protests, with members of the disability rights group Not Dead Yet chaining themselves to administration buildings.

Such vehement responses to a philosophical argument are foreign to the distinguished individuals gathered at Simpson's, some of whom merely shift uncomfortably in their seats as Singer details the costs to others of their lifestyles. One audience member asks whether, on Singer's view, failing to spend much of one's income on saving lives is tantamount to murder. If so, the questioner adds, doesn't it follow that Singer's view is clearly mistaken, since failing to save and killing are obviously not morally equivalent? Singer is often asked this question, and responds to the questioner as follows.

> Do I really regard as morally equivalent someone who fails to give £100 to Oxfam because he wants a new sweater that he doesn't really need and another person who travels to Africa and maliciously kills a farmer? Of course not. Several factors make it useful to distinguish between the two. For one, these people's motivations are completely different—one simply wants to look fashionable, while the other is malevolent. Moreover, someone who will take the trouble of going to Africa to kill someone is probably far more dangerous to others. Finally, it is usually easier for people to refrain from killing others than to completely focus their lives on saving others from deprivation. So the malicious killer has a more morally monstrous character than the person who just throws the Oxfam letter in the bin and goes shopping. Given the way our societies are organised, the former is violating a minimal standard for acceptable conduct, whereas the latter is simply acting in a way most people think is okay. Still, from the point of view of the person who dies from hunger or a disease that could have been prevented with that £100, it makes no

difference whether he dies through someone failing to take the steps to save him or through someone killing him. So even though spending money on luxuries and thereby failing to save lives is not normally morally equivalent to killing, it *is* a mistake to think, as many people do, that one is not obligated to use one's money for the prevention of suffering. Choosing to aid is not merely admirable; it is required.

Singer's answer draws on differences between failing to save and killing that, though present in this particular case, are not essential to the contrast between the two. I am curious what Singer would say about cases in which only the essential differences are at stake. So after the forum ends and we have walked the few blocks to my office in the London School of Economics, I start our discussion by asking him about a pair of cases proposed by Frances Kamm.

ᔓ

ALEX VOORHOEVE: *Suppose that a driver must choose which of two roads to take home through the mountains: one, a winding road which carries a significant risk of a fatal accident, and another, safe road. In the first scenario, taking the treacherous route would enable the driver to save a stranger who would otherwise die; this person cannot be saved if she takes the safe route. (The person in need of saving is, we are to imagine, located before the dangerous part of the treacherous route, so that the driver will certainly save him if she takes this route.) In a second scenario, there is no one the driver can save by taking the treacherous route, but if she takes the route that is safe for her, she will start a rockslide that will kill someone who lives by the side of the road.*

In both scenarios, we can assume the driver's motivation is simply to get home safely, even if this involves a high cost to another person. There is, moreover, no difference in the difficulty of choosing the safe route in the two scenarios. Nonetheless, intuitively, there is an important difference between the two: while it may be permissible for the driver to take the safe route home when doing so involves failing to save someone, it seems impermissible for her to take the safe route when doing so involves killing someone.

Of course, these intuitions may be mistaken. Still, strong intuitive responses to cases are often quite reliable. For example, if a sentence strikes an educated native speaker as ungrammatical, this usually indicates that the sentence is indeed ungrammatical. Similarly, the inchoate feeling that someone is not quite trustworthy can be a useful (though imperfect) indicator of his untrustworthiness. Or, to take another example, a chess master might get a sinking feeling when contemplating the board and rightly take this as an important sign that she is in a losing position. So shouldn't we take our intuitions about these moral cases as presumptive evidence that there is a significant difference between failing to save and killing?

PETER SINGER: Well, I think people probably have these intuitions because we are brought up in an ethic that tells us that we must not kill, but normally need not devote much of our energies to saving others. And I think it is no accident that society has this rule and that we are generally disposed to conform to it. Society depends for its functioning on people accepting restrictions on most kinds of killings; it does not similarly depend on people being strongly motivated to save distant strangers. It is therefore important that people find killing especially abhorrent. But though it is understandable that we have these intuitions, I don't think they point to a relevant moral difference in these cases. Morality demands that we take an impartial point of view, from which it is just as bad if the person dies because no one is there to save him as it is if he gets killed in a rockslide.

ALEX VOORHOEVE: *I admit that it isn't easy to find a wholly persuasive explanation of why killing is worse than letting die. But that doesn't show that there isn't a morally relevant difference between them. Shouldn't we think that there may be a deeper rationale for our everyday judgements that we simply haven't found yet, and so be sceptical of our theoretical reasoning when it ends up being so at odds with the verdicts of our moral sense?*

PETER SINGER: Some scepticism is indeed in order, but I'm not sure what you're suggesting. Are you saying that because we have reason to be sceptical about our conclusions in moral theory, we should simply stick to inherited social rules? That doesn't follow!

ALEX VOORHOEVE: *I'm saying that it seems hubristic to break so radically with our ordinary moral sense without taking seriously the possibility that there is something to our intuitive responses. Take, for example, Dostoevsky's* Crime and Punishment; *the story seems to illustrate the folly of overruling our sense that killing is especially wrong for the sake of a moral theory.*[1]

PETER SINGER: I regard *Crime and Punishment* as a great novel in terms of representing something in our experience: the rule against killing comes to us with mysterious force—it has authority, but at the same time the source of its authority is mysterious. Dostoevsky's

---

[1] In the novel, Raskolnikov, a down-and-out university dropout, overhears a student in a tavern reasoning as follows about an old, miserly pawnbroker:

> '[A] hundred, a thousand good deeds and undertakings...could be arranged and set going by [her] money...Hundreds, maybe thousands of lives put right; dozens of families saved from destitution, from ruin, from depravity, from the venereal hospitals—all on her money. Kill her and take her money, so that afterwards with its help you can devote yourself to the service of all mankind...One death for hundreds of lives—it's simple arithmetic!'

This utilitarian analysis strikes Raskolnikov as impeccable. He is aware that for a man of ordinary sensibilities, murdering the pawnbroker is a horrifying prospect, so that to transgress the bounds of ordinary morality in this way requires uncommon confidence in the correctness of one's moral reasoning and an iron resolve. Raskolnikov admires men who are possessed of such qualities, and out of both humanitarian motives and the desire to prove his strength of mind, Raskolnikov bludgeons the pawnbroker to death with an axe and takes her money. Afterwards, he falls into a feverish state, in which he is tormented by thoughts of his crime. Finally, he confesses to the police and is sentenced to penal servitude in Siberia. The book ends with what Dostoevsky describes as Raskolnikov's redemption: under the influence of his suffering in the prison camp and the love of a devout woman, a humbled Raskolnikov comes to accept traditional morality.

analysis of Raskolnikov's feelings is compelling. Still, I do not regard it as a great novel in terms of its moral message — that Raskolnikov is only redeemed when, through faith, he submits to moral rules that he cannot justify through reasoning.

From a utilitarian perspective, one *might* say that Raskolnikov's mistake was to put too much weight on his independent judgement of the expected consequences of his actions. Some utilitarians have claimed that normally, we should stick to the rules that people live by in our society because we have reason to believe that the process of social development has a tendency to select rules that have better consequences than other possible social rules. We should therefore realize that we may be in error when, in a particular case, it seems to us that it would be for the best to break the ordinary rules of social life.

I have some sympathy for this view. And one might say that the story illustrates it: Raskolnikov was mistaken about how strongly he would be affected by the crime, and how he would be driven to confess rather than use the money for good purposes. He also didn't take into account other bad consequences — for example, that killings typically undermine people's sense of security and their trust in others, which are essential for social life. Still, I do not conclude from this that we should stick to the everyday rule even when we *do* know the consequences of our actions and the utilitarian calculus tells us to break it. If we imagine that Raskolnikov really knew that he would use the pawnbroker's money to do greater good and that there would be no further bad consequences, then he would have been right to kill her.

I know that, at this point, some people will wave their hands in shock and horror and say: 'You've just said we should kill an old woman to use her money to save others!' My response to this would be: Yes, I've said that in a *fictitious* world. And I don't think that reactions of shock and horror have much relevance, since they are based on the thought that I would recommend this in typical circumstances in *this* world, which is not the case.

ALEX VOORHOEVE: *In some cases, though, you do recommend changes to our everyday practices that many find counterintuitive — with respect*

to the treatment of animals and infants with disabilities, for example. In those cases, too, you dismiss our intuitive judgements. Why do you do so, and how do you think we should engage in ethical reasoning, if not by appealing to our judgements about cases?

PETER SINGER: I don't place much weight on these judgements, because it seems possible that they derive from untrustworthy sources. We are raised in traditions and habits of thinking that are shaped by religious systems, and even if we no longer regard these religions as sources of moral authority, we may find it hard to shake off essentially religious views of the sanctity of human life that we have absorbed from our parents and teachers, and from the broader culture. This may make our intuitions about such things as abortion, suicide, and voluntary euthanasia entirely unreliable. We are also raised in a culture that has historically oppressed and maltreated women, homosexuals, and people of different races, and invented supposed justifications for this maltreatment. The 'moral intuitions' of those who engaged in such practices were warped by prejudice; and I think many people's 'intuition' that it is okay to use animals in ways that cause them needless pain is equally warped by prejudice. Still other judgements stem from being raised to accept social conventions that lack moral justification, such as the convention that it is okay to do with our money what we like. Finally, some other moral judgements may simply stem from our evolutionary inheritance — our ideas about the importance of reciprocity, for example, may have biological origins but also lack any deep justification. Therefore, it seems to me a good idea to place little weight on our particular moral judgements.

ALEX VOORHOEVE: *So how should we proceed instead?*

PETER SINGER: I think we should start from certain basic and immediately appealing moral ideas. Now, what these ideas are is a difficult question. I would like to find judgements that appeal to self-evident principles that any rational being would have to accept.

I am not sure that there are such principles; still, the following ideas seem to me compelling. First, the thought that, from a moral point of view, the interests of every sentient being count equally. Second, that the right way to spell out what it means to count them equally is to weigh each interest as you would your own — that just as, from a self-interested perspective, you would pursue the maximum satisfaction of your interests, from a moral, impartial perspective, you should pursue the maximum satisfaction of the interests of all beings. Now, what is interesting is that this idea of giving everyone's interests equal weight, this kind of broad-based altruism, is not something that you would expect to have evolved. So it appears that when we think of things in this way, we are not just reporting our intuitions, but rather a reasoned response to things that we recognize are of value.

ALEX VOORHOEVE: *It seems, though, that one could accept the first of these basic ideas — that the interests of every being matter equally from the moral point of view — without accepting the second — that the way to respect this equality is to maximize the total satisfaction of interests in a given population. For focusing only on the sum of well-being leads one to ignore how this well-being is distributed among different individuals — and the latter seems relevant. Suppose, for example, that we could treat either a person who has a minor disability (say, being unable to walk more than short distances) or a person with a very severe disability (say, being generally bedridden and needing the help of others to sit up); we cannot treat both. Suppose further that the treatment for the minor disability would offer a slightly larger increase in well-being than the treatment for the very severe disability: while the treatment for the minor disability would lead to a complete cure, the treatment for the very severe disability would only somewhat alleviate that condition — the person would still need the help of others to move around, but would be able to sit up on his own. In this case, a utilitarian would have to say that we should treat the person with the slight disability. But this seems wrong; given that the two treatments offer nearly the same increase in well-being, the worse-off person would seem to have a stronger claim to be treated.*

PETER SINGER: I do not agree that the person who is worse off has the greater claim in this case. I think our intuitive responses to these examples turn on applying mentally the law of diminishing marginal utility.[2] We think, 'Well, if you are that much better off, an increase in mobility will create a small increase in your well-being, but if you are badly off the relief would be huge.' So in a way, we have difficulty accepting the description of your example, in which the size of the benefit one can give to the better off is slightly larger than the size of the benefit one can give to the less well off. The right way to take in the relative size of the benefits to each person would be to imagine that we had to decide who should get the treatment from behind a veil of ignorance. Behind this veil, we would know that we will be one of these two people once the veil is lifted, and we would believe that we had an equal chance of being each. If your description of the example is correct, then, from behind such a veil, we would want the treatment to be given to the person with the minor disability, since this would do us the greatest expected good.[3] If this were the case, then I can't see how people could argue that this is not the right distribution.

ALEX VOORHOEVE: *Many would say, however, that it is inappropriate to use this kind of veil of ignorance for deciding on distribution among different individuals, because it takes the perspective of a single person with two possible, equally likely futures (one in which he is slightly disabled, and one in which he is very severely disabled) as a model for*

---

[2] This 'law' is an empirical generalization about the way resources contribute to a person's well-being. It states that a given improvement in a person's command over some resource is typically more important the less he has of that resource. This is clearest in the case of money: an additional £100 is typically less important, for example, to a person who has £1,000,000 than to a person who has £1,000.

[3] In other words, we would prefer the treatment for the minor disability, because a 50 per cent chance of receiving the larger benefit if and only if we ended up being the person with the minor disability would outweigh the 50 per cent chance of receiving the smaller benefit if and only if we ended up being the person with the very severe disability.

evaluating the moral claims of two separate *people, one of whom is slightly disabled and another of whom is very severely disabled. This seems inappropriate, because when we are considering a single person's (potential) well-being, there is a unified perspective on what is good for this person that is lacking in the case of two* separate *people. As John Rawls put it, by treating these separate people as if they were all equally likely potential futures of a single person, utilitarianism ignores the separateness of persons.*

For example, take a single person, who is now in good health, but who we know will shortly develop either the slight disability or the very severe disability and is equally likely to develop either. Suppose this person may receive only one of the aforementioned treatments, and prefers the treatment for the slight disability because this would do him more expected good. If we give him this treatment and he subsequently develops the very severe disability, we could still maintain that, in treating him for the slight disability, we were acting in the way that we believed would do him the most expected good. This would seem to fully justify treating him for the slight disability. In the two-person case, however, when we deny the less well-off person the treatment because the better-off person would benefit slightly more, we cannot say to the less well-off person, 'We acted in your interests.' Moreover, it would seem reasonable for the worse-off person to ask, rhetorically, 'How can you treat the person who is already better off in order to make him better off still, when by treating me instead you could give me a benefit almost as large and which, after treatment, would still leave me less well off than the person with the (untreated) minor disability?'

This is not merely a point about our moral intuitions about cases. Instead, it is a point about the nature of the impartial, moral perspective: from this perspective, it would seem, there is not a single, unified total amount of (prospective) well-being. Instead, there are just separate individuals, each with her or his (prospective) well-being. And when separate persons have competing claims on a resource, the relative strength of their claims depends not just on how much good this resource would do for them, but also on how well off each of them is compared to others.

PETER SINGER: I disagree. I think there *is* this single perspective from which we can evaluate how important various benefits to different people are; furthermore, I believe that people can readily understand appeals to this perspective. If I am the person with the very severe disability, and you are the person with the slight disability, and I properly imagine myself as potentially being in your situation, then I can see that when the two are weighted equally, your improved situation compensates for the smaller improvement that I will forgo.

Now, on the view you are suggesting, we should give some additional weight to benefits that accrue to those who are worse off. The question I have for people who hold this view is: How much priority do you want to give to the worst off? You mention Rawls — he proposed that we give *complete* priority to the worst off, preferring any gain to the worst off, no matter how small, over any gain to the better off, no matter how large. This is an unattractive view; in your example, it would involve treating the severely disabled person rather than the person with the minor disability, even if we could only offer a barely significant improvement in the former's situation, while we could fully cure the latter. So Rawls's view must be wrong. How much priority, then, should we give the worst off? It turns out that it is completely arbitrary; there is no principled answer.

ALEX VOORHOEVE: *Well, I suppose we must engage in some kind of intuitive balancing in cases of this kind between, on the one hand, the size of the benefit and, on the other, the relative levels of well-being of the two people.*

PETER SINGER: I don't have much faith in intuitive balancing. As I said, I think that the part of people's intuitions that your argument appeals to can be explained by a natural focus on those who are very badly off. We focus our attention on them, because often they are the ones for whom we can do the most good with given resources. So I think our intuitions are based on facts that are generally true about the real world, but I don't think that they necessarily reflect any deep commitment to the view you're proposing.

ALEX VOORHOEVE: *I'd like to turn to your understanding of the interests of humans and non-human animals, and the moral conclusions you draw from your characterization of these interests. You argue that a being's interests are determined by the capacities it possesses: a being with only a bare capacity for the pleasures and pains of the moment, such as (let us suppose) a chicken, has an interest in enjoying such pleasures and avoiding such pains as it is capable of. But, since it lacks a conception of itself as existing through time, it has no interest in its continued existence (there would not, after all, be a single consciousness to whom this additional time alive would mean anything). By contrast, an animal with an enduring self, such as (it would appear) an ape, has an interest in continued existence under favourable conditions, because it would benefit from this extra time alive. Finally, you argue that the interests of beings with both a persisting self and the capacity to rationally evaluate what they want (such as most adult humans) are determined by their preferences — the things that, after due consideration with full relevant information, they decide they want from life.*

One of the striking aspects of your view is that only the capacities that a being actually possesses determine its interests; the capacities it might develop, you claim, are irrelevant. It follows that a newborn, which has the capacity for pleasure and pain, but which lacks rationality and a sense of itself as persisting over time, has an interest only in experiencing pleasure and avoiding pain; it has no interest in continued existence. It follows that a newborn is not harmed if it is painlessly killed. Moreover, since, in a utilitarian view, the wrongness of killing is entirely founded on the harm it would do, it also follows that killing an infant does not wrong it (although killing the infant may harm, and therefore wrong, people who care about it). But can this view really be correct? After all, we speak of doing things for the sake of a newborn, and these are things that secure the conditions of its future healthy development. We also commonly say of an infant that it has a great future ahead of it. Doesn't it harm a newborn to rob it of that future?

PETER SINGER: I think this is an understandable, but nonetheless misleading way of thinking about newborns. Parents who want a child naturally think of the person the infant will become, and they want that person to do well. But the newborn is not this person; it is merely the biological basis of this future person. Now, some philosophers have proposed something similar to what you seem to be saying. Don Marquis, for example, has argued that both abortion and infanticide are wrong when and because both embryos and newborns have what he calls 'a future of value'—if they would go on to have a full, good life, then by aborting or killing them, we are robbing them of this life's goods. But, as I said, I don't think that either embryos or infants are identical, in the relevant sense, with the person whose life this would be. I don't think, for example, that *I* was born; rather, I came into being at a later stage, when the newborn that became me developed certain capacities.

Moreover, strange conclusions follow if one supposes that the embryo *is* identical with the person it can become, so that it can have a future of value. For example, take a test-tube embryo that consists of eight cells. At this stage, these cells are totipotent—if split from the other cells, each of them has the potential to develop into a whole individual. Now, we have the technology to split these eight cells into separate cells, which, after allowing them to develop further in separate Petri dishes, we could implant in women volunteers. If each of these developing cells is identical with the person it can become, it would seem that we *should* split these cells and find volunteers to carry them to full term, since otherwise we would be failing to give each of them a future of value.

ALEX VOORHOEVE: *I admit that it is difficult to spell out a plausible view of how, precisely, the embryo's or infant's potential future makes a moral difference. Still, your view also has unpalatable implications. Suppose, for example, that we can save either a newborn orphan (for whom no one has special concern) or two dogs from painful death in a fire, and we cannot save all three. It seems you would be committed to saying that, if their deaths would be equally painful, we should save the two dogs, since this prevents more suffering.*

PETER SINGER: I'm not sure about that. We cannot isolate the case in this way. There might be other people who want to care for the orphan, or adopt it, and this might make a big difference.

ALEX VOORHOEVE: *But leaving aside other people's feelings for the orphan . . .*

PETER SINGER: [*pauses*] Leaving aside other people's feelings . . . If we really assume that there is no one who especially desires to care for the infant and that the world has as many people as we want it to have, then *maybe* I would come to the conclusion that we should save the dogs. But in a life-saving situation of this sort, I think we would find it emotionally difficult to abandon the infant. It is understandable why we should feel this way. So a general recommendation that we should do something that cuts against these feelings . . . I do not want to give that. But if someone saved the dogs, and said by way of justification, 'For me, it was just as emotionally hard to leave the dogs as it was to leave the infant because I care a lot about dogs,' then I would think that for that person, saving the dogs was an acceptable thing to do.

ALEX VOORHOEVE: *Whether or not it captures everything that is morally relevant in the case of infants, I wonder whether your interest-based account adequately captures everything that is morally relevant in the case of adults. For example, there is no place in your account for the value of autonomy.*

PETER SINGER: Well, autonomy is valuable because it helps you satisfy your preferences.

ALEX VOORHOEVE: *But a person can be autonomous and take actions that do not optimally satisfy her considered, well-informed preferences. She* *might, for example, fully autonomously take hallucinogenic mushrooms that she knows are harmful, simply on a whim. And respect for her autonomy appears to give us reason not to override her will paternalistically in this case. So it doesn't appear to be the case that autonomy is valuable only when it helps a person satisfy her preferences.*

PETER SINGER: I don't agree. To the extent that we believe that people will typically use their autonomy to make choices that do not further their own well-being or their own plans — to that extent we think that autonomy is not a good thing, and we limit it. This is the case with children, the mentally ill, and so on.

ALEX VOORHOEVE: *It seems, though, that a rational adult has a special responsibility for her own life. One consequence of recognizing this responsibility is that we respect her will in decisions that concern her alone, even when she may not always make the best decisions. Another consequence is that we think a person may have a less weighty claim to aid when she comes to harm through her informed, free choice than when she comes to harm through no choice of her own. For example, suppose we are deciding how to use next year's health budget. We know that in our community, every year one person becomes ill through the (legal) use of hallucinogenic mushrooms, and another person will develop kidney failure because of a congenital condition. Both conditions, if untreated, are equally bad. Suppose that we can invest in only one piece of medical equipment: we can either buy a machine that will cure the patient poisoned by the mushrooms or we can invest in the facilities that will enable us to perform a transplant that would cure the patient with kidney failure. Other things equal, it would seem that we should invest in the transplant facilities, because the person who comes to harm only because of her choice has a lesser claim than the person who could not avoid coming to harm. (This is not to say that the former has no claim to aid; nor is it to say that she deserves to be badly off.) Do you deny that people have this special responsibility for their own well-being?*

PETER SINGER: Obviously, I think it is good to encourage people to take responsibility for their own well-being, since that reduces the burden on others to repair the damage they would otherwise do to themselves. And I accept at least some of John Stuart Mill's arguments in *On Liberty* for restricting the powers of the state to interfere with individuals for their own good. Mill was a utilitarian, after all, and his arguments are based on the good consequences of restricting the powers of the state to tell individuals what is in their own interests. I don't, however, think this is an absolute principle.

But apart from those utilitarian considerations, I deny a fundamental role for the notion of choice — for the idea that someone could have done otherwise than she did. And this brings in something that we haven't talked about yet, namely free will in a deep sense. I doubt that we have this. I mean, the more we know about the causes of behaviour, the more difficult it is to believe that we have it. Take the well-known study by Walter Mischel, in which four-year-old children were given a marshmallow, and told that they could eat the marshmallow now or could wait for the experimenter to return from an errand and get two marshmallows instead. Each child was then left alone in a room with the single marshmallow for up to twenty minutes. Some children ate the single marshmallow immediately; others waited the entire time for the experimenter to return. Mischel then investigated how the children were doing at eighteen. He reports that the children's behaviour was a very strong predictor of how they were doing: the children who were willing to wait for the second marshmallow did far better in school, for example. This seems to me relevant to your example of the woman who took the harmful mushrooms because it indicates that people's dispositions to choose wisely are a matter of luck. It seems to me that the woman who took the mushrooms on a whim was unlucky in the same way the person with the congenital illness was unlucky.

All this doesn't mean, of course, that utilitarianism is premised on the falsity of free will; one could believe in freedom of the will and be a utilitarian. But I think utilitarianism is more congenial if you don't believe in free will.

ALEX VOORHOEVE: *In closing, I'd like to ask about the reasons you think we have to act as utilitarianism demands. You mentioned previously that utilitarianism was based on a form of broad-based altruism. But ordinary altruistic feelings don't extend equally to all, as it would seem they would have to if we are to be motivated to act on utilitarian morality. It appears that David Hume was right to observe that the typical person cares more about his own well-being than about the well-being of any other, and cares more about the well-being of those close to him than about distant strangers. Even the behaviour of utilitarians like yourself seems to bear out the truth of Hume's view: though you are a vegetarian, and give a substantial part of your income to charity, like most of us, you fall short of doing everything that utilitarianism demands. Can we really be motivated to act from the utilitarian point of view?*

PETER SINGER: It is true that very few, if any, of us have a concern for every being's interests that is strong enough to make it the dominant influence on our behaviour. Still, I think we can cultivate this concern and can increase its motivational power. We do so when we make people attentive to the preventable suffering in the world. There is something in our nature that is capable of responding simply to the thought that there is another human being, just like us, who is suffering preventably.

I do not think, however, that to be rational we *must* take up and act from the utilitarian point of view — what the utilitarian philosopher Henry Sidgwick called 'the point of view of the universe'. I agree with Sidgwick that it is rational to care more about your own interests and the interests of those close to you than the interests of others. (That is *not* to say it is *irrational* to act from the moral point of view, since more than one way of acting may be rational.)

But even though moral considerations do not necessarily trump non-moral considerations, I think that the two kinds of reasons are not always at odds with each other. For our psychology is such that we will often be happier and lead more fulfilled lives if we do not care only about our own happiness or personal fulfilment. This is the ancient 'paradox of hedonism': in order to lead a happy life, you often need to develop attachments to things other than your own happiness. And one of the things that you can develop an attachment to is the reduction of suffering in the world and the promotion of others' well-being. And, as I write in *How Are We to Live?*, I think that aiming at things like better treatment of animals, the alleviation of widespread malnutrition, and a reduction in the thousands of daily deaths due to easily preventable diseases is a good way of leading a life that you will find meaningful. The reason is that, typically, the more you reflect on the value of these causes, the more compelling they become. I think this is not always true of other aims, like being fashionable or driving a better car, because you can ask of each of these, when you consider it from a more general, less personal perspective, whether it really is important. I mean, when you start with purely personal goals, and you say to yourself: 'What I really want is to have an enjoyable life and drive a fast car,' you can reflect on this, and ask whether these things are really of value, and whether a life devoted to them amounts to anything. And it would seem that, in part because of our ability to take up the impartial perspective, the answer is often going to be 'No'. By contrast, at the end of an activist life, you can say: 'I've done my bit to make the world a better place.'

So I think we are not sufficiently reflective, and, as a consequence, we often pursue things that we think will be interesting and rewarding when they're not. I also think that if we choose to be moral and devote ourselves to some important cause, that we will be fulfilled. Still, many people say to me: 'What I am really concerned about is a much smaller community, including my family and friends, and my football club.' And this is true, even after they reflect on it. So though the moral life is *one* way of achieving fulfilment, it is certainly not the only way. The moral life also can be depressing, of course: once you take up the impartial perspective, you become aware of how much more there is to do. So I don't think the argument for the idea that it is in our interest to lead a moral life is as solid as I would like it to be.

ALEX VOORHOEVE: *As you say, close relationships with people we love are typically part of what makes our lives meaningful. But these relationships require partial concern, which seems at odds with utilitarianism — can a committed utilitarian give them any place in his life?*

PETER SINGER: I agree that a good part of our happiness must come from close, loving relationships. Psychological evidence shows that good relationships of this kind are the main reason why contented people are so. That is just the kind of beings that we are; we can't do without such relationships. But the thought that morality is at odds with some elements of our nature is not peculiar to me. Kant, of course, saw morality as a rebellion of our rational nature against our empirical, desirous nature. I don't want to go that far, because I think there need not always be a deep conflict between morality and the demands of particular relationships. Given their contribution to human well-being, we have moral reasons to cultivate these relationships. Moreover, I think that these relationships are stronger when the people involved respect each other's values and recognize that each person's self-respect is tied up with pursuits that he or she regards as worthwhile. Still, there is some truth in Kant's view. I would say that our rational nature enables us to see that we are just one among others; that, from the impartial point of view, there is no reason why our lesser interests or the lesser interests of those close to us should outweigh the greater interests of others. But close relationships require that you give greater weight to the interests of those close to you. So of course there is conflict.

References and further reading

Peter Singer has written widely on ethical theory, bioethics, and applied ethics, as well as on figures in the history of thought. Some of his best-known works are *Animal Liberation* (New York: Random House, 2nd edn 1990), *Practical Ethics* (Cambridge: Cambridge University Press, 2nd edn 1993), *How Are We to Live?* (Oxford: Oxford University

Press, 1997), and *Rethinking Life and Death* (Oxford: Oxford University Press, 1995). *Writings on an Ethical Life* (New York: Ecco, 2000) is a collection of his writings. *The Life You Can Save* (New York: Random House, 2009) develops his views on our obligation to help the world's poor. *Singer and His Critics*, ed. Dale Jamieson (Oxford: Blackwell, 1999) and *Peter Singer Under Fire*, ed. Jeffrey Schaler (Chicago: Open Court, forthcoming) are good starting points for further discussion of his views. For Singer's criticism of the use of intuitions in moral theory, see 'Sidgwick and Reflective Equilibrium', *The Monist* 58 (1974): 490–517 and 'Ethics and Intuitions', *Journal of Ethics* 9 (2005): 331–52.

The claim that utilitarianism fails to respect the separateness of persons was made forcefully by John Rawls in *A Theory of Justice* (Oxford: Oxford University Press, 2nd edn 1999): sects 5, 6, 30. For further discussion of the implications of the separateness of persons for moral theory, see Thomas Nagel, 'Equality', in his *Mortal Questions* (Cambridge: Cambridge University Press, 1979): 106–27, and Michael Otsuka and Alex Voorhoeve, 'Why it Matters that Some are Worse Off than Others', *Philosophy and Public Affairs* 37 (2009): 171–99. The 'veil of ignorance' model that Singer mentions was first proposed in John Harsanyi, 'Cardinal Utility in Welfare Economics and the Theory of Risk-taking', *Journal of Political Economy* 61 (1953): 434–5. See also his *Rational Behaviour and Bargaining Equilibrium in Games and Social Situations* (Cambridge: Cambridge University Press, 1977), ch. 4. Rawls offered a different interpretation of the veil of ignorance in ch. 3 of *A Theory of Justice*. See also Chapter 6 of this volume for further discussion of this idea.

Singer's views on the interests of newborns and the permissibility of infanticide draw on Michael Tooley, 'Abortion and Infanticide', *Philosophy and Public Affairs* 11 (1972): 37–65. Singer mentions the opposing views expressed in Don Marquis, 'Why Abortion is Immoral', *Journal of Philosophy* 86 (1989): 183–202. For an account of how Singer's work is received among people with disabilities, see Harriet McBryde Johnson, 'Unspeakable Conversations', *New York Times*, 13 February 2003.

The 'marshmallow test' is reported in Y. Shoda, W. Mischel, and P. K. Peake, 'Predicting Adolescent Cognitive and Self-regulatory Competencies from Preschool Delay of Gratification', *Developmental Psychology* 26 (1990): 978–86. Hume discusses altruistic motivation in his *Treatise of Human Nature*, ed. P. H. Nidditch (Oxford: Oxford University Press, 1978), book 3, part 2, sect. 2. Sidgwick discusses the reasons one has to be moral and their conflict with self-interested reasons in *The Methods of Ethics* (Indianapolis: Hackett, 1981), book 2, ch. 5.

3
DANIEL KAHNEMAN

CAN WE TRUST OUR INTUITIONS?

Daniel Kahneman is the world's pre-eminent investigator of
the ways in which the limits of our cognitive abilities shape
our judgements. Since the late 1960s, his work, much of
which was carried out in close collaboration with the late
Amos Tversky (1937–1996), has focused on our intuitive judgements.
One of Kahneman and Tversky's favoured methods of studying such
judgements involves asking subjects relatively simple questions about
cases. An example is the famous 'Linda Case', in which subjects are
given the following description of the protagonist:

> Linda is 31 years old, single, outspoken and very bright.
> She majored in philosophy. As a student she was deeply
> concerned with issues of discrimination and social justice and
> also participated in anti-nuclear demonstrations.

Subjects were then given a list of eight possible outcomes describing
Linda's present employment and activities. Besides a number of miscel-
laneous possibilities (e.g. elementary school teacher, psychiatric social
worker), this list included the descriptions 'Linda is a bank teller' and
'Linda is a bank teller active in the feminist movement'. Subjects were
then asked to rank these descriptions by the probability that they were

true. A large majority responded that Linda was less likely to be a bank teller than a bank teller active in the feminist movement. This is an obvious mistake, since it cannot be more likely for Linda to possess attributes X and Y than for her to possess attribute X. The explanation Kahneman offered for the erroneous majority judgement was that respondents were implicitly using a heuristic — a mental short-cut — to arrive at their judgements. This particular heuristic involved replacing the attribute that was the target of the question (the relative probability of the description's truth) with an attribute that comes more easily to mind (the relative resemblance of the description to the introductory statement about Linda). In other words, respondents were using the degree to which the description of her current activities resembled Linda as a quick way of judging the likelihood that the description was true.

The Linda Case illustrates several aspects of intuitive judgements: they typically spring to mind quickly and automatically, without much effort, and are difficult to control or modify, even in the face of conflicting evidence. (As the biologist Stephen Jay Gould wrote about this example: 'I know [the right answer], yet a little homunculus in my head continues to jump up and down, shouting at me, "But she can't just be a bank teller, read the description!"') Moreover, while the heuristics that give rise to such judgements may generally be useful — they economize on our mind's scarce computing time and ability — they can also lead us astray.

Kahneman and Tversky also famously drew attention to another way in which our intuitive judgements may fail to conform to rational principles: irrelevant variations in the description of alternatives can evoke a change in judgement, because each description elicits a different intuitive mental representation of the alternatives. An example is their Asian Disease Case:

> Imagine that the United States is preparing for the out-break of an unusual Asian disease, which is expected to kill 600 people. Two alternative programmes to combat the disease have been proposed. Assume that the exact scientific

estimates of the consequences of the programmes are as follows:

> If programme A is adopted, 200 people will be saved.

> If programme B is adopted, there is a one-third probability that 600 people will be saved and a two-thirds probability that no people will be saved.

Which of the two programmes would you favour?

In this version of the problem, a substantial majority of respondents favours programme A. Other respondents, however, received the same cover story followed by two differently described options:

> If programme A* is adopted, 400 people will die.

> If programme B* is adopted, there is a one-third probability that nobody will die and a two-thirds probability that 600 people will die.

Given these options, a clear majority favours programme B*. Of course, A and A* are identical, as are B and B*. Nonetheless, subjects are significantly more likely to choose the option in which 200 people will certainly be saved and 400 will certainly die over the risky option when the description draws attention to lives saved rather than to lives lost.

Kahneman and Tversky explained this pattern as a result of people's intuitive tendency to represent outcomes as involving 'gains' or 'losses' relative to an imagined baseline and apply different decision-making rules depending on whether outcomes are represented as gains or as losses. The first description of the problem draws attention to lives saved, eliciting a 'gain' representation relative to a baseline in which everyone dies. The second description draws attention to lives lost, eliciting a 'loss' representation relative to a baseline in which everyone survives. Now, when considering *gains*, people are generally *risk-averse*: they favour a certain gain of a given number of lives over a gamble in which the sum of probability-weighted lives gained is just as great. This makes the certain gain in A of 200 lives seem attractive relative to the gamble in B, which involves a one-third probability of saving 600 lives and a two-thirds probability of saving no lives at all. (The sum of probability-weighted lives saved in B is therefore $(1/3 \times 600) + (2/3 \times 0) = 200$, which is equal to the number of lives saved for certain in A.) When considering *losses*, however, people are generally *risk-seeking*: to avoid a certain loss, they will take a gamble in which the sum of probability-weighted lives lost is just as great as the number of lives lost in the certain option. This makes a risky option like B*, which involves a one-third chance of no loss of life and a two-thirds chance of a loss of 600 lives, relatively attractive when compared to A*, which involves a certain loss of 400 lives. Kahneman and Tversky described the resulting difference in people's preferences as a 'framing effect': different ways of presenting the same decision problem elicit different responses, even though rationality requires the same pattern of response.

Kahneman and Tversky's work on a variety of heuristics and framing effects, and their innovative theory of how people choose in risky situations, spawned a huge research programme in psychology and economics, and earned Kahneman the Nobel Prize in Economics in 2002. Since the mid-1980s, Kahneman and others have also investigated the use of heuristics and the existence of framing effects in moral judgements. This work is relevant to moral theory because one common procedure of moral enquiry is to employ the method of reflective equilibrium, which involves working back and forth among our intuitive judgements about particular cases and the principles we believe to govern them, revising any of these elements wherever necessary in order to achieve an acceptable coherence among them. We reach reflective equilibrium when our intuitive case judgements and moral principles are consistent with each other and some of these judgements and principles provide support for or provide a best explanation of others. For those who employ this method, it is obviously important to find out when these case judgements are liable to error, and if they are, what, if anything, we can do to correct them.

I meet Kahneman to discuss these issues in London in September 2006. I am immediately struck by his energy and the sense of excitement with which he approaches his work. We've arranged to meet following an afternoon seminar at a central London think tank. The seminar runs late, and most participants push out of the crowded, airless room looking exhausted. Kahneman, however, emerges with a spring in his step. During our walk through Covent Garden to my office at the London School of Economics, he enthusiastically recalls his meeting earlier that day with a Ph.D. student, Benedetto De Martino, at the nearby Wellcome Department of Imaging Neuroscience. De Martino had studied the areas of people's brains that become active while they are making choices. He had found that subjects who are strongly susceptible to the aforementioned gain/loss framing effects have higher activity in a part of the brain associated with emotional processing (the amygdala), whereas subjects who are less susceptible to such effects display higher activity in parts of the brain associated with analytical processing (areas in the prefrontal cortex). The study therefore offered some support for the view that the intuitive processes that Kahneman and Tversky had uncovered operate in a distinctive part of the brain and determine judgement unless overridden by more deliberative reasoning. As Kahneman is explaining the suggestions he made to De Martino for further research, we cross the wide, busy Kingsway. In the middle of the pedestrian crossing, he stops short, oblivious to the approaching traffic, and exclaims 'Damn! I made a mistaken suggestion. I need to e-mail this guy right away!' A few minutes later, after he has fired off a quick message to De Martino, I start the interview by asking how he became interested in moral questions.

~

DANIEL KAHNEMAN: In my teens, I was interested in philosophical questions — God's existence, the reasons not to do what people think is wrong. But I discovered very early on that I was more interested in what made people believe in things than in the correctness of the beliefs themselves. For example, I was more curious about what made people believe in God than whether He really existed, and was more occupied with the origins of people's moral intuitions than with moral philosophy.

ALEX VOORHOEVE: *'Intuition' is a vague term. How would you define it?*

DANIEL KAHNEMAN: I haven't always been consistent in my use of the term. The first time that I used it in print, I think, was in a paper with Amos Tversky on the 'Law of Small Numbers'.[1] In that paper, we wrote something to the effect that 'the Law of Large Numbers is not part of the repertoire of human intuition'. What we meant there by 'intuition' was a descriptive generalization made by an objective observer about the rule that appears to generate the judgements of an individual about specific cases. And this can be an accurate description by the outside observer, even if the individual would reject this rule if he were to consider it.

I have also used the term to describe an intuitive *system*, a way of generating thoughts that are called intuitive thoughts. The operations of this system are typically automatic, quick, effortless, associative, and often emotionally charged. Usually, they are not open to introspection, and difficult to control or change. This intuitive system generates involuntary impressions that come to mind spontaneously, like percepts. Intuitive judgements directly reflect these impressions with little modification from the reasoning system, which functions very differently from the intuitive system: the reasoning system's operations are step by step,

[1] The Law of *Large* Numbers holds that given a sample of independent and identically distributed random variables with a finite expected value, the average of these observations will eventually approach and stay close to the expected value. 'Expected value' here does not mean what it does in ordinary English; it is the sum of the possible outcomes weighted by the probability that they will occur. For example, if one rolls a fair die, the expected value of the outcome is $(1 + 2 + 3 + 4 + 5 + 6)/6 = 3.5$. The Law of Large Numbers predicts that the average stabilizes around the expected value of 3.5 as the number of times one rolls the die becomes large. The Law of *Small* Numbers is a psychological tendency to treat small samples as if they were large samples.

slow, effortful, and more likely to be consciously controlled and flexible.

ALEX VOORHOEVE: *There appears to be a difference between what you call intuitive judgements, understood as a product of the intuitive system, and the type of case judgements that philosophers use to build and test their moral theories, which they also sometimes refer to as 'intuitions'. Philosophers typically take these to be considered case judgements, that is, judgements that arise after reflection on the case and on our reasons for judging it as we do, whereas your category of intuitive judgements does not appear to involve such extensive reflection. Perhaps the relation between the two types of judgements is as follows. Philosophers start with a judgement about a case that comes to mind quickly and automatically and that may be emotionally laden — what you would call an intuitive judgement. They then examine whether they can find reasons to regard it as unreliable or biased. If they find no such reason, it is presumptively treated as a valid case judgement, and they try to find principles that explain the judgement, in part by reflecting further on what caused them to arrive at the judgement in question. An example of someone who uses this approach is Frances Kamm, who, in conversation, describes her method as follows:*

> I don't really have a considered judgement about a case until I have a visual experience of it. I have to deeply imagine myself in a certain situation with an open mind. It is almost as if you are looking at something with no preconceptions. You have to attend to it, and then things will pop out at you. First you may get the intuitive judgement of what you really should do in the circumstance you are imagining. Then you wonder, 'Why am I reaching this conclusion?' And your inner eye focuses on one factor as driving this judgement.

What do you think of this method of arriving at considered case judgements?

DANIEL KAHNEMAN: Well, there is a very interesting contrast between the way a psychologist would go at it and the way a philosopher
would go at it, and it has a lot to do with the idea that the philosopher
can know *why* she is reaching this conclusion. A basic assumption
in psychological analysis is that you first have an intuition in a given
situation. Then, when you ask yourself why you have it, you tell
yourself a story. But the story you come up with does not necessarily
identify the cause of your intuitions, because you typically do not
have access to what causes your intuitions. Moreover, in her work,
Kamm seems to assume that the cause of her intuitive judgement
is the recognition of something that counts as a reason. But this
need not be true. For example, the psychologists Dale Miller and
Cathy McFarland asked subjects to determine the appropriate level
of compensation for a man who was shot in the arm during the
robbery of a grocery store. Some respondents were told that the
robbery happened in the victim's regular store; others were told that
the victim was shot in a store that he visited for the first time that day,
because his usual store happened to be closed. The second version
is more poignant, because it is easier to imagine the counterfactual
undoing of an unusual event than of a regular occurrence. This
difference in poignancy led to a difference of $100,000 in the median
compensation that respondents awarded, so it was a clear cause of
the size of the award. But further research showed that subjects do
not regard poignancy as a good reason to award higher compensation
in such cases. So I would very sharply separate the different phases in
Kamm's description of her method: the first phase, where she knows
what she would do, and the second phase, in which she thinks deeply
as to why she would do it and comes up with a reason. It is at least
possible that the reason she comes up with was not the cause of her
judgement.

  You know, many psychologists believe that consciousness is a story
that we tell ourselves about ourselves. And in many cases, the story
does not correspond to reality. I mean, it is very easy to create cases
where you know the story isn't true. Let me give you an example, just

to push the point a little. There are experiments with post-hypnotic suggestion, where you tell somebody, 'I'll clap my hands and then you'll get up and open the window.' The person wakes up, you clap your hands, and he gets up and opens the window. If you ask him, 'Why did you open the window?' he'll say something like, 'The room felt very warm.'

ALEX VOORHOEVE: *But aren't these cases of hypnosis simply pathological?*

DANIEL KAHNEMAN: No, they are the best examples! The beauty of these examples is that you know why the subjects are doing it. They are doing it because they were given the instruction, and then somebody clapped his hands. But they have a completely different experience of why they are doing it. What's more, people are never at a loss for a reason why they did it. They can be made to do absolutely absurd things with post-hypnotic suggestion, and yet these things seem to make sense to them when they do them. The conclusion I draw from this is that the mental operation of making sense of our intuitive judgements is a very different cognitive activity from having these intuitions. This takes us to the core of my disagreement with Frances Kamm. To me, her confidence is very much like the confidence of the hypnotic subject who claims he knows why he opened the window.

ALEX VOORHOEVE: *Still, the case of the hypnotic seems to show only that we cannot always trust our introspective judgements about why we act or judge as we do; it doesn't show that we can never trust these judgements. And the method employed by Kamm and others involves more than simple introspective judgement about what is driving our judgements in isolated cases. Philosophers employing this method go on to consider whether the reason they think they might be responding to in a particular case determines their judgement in other cases also.*

DANIEL KAHNEMAN: But this raises another methodological problem. There is a distinction between what I have called the 'within-subject' and the 'between-subject' method of considering cases. The within-subject method involves noting the intuitions a given subject has when she is considering multiple contrasting cases. The between-subject method involves noting the intuitions a subject has in a single case without engaging in explicit comparison with other cases. The two methods can elicit very different intuitions about the cases considered. Now, because its aim is to find rules that are applicable across different cases, moral philosophy is, by its nature, restricted to the within-subject method. That is, a moral philosopher is always conscious of two or more cases and has intuitions about the differences in the two cases and about whether these differences are relevant to how she should respond. And I think this is a major limitation of moral philosophy, because, in their everyday life, people are confronted with problems one at a time, so their relevant intuitions are about cases that occur one at a time. And the moral philosopher's stance prevents her from identifying the moral intuitions that are relevant to individuals who live their lives in this way. For this purpose, the between-subject approach, which involves asking one group of people about one case and another group of people about another case, is superior.

ALEX VOORHOEVE: *That's very interesting... I suppose I see how people's tendency to respond differently to the same case depending on whether it is framed as involving gains or losses, as in the Asian Disease Case, would only clearly emerge in a between-subject experiment. Can you give some other examples of cases in which the two methods lead to different judgements?*

DANIEL KAHNEMAN: Let me give you two examples. First, the intuitive judgements in the grocery store cases I mentioned before, which revealed the effect of poignancy on financial compensation for the victim, could only have been elicited by the between-subject method. For if one considers the two cases side-by-side, whether the victim was at his regular grocery store or not would have appeared irrelevant, and so would have made no difference to the compensation awarded. Second, in research I carried out with Cass Sunstein, David Schkade, and Ilana Ritov, we found that the punishments people thought appropriate when considering in isolation cases of business fraud differed significantly from punishments they thought appropriate when they compared cases of business fraud with wrongdoing involving bodily injury. Our hypothesis was that outrage at an act was a significant contributor to the size of the punishment people judged appropriate. When they considered a case of business fraud in isolation, people implicitly compared the case to other cases of business fraud, so their level of outrage was determined by how egregious the conduct was as compared to other cases of business fraud. A particularly egregious case of business fraud would therefore be very heavily punished. However, in comparing cases of business fraud with cases of a different category altogether, like bodily injury, the relative importance of the category to which the wrongdoing belongs became relevant as well. Since bodily injury was regarded as generally worse than fraud, this could make the same case of fraud seem less worthy of severe punishment.

ALEX VOORHOEVE: *But these cases seem to vindicate rather than undermine the within-subject approach used by philosophers. For in these cases, the within-subject approach of having a single person consider multiple cases side by side seems to prevent mistakes that would occur if we considered each case separately.*

DANIEL KAHNEMAN: Well, to some extent I agree, and in that paper with Sunstein, Schkade, and Ritov, we indeed try to argue that the within-subject comparison has an advantage because it gives you a better shot at approaching a consistent view of the world than judging single cases in isolation would, even though it doesn't always work. But when we are thinking about policies and about applying moral rules to people, then it's important to remember that these people will experience cases as participants in the between-subject experiment. What is morally compelling to us as we consider the contrast between the two cases may not seem morally relevant to them at all, and so the rules we may wish to impose on them may not seem relevant to them. There is, I think, a genuine dilemma here between the demands of coherence and the need not to impose on people principles that violate their judgements. A solution that we arrived at in that paper is to partially accommodate both demands. So our recommendation was to measure outrage at the wrongful behaviour, considered in isolation, and use outrage as an input in determining the severity of punishment. We would not recommend allowing outrage alone to determine punishment, as it appears to do in some jury trials. Our thinking was that while a public policy that merely reflects outrage is grotesque, a policy that is insensitive to outrage is not going to be acceptable to people. So public policy should be sensitive to outrage, but not dominated by it. That is the best we could do. It is not a unique solution, but it acknowledges that moral intuition about a specific case can neither be trusted nor altogether ignored.

ALEX VOORHOEVE: *This proposed solution seems to treat people's emotions and judgements as simply given, when they are not. As you said, moral emotions like outrage are judgement-sensitive; how outraged we are depends on how awful we consider the wrongdoing to be. So if people's sense of outrage is based on a mistaken judgement of the turpitude of the crime, then that judgement needs to be corrected rather than accommodated.*

DANIEL KAHNEMAN: I think that is an excellent point, and I think that intuitions are indeed malleable to some extent and in some cases can change through education. Here's a nice example. We did a survey once in Canada where we found that people are truly offended by the fact that car accident insurance rates are determined by where they live, so that if they live in an area where there are many accidents, they pay a high insurance rate. People initially thought that was deeply immoral, because they felt that insurance rates should be determined by the driver's behaviour alone. But this is an intuition you could train people to recognize as mistaken. For they recognized that the insurance rate it is proper for people to pay is proportional to the probability of their being in an accident, even if they don't cause it, and they saw that the area they lived in affected the probability that they would be in an accident. But not all intuitions are malleable in this way.

ALEX VOORHOEVE: *Can you give an example of a case in which you think our intuitions are not responsive to reflection?*

DANIEL KAHNEMAN: Take moral philosophers' favourite pair of so-called 'trolley cases'.[2] The case of the fat man on the bridge is an example where I think it is clear that people's intuitive judgements follow the rule that using direct physical violence against an innocent person is unacceptable, and the more directly physical the violence is, the more unacceptable it is. Now, on reflection, this looks like a poor rule — it doesn't seem to pick out a morally relevant factor. But applied to individual cases it is going to be powerful every time. You (or at least I) could blame an individual who did not divert the trolley, but I cannot imagine blaming anyone for not throwing the fat man in front of the trolley.

ALEX VOORHOEVE: *I agree that in the form in which the case of the fat man is traditionally stated, the harmful direct physical contact may play some role in generating people's intuitive judgement that pushing him is wrong. But my guess would be that the judgement that it is wrong to use him to stop the trolley would persist if the case was described as one in which one had to press a lever which opened a trapdoor and dropped him into the path of the trolley. So our judgement in the two contrasting trolley*

---

[2]   In the Side-track Case, a runaway trolley is headed towards and will kill five people unless a lever is pulled which will divert it onto a dead-end side-track where it will kill one person. Most people intuitively believe it is permissible — and some believe it is obligatory — to divert the trolley in this case. In the contrasting Bridge Case, the trolley will kill the five unless you push a large bystander, whose weight is sufficient to stop the trolley, off a bridge and into its path, thereby killing him. Most people intuitively believe it is impermissible to push the large man in this case. This pair of judgements stands in need of explanation, since both diverting the trolley and pushing the bystander involve taking an action that will kill one and save five.

cases appears to be better explained by the following general principle: while it may be permissible to pursue the greater good in ways that have lesser harm as a side-effect (as one would do if one diverted the trolley onto a side-track where it kills the one), it is impermissible to use someone harmfully as a means to a greater good (as one would do if one used the fat man to stop the trolley). Something like this principle would seem to make more sense than the 'Don't use direct physical violence against innocents' rule you cited, because it seems to incorporate a significant moral idea, which is, roughly, that innocent people are not to be used harmfully as a means to others' ends without their consent.

DANIEL KAHNEMAN: I am sceptical about the potential of this idea to explain and justify this intuitive judgement. The aversion to pushing the fat man is linked to intuitions about *causes* — you feel you have a more direct causal role in the man's death if you push him, or push a lever that moves him toward the train, than if you move a lever that moves the train toward him. When you call the killing of the single person in the latter case an unintended side-effect, you draw on an intuition about causality that I do not find morally compelling. So I find it hard to believe that the two cases differ in morally relevant ways. However, since the fat man scenario evokes an extraordinarily powerful intuition, you should not have a rule that ignores it. That is, if anyone had a system that would condone pushing the bystander to save the five, then that system would not be viable, that system would not be acceptable. Because pushing him is just deeply repugnant. When I say this, I am not stating a piece of moral knowledge; I am simply making a sociological and psychological prediction.

ALEX VOORHOEVE: *Well, what would 'work' in practice — in the sense of finding a rule that people would accept and act on — is a pragmatic question. But I am interested in whether it really is morally permissible to use the fat man to save the five, whether or not I can get others to agree to it. You seem to think there is no justification for your intuitive judgement that it is impermissible to use him harmfully as a means in this case. You also seem to think that rationally, the case where we use him* *to stop the trolley is just like the case where we divert the trolley onto the side-track, because both involve taking an action that will kill one in order to save five. If you also think that you should divert the trolley because this brings about the greater good, then I think you should simply revise your judgement that it is impermissible to push the fat man. Should you ever be confronted with a case like that, then you should tell yourself, 'I should overcome my irrational repugnance, and push him.'*

DANIEL KAHNEMAN: I find that unconvincing. My intuitions about abstract theories like consequentialism that tell you always to pursue the greater good are just weaker than my intuitive judgements about cases. To me, consequentialism is just a story, and a pretty good story at that, even though it has some holes in it, but it doesn't have the power of our intuitions about particularly compelling cases.

ALEX VOORHOEVE: *You believe, however, that we can sometimes be motivated to abandon our initial intuitions if we come to believe they are generated by morally irrelevant factors, as in the grocery store cases, or if we realize that they result from insufficient consideration of relevant information, as in the business fraud versus bodily harm cases and the accident insurance cases. So you believe we have the ability to revise our intuitive case judgements in the process of searching for reflective equilibrium, at least in certain cases. Why don't you think that can happen in this case?*

DANIEL KAHNEMAN: I don't dispute that reflective equilibrium is something we must strive to achieve. But we start the search for reflective equilibrium from a position in which our basic intuitions appear inconsistent. That is to say, we start out with strong, basic intuitions, which are accompanied by powerful emotional reactions, and which strike us as self-evidently correct, so that we think that we can generalize fairly naturally from them. However, we find that when we generalize from our intuitions we hit a point where other intuitions, naturally generalized, will lead us to contrary conclusions. This is true in many areas, including judgements of probability and non-moral decision-making. So what we do then is construct systems that ultimately suppress some of these contradictory intuitions and build mostly on others. My expectation is that there is no uniquely reasonable way to do this, and that rhetoric, reigning cultural habits, and so on are going to play very important roles in determining how we do this. Part of the rhetorical success of a system stems from its ability to sustain the conviction that comes from some of the basic intuitions and to generalize from those intuitions whilst drawing people's attention away from conflicting intuitions. For example, the motivational force of the consequentialist story depends heavily on the rhetoric you use to back it up and on the ability to anchor yourself in some intuitions and draw on the emotional and motivational powers of those intuitions, while keeping your mind away from other intuitions. And some consequentialists, like Peter Singer, are very good at this. But it is clear to me that you can start with one set of intuitions or with another set, and that depending on where you start and on the rhetoric you employ, you are going to end up in a different place. In some sense, this makes the enterprise unending, because there is no unique solution. So, given that we have powerful but profoundly inconsistent intuitions, and given that there appears to be no uniquely compelling way to resolve the inconsistencies, I am sceptical about the hope of achieving a unique and fully satisfactory reflective equilibrium.

ALEX VOORHOEVE: *Are you saying that if we are clear-headed enough to see that there is no uniquely compelling and coherent system of moral thought, we will not be sufficiently confident about the rightness of our more general principles to override strong intuitions that are inconsistent with those general principles? Is that why you could not see yourself as ready to revise your intuitive judgement that pushing the fat man is impermissible in the light of a general principle that it is always better to act in a way that kills one and saves five?*

DANIEL KAHNEMAN: Obviously, I am quite aware that my position is not internally coherent. But I have a reason not to try to achieve coherence: I believe coherence is impossible. Some moral quandaries evoke intuitions that have the form of a sensible rule—the case where you turn the trolley onto a side-track is an instance. Other cases evoke intuitions that do not have the form of a sensible rule but that are easily abandoned when they conflict with sensible rules or with other intuitions. (The grocery store cases are of this kind.) Cases of a third kind, however, evoke powerful intuitions that do not suggest a sensible rule and that nevertheless do not yield to conflicting rules or intuitions. The fat man scenario is a prime example. I do not believe a sensible rule is generating the intuition that one shouldn't push the fat man, nor do I believe one could be invented to justify it; nonetheless, I find pushing the fat man deeply repugnant. Because of this third class of cases, our basic intuitions are likely to contain contradictions that cannot be resolved. I believe that the search for coherence is admirable, and that it should be diligently pursued. But I also believe it is important to remember that it will inevitably fail.

References and further reading

For an overview of Daniel Kahneman's work, see his Nobel Prize Lecture, 'A Perspective on Judgement and Choice: Mapping Bounded Rationality', *American Psychologist* 58 (2003): 697–720. His autobiography is published online at <http://nobelprize.org/nobel_prizes/ economics/laureates/2002/kahnemanautobio.html>. The quotation by Stephen Jay Gould is from *Bully for Brontosaurus: Reflections in Natural History* (New York: Norton, 1991): 469. The brain imaging research mentioned is reported in Benedetto De Martino, Dharshan Kumaran, Ben Seymour, and Ray Dolan, 'Frames, Biases and Rational Decision-making in the Human Brain', *Science* 313 (2006): 684–7.

The method of reflective equilibrium in moral theory was first proposed in John Rawls, *A Theory of Justice* (Oxford: Oxford University Press, 2nd edn 1999), sect. 4. See also Norman Daniels, 'Reflective Equilibrium', in *The Stanford Encyclopaedia of Philosophy Online* (2003).

The research on poignancy as a determinant of compensation is reported in Dale Miller and Cathy McFarland, 'Counterfactual Thinking and Victim Compensation: A Test of Norm Theory', *Personality and Social Psychology Bulletin* 12 (1986): 513–19. For a discussion of the ways in which we construct erroneous *post hoc* justifications for our intuitive judgements, see Jonathan Haidt, 'The Emotional Dog and Its Rational Tail: A Social Intuitionist Approach to Moral Judgement', *Psychological Review* 108 (2001): 814–34. The study on intuitions about punishment to which Kahneman refers is Cass Sunstein, Daniel Kahneman, David Schkade, and Ilana Ritov, 'Predictably Incoherent Judgements', *Stanford Law Review* 54 (2001/2): 1153–215. For other discussions of moral heuristics see Daniel Kahneman, Jack Knetsch, and Richard Thaler, 'Fairness as a Constraint on Profit-seeking: Entitlements in the Market', *American Economic Review* 76 (1986): 728–41, Kahneman's Tanner Lecture on Human Values, 'The Cognitive Psychology of Consequences and Moral Intuition' (unpubl. ms, 1994), Tamara Horowitz, 'Philosophical Intuitions and Psychological Theory', *Ethics* 108 (1998): 367–85, Frances Kamm, 'Moral Intuitions, Cognitive Psychology, and the Harming/Not-Aiding Distinction', in *Intricate Ethics* (Oxford: Oxford University Press, 2006): 422–49, and Cass Sunstein, 'Moral Heuristics', *Behavioural and Brain Sciences* 28 (2005): 531–73. The ways that people respond to trolley cases are reported in Marc Hauser, *Moral Minds* (New York: HarperCollins, 2006): ch. 3.

II

VIRTUE AND FLOURISHING

4
PHILIPPA FOOT

THE GRAMMAR OF GOODNESS

Philippa Foot was born in 1920 and was educated mainly at home before going to Somerville College, Oxford in 1939 to study Politics, Philosophy, and Economics. She graduated in 1942 and worked as a government economist during the remainder of the Second World War, before returning to Somerville to take her M.A. In 1949, she became a Fellow of the college. In the 1960s and 1970s, she was an itinerant philosopher, holding visiting professorships at Cornell, MIT, UCLA, Berkeley, and the City University of New York, before settling at UCLA in 1976. She is now an Honorary Fellow of Somerville.

At the start of our conversation, Foot reflects on how she would characterize herself as a philosopher. 'I'm not clever at all,' she remarks. 'I'm a dreadfully slow thinker, really. But I do have a good nose for what is important. And even though the best philosophers combine cleverness and depth, I'd prefer a good nose over cleverness any day!'

Foot describes her career as one of slow progress in developing a distinctive line of thought on two questions: the nature of moral judgement and the rationality of acting morally. At first, the position she opposed was moral subjectivism: the idea that moral judgements merely express a person's evaluative attitudes and intentions to act, and that knowledge of the facts about a particular case is not sufficient for moral judgement, but that people must also place a value on these facts. Radical subjectivism holds that nothing about the facts of the case under consideration constrains people in this evaluative judgement. In her first articles, later collected in *Virtues and Vices*, Foot took issue with this 'free-for-all' version of subjectivism. The rules of moral discourse, she argued, required that only things relating to human good and harm could count as moral considerations. She further undermined the subjectivist distinction between facts and values, or 'description' and 'evaluation', by drawing attention to moral concepts like temperance and courage, which, she claimed, do not allow for a separation of descriptive and evaluative elements in moral judgement. For, Foot argued, these concepts are evaluative, but have a necessary connection both with facts about human good and harm and with the presence of a particular set of factual circumstances and dispositions of the will. The virtue of courage, for example, exists because people may find themselves in circumstances where they have to resist giving in to their fears. Courage thus requires constancy in the pursuit of a good aim in the face of knowledge of threats or risks. Prompted by the thought that virtues like courage provided a way towards a more objective view of moral requirements, Foot gradually became convinced that sound moral philosophy should start from a theory of the virtues and vices.

The question of the rationality of acting as morality requires has also dogged Foot throughout her career. The issue is key to any theory of morality, since, as David Hume stressed, morality is necessarily practical, serving to produce and prevent action. At first, Foot argued that everyone has reason to cultivate at least the virtues of temperance, courage, and wisdom, since their possession is advantageous whatever one's interests and desires. In later work, she took a different tack, arguing that just as one can recognize the requirements of etiquette and have no reason to adhere to them, one could recognize moral norms and have no reason to act as they require. In her latest work, *Natural Goodness*, Foot once again formulates a new answer to this question, arguing that recognizing and acting on certain reasons, among which are moral reasons, is simply part of practical rationality. If she is right, the question of the rationality of acting morally simply cannot arise, since it is akin to asking, 'Why should one do what it is rational to do?', and this is, as she puts it, 'to ask for a reason where reasons must *a priori* come to an end'.

In addition to her work on these foundational questions, Foot has written widely acclaimed pieces in medical ethics, some of which are reprinted in her collection *Moral Dilemmas*. Aside from a style which is both straightforward and elegant, what unifies her work is an awareness of the ways that the terms in which we think about moral questions in the course of our philosophical debates can lead us astray. Foot is wary of assuming that questions commonly raised in philosophical discourse, such as 'How good is this state of affairs?' or 'Why should I do what is right and good?', make any sense. In a manner reminiscent of Ludwig Wittgenstein's approach in his *Philosophical Investigations*, Foot tries to break the spell of certain ways of thinking in moral philosophy by bringing terms such as 'a good state of affairs' back from an abstract sphere of moral evaluation to their everyday use in a characterization of the kinds of things a benevolent person should want. It is in this project, too, that Foot believes that thinking in terms of virtues and vices can help.

All three of Foot's principal concerns — subjectivism, the rationality of acting morally, and the need to be wary of the terms in which we express ourselves when we are doing moral philosophy — come together in *Natural Goodness*. In this book, Foot isolates a form of evaluation that belongs only to living things and argues that moral judgement belongs to this form of evaluation. I speak with her about this idea at her home in Oxford in September 2002.

While we are chatting over coffee, she brings up a remark Wittgenstein once made to a speaker who realized that what he was about to say was both compelling and clearly ridiculous.

ɷ

PHILIPPA FOOT: Wittgenstein said to this man, who was trying to say something sensible instead: 'Say what you want to say! Be crude, and then we shall get on.' I open my book with this remark, since I have found it excellent advice. Whenever I find myself tempted to pass over an odd thought, I press myself to do the opposite. So I'd say, 'Stick with the odd thought, it's gold.'

ALEX VOORHOEVE: *How do you mean, 'It's gold'?*

PHILIPPA FOOT: I am sure an analogy will help, though one must always be careful of analogies. If you are working with a therapist, and you find yourself about to say something disreputable, the last thing you should do is substitute something respectable for it. It is the same with our philosophical thinking: the philosophical interest is where the *trouble* is. And that is why we must focus on the odd or crude thought which we are tempted to have. At the beginning of *Natural Goodness*, I give the example of being puzzled by the expression 'If I were you'. I remember someone saying to me when I was a child, 'I'd take my medicine if I were you!', and thinking, 'No you wouldn't, for I am not going to take it!' I later realized that my puzzlement at this expression was in effect a philosophical problem.

By contrast, we don't have a philosophical difficulty when I ask you, 'Do you take your coffee black?,' and one would have to think quite hard to find a difficulty in this. One *might* be able to . . . if one had a funny picture that one consults a little book in one's head to see what one would like, *then* one would be off into the philosophy of mind.

Perhaps it is because of this peculiar nature of philosophical questions that philosophy is very difficult to explain to non-philosophers. You know, someone once said, 'One lesson in philosophy is as much good as one lesson in piano-playing,' and I think that's right!

ALEX VOORHOEVE: *How did you become interested in philosophy, and how did you come to study it?*

PHILIPPA FOOT: I had no formal education as a child. I lived in the sort of milieu where there was a lot of hunting, shooting, and fishing, and where girls simply did not go to college. But one of my governesses, who herself had a degree, said, 'You could go to university, you know.' And so I decided to work for it. I was extremely ignorant, which is not surprising because most governesses weren't highly educated, even though they were supposed to be able to teach you everything! Anyway, I took some correspondence courses and to my surprise was accepted by Somerville. I had put in for Somerville because I had heard that it was a college that was intellectually but not socially snobby, and I was working my way out of this socially snobby background. I decided to do the course in Politics, Philosophy, and Economics because I wanted to do something theoretical. I couldn't do mathematics, by lack of education and talent. So I thought economics and philosophy would be the theoretical subjects I could do.

ALEX VOORHOEVE: *Why did you focus on moral philosophy?*

PHILIPPA FOOT: I was always interested in philosophy. But it was significant that the news of the concentration camps hit us just when I came back to Oxford in 1945. This news was shattering in a fashion that no one now can easily understand. We had thought that something like this could not happen. This is what got me interested in moral philosophy in particular. In a way, I was always more interested in the philosophy of mind, and I still am very interested in it. But in the face of the news of the concentration camps, I thought, 'It just can't be the way Stevenson, Ayer, and Hare say it is, that morality is just the expression of an attitude,' and the subject haunted me.

ALEX VOORHOEVE: *What was it about the idea that morality is simply the expression of an attitude that seemed to you so wrong in the face of the Holocaust?*

PHILIPPA FOOT: What these theorists tried to do was construe the conditions of use of sentences like 'It is morally wrong to kill innocent people' in terms of a speaker's feelings or attitudes, or of his or her commitment to acting in a certain way. And this meant that, according to these theories, there is a gap between the facts or grounds for a moral judgement and that judgement itself. For whatever reasons might be given for a moral judgement, people might without error refuse to assent to it, not finding in themselves the relevant feelings or attitudes. And this is what I thought was wrong. For, fundamentally, there is no way, if one takes this line, that one could imagine oneself saying to a Nazi, 'But we are *right*, and you are *wrong*', with there being any substance to the statement. Faced with the Nazis, who felt they had been justified in doing what they did, there would simply be a stand-off. And I thought, 'Morality just cannot be subjective in the way that different attitudes, like some aesthetic ones, or likes and dislikes, are subjective.' The separation of descriptions from attitudes, or facts from values, that characterized the current moral philosophy had to be bad philosophy.

ALEX VOORHOEVE: *Before we turn to your response to subjectivism, I would like to dwell a bit longer on your early influences in moral philosophy. When one reads your work, one clearly sees the influence of Elisabeth Anscombe and Wittgenstein. How would you say they have influenced your work?*

PHILIPPA FOOT: Anscombe, above all, influenced me. My excellent tutor, Donald MacKinnon, was more of a theologian than a philosopher, really. He taught me about Hegelian philosophy. And about Kant, which was wonderful. But MacKinnon didn't really believe in modern, analytic philosophy. So it took Anscombe to get me to see the good in that. She was a difficult character, not quite the person to be a college tutor and help all the undergraduates through their exams. So she was hard to fit into the Oxford setup. But, happily, Somerville saw her merits. They thought she was marvellous, and found one research fellowship after another for her, not wanting to let her go. This was marvellous for me because it was natural for us to talk together day after day. After lunch in college, we would sit down and talk philosophy. She would propound some topic, and, although she hardly ever agreed with what I said, she was always willing to consider my objections, and to wonder why I had made them. At one crucial moment, I remember describing some sentence as having a mix of descriptive and evaluative meaning. And she said, 'Of what? What?' And I thought, 'My God, so one doesn't have to accept that distinction!'

So, you see, my position was incredibly privileged because Anscombe is one of the very best philosophers of our time. And moreover, she must have been putting to me the problems that Wittgenstein had put to her; she must have had discussions with Wittgenstein on topics like the ones that I was discussing with her. She didn't talk about Wittgenstein, but she was teaching me something of his way of thinking. I am sure she didn't think of herself as teaching me, but that's what was going on. She would often come to my seminars, and I would always attend hers, where I usually opposed nearly everything she said. Naturally, I was regularly defeated. But I would be there, objecting away, the next week. It was like in those old children's comics where a steamroller runs over a character who becomes flattened — an outline on the ground — but the character is there in the next episode, unscathed. I was like one of those characters.

This went on for about five years, I think. Then Norman Malcolm gave a talk which got me interested in Wittgenstein's *Philosophical Investigations*. So I began reading it, I mean *really* reading it, and I said to Anscombe, 'Why didn't you tell me?' And she said, 'Because it is very important to have one's resistances.' She thought that it was very important *not* to accept what Wittgenstein wrote, but rather to try everything against it. She would not have liked it if I had too easily agreed with anything that she said, either. On a personal level, we were friends of course. She was, as you know, more rigorously Catholic than the Pope, while I am a card-carrying atheist, so we didn't agree on ideological grounds at all. But we had these marvellous discussions, and her children used to visit me quite often.

ALEX VOORHOEVE: *You approach moral philosophy by focusing on the virtues. What attracted you to this way of doing moral philosophy?*

PHILIPPA FOOT: I believe that it was reading Aquinas that got me started. I was on leave, and Anscombe had said, 'I think you ought to read Aquinas.' I got interested in the second part of the *Summa Theologiae*, which is about particular virtues and vices. And it struck me that there were always good reasons for saying of something that it was a virtue or a vice. I recall reading the bit where Aquinas calls loquacity a vice, and thinking, 'What an extraordinary idea!' But if you take seriously a particular question about a particular virtue, you see that it isn't just subjective, that you can't say anything you like. There must be a *reason* why this is a vice, if indeed it is a vice. I put this question to a pupil of mine—'Why on earth should loquacity be a vice?'—and she said, 'Well, if one is always talking, one doesn't have time to think.' This wasn't Aquinas's reason, but it seemed right to me. I repeated what she had said in a lecture; and a young man caught me on the way out and said, 'But perhaps *my girlfriend* doesn't need to think.' (This was a long time ago, you know.) And I said, straight out, '*Everybody* needs to think!'

That kind of approach is the key to all my work right down to the writing of *Natural Goodness*. One doesn't just have to say, 'There *must* be grounds for moral judgements.' For it was obvious in the case of individual virtues and vices that one could ask *what grounds there were*. One could ask, for instance, 'Is there a virtue of chastity, and, if so, what might the grounds for it be?' And with this, the whole subject of moral philosophy thickened up in my mind. Before that, I had simply thought, 'There *must* be objective grounds for moral judgement,' without being able to say much except that they would have to be connected to human welfare or something like that. But looking in detail, as Aquinas made me do, made me see that a virtue/vice point of view provided an excellent way to make an idea of objectivity in moral judgement concrete. A proposition such as 'This act is wrong' didn't lead one on to particular reasons or judgements in the way 'Loquacity is a vice' did.

However, after this discovery, I still didn't have the general conception of goodness as pertaining to the capacities, dispositions, and actions that are necessary for a particular way of life, which forms such an important part of my arguments about the grounds of moral requirements in *Natural Goodness*. For a long time, I couldn't find such a general basis for morality, and I was too lazy to write more than a few articles with my inconclusive thoughts. So I went on to medical ethics, which was very much in demand. I didn't despise the subject, but I left it as soon as I could see how to approach the foundational questions that I address in *Natural Goodness*. That wasn't until the mid-1980s. And it took me a long time after that to get around to publishing the book. At the launch of *Natural Goodness*, my editor, Peter Momtchiloff, picked up on the line from Wittgenstein with which I open the book — the one that says that it is difficult to do philosophy as slowly as it should be done — and he said, 'Well, that is a problem that Philippa seems to have solved.'

So that was the progression of my thought: from thinking that subjectivism must be wrong to thinking that when we look at the individual virtues and vices we can actually begin to see an objective basis for particular moral judgements, and on from there.

ALEX VOORHOEVE: *You didn't see this basis for morality in other foundational concepts used in contemporary moral philosophy, like the ideas of 'good states of affairs' or rights and obligations?*

PHILIPPA FOOT: Exactly. You see, all I could do at first was to reject subjectivism and insist that somehow there was objectivity in moral judgement, and that it had something to do with human welfare, without sinking into utilitarianism. But I couldn't get my feet on the ground with concepts like 'the best state of affairs' or 'good' in the abstract, whereas concepts like virtues and vices made sense to me. I realized, however, that to really answer those who had a different theory of morality, I needed a whole alternative theory of moral judgement.

ALEX VOORHOEVE: *So where did you find this alternative?*

PHILIPPA FOOT: I found a new beginning by thinking about plants and animals. Not that I thought that you could argue from 'Such and such is important to animals' to 'Such and such is important.' Rather, I was saying, 'Look, there is a particular logical category here.' I had an absolutely excellent graduate student at UCLA, Michael Thompson, who is now at Pittsburgh. He had been influenced by Anscombe, even at a distance, because he had very good taste in philosophy. He had this super idea, which he had picked up from her writing, about the proposition 'Humans have 32 teeth.' Very few humans actually have 32 teeth. So what is the logical status of this proposition? It is not that it says, 'All people have 32 teeth.' It doesn't even state, 'Most people have 32 teeth.' Nor does it mean merely, 'Some people have 32 teeth.' So if you think of quantification, you see that it simply doesn't fit the logical categories that we have. It is of a different logical status from propositions like 'Gardens have railings.' Michael Thompson realized that there is a logical peculiarity to the way we talk about living things, and we both started thinking about this special way in which we can talk about them. That is what got my latest work going.

ALEX VOORHOEVE: *You write that this special way of talking reveals itself in our judgements about plants and non-human animals when we think about the way we judge particular members of a species to be either defective or as they should be. You argue that two things enable us to make such judgements about plants and non-human animals: firstly, a set of propositions describing the life-cycle of the species, with particular focus in the case of plants and animals on growth, self-maintenance, and reproduction; and secondly, a set of propositions saying how, for the species under consideration, these things are achieved: how nourishment is obtained, how it defends itself, how development takes place, and how* *reproduction is secured. From these two kinds of propositions, you claim, we can derive norms for individual members of the species. These norms state that the key functions should be carried out by the means specified.*

I'd like to question a few elements of what you call this 'grammar of natural normativity', starting with the idea of certain capacities or characteristics being necessary for the way of life of a certain species. What kind of necessity do you have in mind here? For in the case of teeth, for example, it is not necessary for our way of life, not even of any great consequence, if we do not have a full set of teeth. And yet, this was Anscombe's original example.

PHILIPPA FOOT: Well, it is an imperfection if you have fewer than 32 teeth, since it is typically when the tooth gets knocked out, or gets rotten, that one loses it; so there is still a tie-in with health and disease and accident, even though it isn't always a problem, since one can chew one's food with fewer teeth. I admit that the original example of teeth is not the best one. But I have a different example. Compare the colour in the tail of a peacock with that of a bird I have in my garden, the blue tit. Now, the colour in the tail of the male peacock is necessary: it needs it to get its mate. On the other hand, as far as I know, the little patch of blue in the tail of the blue tit has no such role in the life of that bird. So if it lacked it, it would be an oddity, a rarity, but not a defect.

ALEX VOORHOEVE: *Does the concept of necessity you are using depend on the particular circumstances in which the species in question finds itself? Would one say that in humans a lack of natural teeth used to be a defect, but that it has ceased to be one because of the availability of false teeth?*

PHILIPPA FOOT: I think that there is a certain amount of play here. It isn't easy to draw the line, for one occasion doesn't change what counts as a defect in a member of a species. Certainly, things change all the time. Now that foxes are becoming urban creatures, they need different things, speed being, for example, less important because food can be obtained without it. But this doesn't mean that you can narrow down the reference situation for an attribution of natural goodness as much as you might like. For example, the characteristics animals need in a zoo may actually be defects. For it might be useful for a predatory animal kept in a zoo to lack fierceness. So one must realize that the conditions one can use must not be too limited. And after all, it is only a very small proportion of the human race that has false teeth and a very small proportion of predatory animals that live in zoos, which are not their natural habitat.

ALEX VOORHOEVE: *Why should we look only at the way of life of a species? Why not of a group, or troupe, or herd, a society, a family, or an individual? What privileges the species in the account of natural normativity?*

PHILIPPA FOOT: In the case of urban foxes, one might come up with different necessities than one would for their non-urban counterparts. But it doesn't really matter where precisely this kind of grammar begins to lose its grip, as long as it is recognized as a general category of judgements about goodness.

ALEX VOORHOEVE: *Still, focusing on the species for the derivation of natural norms seems particularly odd in the case of human beings. For you derive natural norms from the fact that certain things are necessary for a way of life. But in humans, the phrase 'way of life' is often used not to refer to the species as a whole, but rather to refer to a society or group with a shared set of institutions, practices, and outlook.*

PHILIPPA FOOT: Again, perhaps there are no strict boundaries here. This is not of very great importance. Some things are species-wide in our way of life. All human beings, for example, need courage to face danger, challenges, and loss. There are many things that all humans need, though some amount of relativity does emerge from different ways of life in different times and places and different social, economic, and cultural circumstances. I think it is one of the advantages of this approach that it doesn't have to claim that all moral norms are the same for all human beings. But we mustn't lose sight of the fact that there are many things that are absolutely basic human needs.

ALEX VOORHOEVE: *You mentioned moral norms. How is this kind of natural goodness related to moral goodness?*

PHILIPPA FOOT: Starting again from plants and animals, we see that all kinds of things are necessary for them in their normal way of life, such as certain kinds of roots for certain kinds of trees or good night vision for an owl. Now, humans have an entirely different range of activities and capacities that are part of their way of life. A corresponding different set of defects is possible, most obviously those defects relating to specific human capacities such as language, imagination, and the will. Human beings can know, for example, that certain things are bad for them. And while animals that liked alcohol and that were supplied with enough of it would probably drink themselves to death, humans can realize its effects and may control their urge for it. Thus, humans need and can develop the virtue of temperance, whereas an animal cannot. But where have I moved on to something grammatically different in this progression? Why make *that* kind of distinction between the way temperance is needed by a human being and swiftness is needed by a deer?

ALEX VOORHOEVE: *So you would say that moral goodness and badness, the virtues and vices, are a subclass of the general class of ascriptions of natural goodness and badness?*

PHILIPPA FOOT: Exactly. The move from plants to animals and the move from animals to human beings are similar. You have different possibilities, different ways of managing, different needs, and there is not the slightest ground for saying, 'Oh, *moral* goodness — now that must be something we judge quite differently.' It is very important, of course, that the subset of the class of ascriptions of natural goodness in human beings that we call 'moral' has to do with the goodness of the will and with practical rationality. Virtues, after all, are intelligent dispositions to take certain things as reasons for action, and vices are defects of the will. Note, however, that I am not too keen on the word 'moral' to mark out this subclass, since it has a certain association with concern for others that separates out things that I should like to bring together. For example, the defect of not looking after oneself, which usually isn't thought of as a moral defect, is equally a defect of the will.

ALEX VOORHOEVE: *How does this way of thinking help us to determine what morality and justice require of us? The virtue of justice requires that we respect others' rights. But it is a disputed question just what these rights are.*

PHILIPPA FOOT: I must admit that I have never thought as much as I should about issues in political philosophy. But I suppose that I would proceed in a way similar to Anscombe in her work on promises, when she stresses how important a practice of promise-keeping is for us to be able to bind one another's will. I don't see any reason why a right, which is a very strong claim — a stronger claim than 'You should help me!' — should not be argued for in the same way, that is, with reference to the good that hangs on it. I mean, society simply depends on certain requirements being strict requirements, like not killing someone and taking their tools. By contrast, one couldn't say, 'You don't have the right to annoy me!' and be taken seriously. Not being annoyed is simply not that important in human life.

ALEX VOORHOEVE: *So in determining which rights we have, you would appeal to the kinds of necessities that exist either for individuals or for society?*

PHILIPPA FOOT: Exactly. I have no doubt that this is the basis of moral requirements.

ALEX VOORHOEVE: *These necessities have changed throughout human history, and they are set to change even more. What does this mean for the category of natural goodness?*

PHILIPPA FOOT: I think I would be very permissive here. Where human beings have changed their environment so that things that were once a defect are now useful, different standards might apply. Of course, a change in what counts as a virtue is only natural when people's way of life changes. It is a good thing to be relativistic on this point. But I stress that, taken as a whole, the approach is radically non-relativistic because there is so much that human beings quite generally need, like courage, temperance, and wisdom. Of course, there are great technological differences between tribal cultures of the world and the modern culture of the 'developed' nations. Yet there is still so much in common between human beings in different cultures, and it is because of this that the idea that there is a universal need for certain character traits and for certain rules of conduct is a strong one.

ALEX VOORHOEVE: *I would like to turn to the topic of practical rationality . . .*

PHILIPPA FOOT: Oh good! Can I tell you why I had to deal with the topic of rationality in *Natural Goodness*? It was part of my attack on the subjectivism that identified moral propositions as expressing some subjective state of mind. In opposition to subjectivism, I argue that moral propositions are about the natural goodness of a human will. And I was open to attack on the ground that I couldn't give a proper account of why anyone should have reason to follow morality. Why? Because subjectivists had the idea that only if you had particular feelings or desires could you have reasons for acting. I myself used to have this view of reasons, and in a notorious article called 'Is Morality a System of Hypothetical Imperatives?' I was brash enough to say that reasons were desire-dependent. As a consequence, I had to explain how one could have reason to do good actions and avoid bad ones, whatever one's aims or desires.

So I needed a better account of what it is to have reasons, and at this point in time I was lucky enough to work with my friend, the late Warren Quinn. He made what I think was an absolutely brilliant suggestion, though perhaps neither he nor others at the time saw the force of it. His move was to ask, 'What would be so *important* about practical rationality if it could be rational to do despicable actions?' Now, this thought was extraordinarily original. For it has been more or less taken for granted in modern moral philosophy that one must first develop a theory of practical rationality in terms of, say, the maximum satisfaction of desires, and then somehow show that even the greatest self-sacrifice could be rational. And no one, not even the cleverest, could do it. But Quinn's remark suggested that one shouldn't tackle it like that at all. One shouldn't think that morality must pass the test of rationality, but rather that rationality must pass the test of morality.

ALEX VOORHOEVE: *The answer to Quinn's question would seem to be that a more limited conception of rationality relating to the consistent pursuit of things a person cares about can easily be shown to be important to that person, since it involves the pursuit of ends that are hers.*

PHILIPPA FOOT: Why would you think that the only way of justifying the claim that it would be rational for a person to do something should make reference to her own desires? If you look closely at the theory of rationality as the maximum satisfaction of your most important desires, you immediately get into a whole series of problems. Is it only present desires that we are concerned with? What of something that you don't want now, but you know that you will want in twenty years' time? Is it irrational to discount the future?

ALEX VOORHOEVE: *Well, all these things still have some connection to what are, or will be, the projects of the person concerned, whereas the pursuit of goodness may not. In your earlier work, you mention the case of the 'cool calculating man', who cares nothing for morality, neither now nor in the future. What good does it do to call this man irrational?*

PHILIPPA FOOT: You are right that 'irrational' may not be exactly the word one would choose to describe him. Nevertheless, he *is* defective — he is failing to recognize and act on something that is a reason. I am curious, though, about your own position. I wonder what *you* would say about a young person who says, 'I don't care about the chance of getting lung cancer due to smoking in twenty years' time.' First, do you call this contrary to practical rationality?

ALEX VOORHOEVE: *Well, it would depend on what this person's attitudes towards the future were, and whether his actions consistently expressed this indifference towards his future.*

PHILIPPA FOOT: What if this young person cares about being well dressed at 40, but not about his health at 40?

ALEX VOORHOEVE: *Although he is being consistent, I might want to say that he is not recognizing something that he should recognize.*

PHILIPPA FOOT: Ah. And where do you get that 'should' from?

ALEX VOORHOEVE: *[pauses] Well, I guess from some idea of normalcy, that it would be normal to care about this . . .*

PHILIPPA FOOT: Normalcy?

ALEX VOORHOEVE: *Perhaps you are right that normalcy isn't the right concept here, since it may be uncommon to care only about living stylishly, but it could still be something someone can rationally pursue . . .*

PHILIPPA FOOT: So I take it that you are conflicted about whether such attitudes and behaviour are indeed irrational?

ALEX VOORHOEVE: *I guess so.*

PHILIPPA FOOT: The problem is — and this is really crucial in this argument — that it is very difficult for someone to deny that it is contrary to rationality not to care about one's future health to the degree that one doesn't when one starts to smoke. For it is difficult to deny that prudence is part of rationality. But then it is very hard to find a basis for our concept of practical rationality that makes prudence a part of rationality and that doesn't make justice or charity a part of rationality. That is what someone in your position has to do. Either you have to accept that it isn't contrary to rationality to imprudently ignore one's future well-being, or you have to accept some conception of practical rationality that makes reference to things other than what one cares about. And I think that you definitely want to say of the young smoker that he is defective with regard to the standards of practical rationality. After all, he is being silly!

ALEX VOORHOEVE: *And 'silly' is a word that points to a defect?*

PHILIPPA FOOT: Absolutely. So this is my challenge: it is going to be difficult for you to find a ground for saying that imprudence is a vice, a defect, but that lack of charity or injustice isn't. Here I think there is something useful in *Natural Goodness*. Because if you treat a defect in the way that it is treated there, they come together. They are different parts of what human beings need.

ALEX VOORHOEVE: *Still, one would say different things to someone who is not acting on reasons for action that he himself accepts than one would say to someone who isn't recognizing something as a reason that you believe he should recognize as such. In the first case, we are concerned with a defect in the way he pursues means to his given ends, while in the second case, we are concerned with his ends. What is the conception of practical rationality that brings together these disparate notions?*

PHILIPPA FOOT: I argue that thinking in terms of natural goodness provides this unity. Both the taking of means to ends in an efficient way and the recognition of relevant reasons are things needed in human life, and a defect in either of these is a defect in practical rationality.

ALEX VOORHOEVE: *In* Virtues and Vices *you write: 'Wise men know the means to ends and know what these ends are worth.' Are practical rationality and wisdom the same?*

PHILIPPA FOOT: Yes. They are absolutely the same. Take someone who says, 'The most important thing in life is to be fashionable.' If you think of the way someone would spend his life if he believed this, of the sort of friends he would have and the celebrities he would try to emulate, well . . . one would have to look into that. I haven't been able to explore this very far, but I think that the question of what is deep and superficial has to come in here. I certainly don't claim to have dealt adequately with this notion of the depth of one's happiness, but it does seem to me that one understands when someone on his deathbed says, 'I have wasted so much of my life on things that didn't matter!' And the idea of being defective in recognizing the weight of reasons seems appropriate here.

ALEX VOORHOEVE: *I feel a resistance to this way of thinking about practical rationality because it seems like preaching—saying to people, 'Such and such is really important, and if you don't see this then you are defective.'*

PHILIPPA FOOT: It *is* preaching! There is good preaching and there is bad preaching. I think a preacher who is worth his salt would be right to say to a fashionable congregation that they are living a very superficial life (though he had better not say it in an offensive way and, in fact, should probably not *say* it at all!). But he might think that they were old enough to know better, being grownups, not teenagers.

ALEX VOORHOEVE: *Still, before you can preach, you must have an idea of the good life for human beings. Aristotle and Aquinas had their own fully developed accounts of what a complete and fulfilled human life was like and could derive from these accounts the reason human beings have to live in a certain way and cultivate the virtues. In Aristotle's and Aquinas's accounts, the virtues would be conducive to and constitutive of a person's well-being, even if he did not see it this way. But we do not share their views of the one correct goal in life. Do you have an alternative account of how a person should live?*

PHILIPPA FOOT: The idea of the 'good' for humans is indeed a difficult one. I think that we can get a handle on the problem by looking at human deprivation. One serious challenge to my view lies, I think, in the idea that happiness is Man's good, and that happiness may be achieved in the pursuit of evil. Now, happiness is a protean concept. But what I want to suggest is that we have *a* conception of happiness (among different possible conceptions) in which it is *the enjoyment of good things*, with 'good things' defined as objects of a good — an innocent — will; and that we have to understand it in that way when we say, 'Happiness is Man's good.' I think that we can approach this concept of happiness indirectly via our idea of what it is to benefit someone. Consider the murderous child abusers Frederick and Rosemary West, and ask what we should say of someone who had made it possible for them to continue getting their horrible pleasures. Should we say that this person had *benefited* the Wests? Surely not!

ALEX VOORHOEVE: *How does one use the notion of benefit as a way into an idea of happiness?*

PHILIPPA FOOT: Benefiting someone means doing something that is for his or her good. If I am right, then the concept of benefiting someone reveals a way of thinking about the human good that excludes the pursuit of evil things, as is shown by my observation of what we should say about prolonging the pleasures of the Wests. But then the concept of happiness that one finds in the expression 'Happiness is Man's good' must also exclude the pursuit of evil. So considering the notion of benefiting someone offers us a glimpse of a way that we have of thinking about happiness that involves goodness.

ALEX VOORHOEVE: *On the final page of* Natural Goodness, *you consider what your arguments mean for moral philosophy. Echoing Wittgenstein, you conclude that your philosophy 'leaves everything as it is'. Wittgenstein, however, was referring to philosophical analysis leaving our everyday activities as they are and wouldn't have thought that our philosophizing could go on as before. So this seems a curious answer to the question about where your approach leaves moral philosophy.*

PHILIPPA FOOT: I was only talking about certain parts of moral philosophy, such as medical ethics, when I said that I would not expect disturbance. Perhaps rashly, I do hope that my approach might — just might — affect the way moral philosophy is done. For my approach is different from that of most contemporary moral philosophers. I do not start with moral judgement, asking directly, 'What is morality?' or 'What is moral goodness?' Rather, drawing on the work of Anscombe and Thompson, I make a general, grammatical point about the evaluation of living things and their parts and features in terms of what I call 'natural goodness and defect', and then suggest that moral judgement is just one case of this kind of evaluation. This is what I think is new, at least to contemporary moral philosophy, and I hope that thinking about moral goodness and badness in this way offers the potential for a change in moral philosophy.

References and further reading

Philippa Foot's principal essays, including all those referred to in the interview, are collected in her *Virtues and Vices* (Oxford: Basil Blackwell, 1978) and *Moral Dilemmas* (Oxford: Oxford University Press, 2002).

Natural Goodness was published with Oxford University Press in 2001. David Hume remarks on the necessarily practical nature of morality in his *A Treatise of Human Nature*, ed. P. H. Nidditch (Oxford: Oxford University Press, 1978), book 3, part 1, sect. 1. The view that moral statements are merely expressions of an attitude is advanced in C. L. Stevenson, *Ethics and Language* (New Haven: Yale University Press, 1944), A. J. Ayer, 'Critique of Ethics and Theology', in *Language, Truth and Logic* (New York: Dover Publications, 1952), and R. M. Hare, *The Language of Morals* (Oxford: Clarendon Press, 1952). A popular edition of Ludwig Wittgenstein's *Philosophical Investigations* was published by Blackwell in 2001 (this edition has the original German and an English translation by G. E. M. Anscombe). Aquinas's *Summa Theologiae* is easily accessible online at <www.newadvent.org/summa>; a more recent, standard edition is the Latin text and English translation by the English Dominicans reissued by Cambridge University Press (2006).

Foot also refers to G. E. M. Anscombe, 'Rules, Rights, and Promises', in *Ethics, Religion and Politics* (Minneapolis: University of Minnesota Press, 1981), and Michael Thompson, 'The Representation of Life', in *Virtues and Reasons*, ed. Rosalind Hursthouse, Gavin Lawrence, and Warren Quinn (Oxford: Clarendon Press, 1995).

5
ALASDAIR MACINTYRE

Alasdair MacIntyre is known as both a radical critic of modernity and of modern moral philosophy, and an advocate of an account of ethics in the tradition of Aristotle and Aquinas. He was born in Glasgow in 1929 and began graduate study in philosophy in 1949 at Manchester University, where he became a lecturer two years later. In the decades that followed, MacIntyre worked in a wide range of areas, contributing to debates on Marxism and Christianity, the philosophy of social science, the philosophy of psychoanalysis, and the history of moral philosophy. He is best known for *After Virtue*, a striking and provocative analysis of the state of modern moral culture, which appeared in 1981. In this work, MacIntyre argued that the condition of contemporary moral discourse was one of interminable disagreement, in the sense that there seemed to be no rational way in which moral disputes could be resolved. What, he asked, could explain this state?

One answer was put forward in the 1930s and 1940s by the philosophers C. L. Stevenson and A. J. Ayer. Referred to as 'emotivists', they held that moral judgements express and are intended to arouse emotions, not beliefs. Saying that an act like lying is wrong was, they argued, akin to saying 'Boo to lying!', Moreover, emotivists held that there is a strict separation between factual judgements and moral value judgements. Factual judgements can be true or false, and in the realm of facts there are rational criteria by which we may come to agree which things are true or false. By contrast, emotivists held that moral value judgements, being mere expressions of attitudes or feelings, are not true or false; they also held that agreement in morals can only be achieved by whatever non-rational means one can use to get people's emotional responses in line. To illustrate: since a person's feelings about lying are not fully constrained by the facts, two people could agree on the facts in a case of lying but have different attitudes towards it. These people could then have different moral judgements about lying without either of them being in error. Moreover, there would seem to be no rational way by which they could come to share the same moral judgements.

MacIntyre came to believe, however, that emotivism cannot be right as an analysis of the meaning of our moral terms, because moral judgements make an appeal to impersonal authority in a way that pure expressions of emotion do not. Early in our conversation, MacIntyre puts his rejection of emotivism as follows:

> During my time as a graduate student, there was a lively debate over emotivism. And it occurred to me that there was something very peculiar about understanding moral language as the emotivists did. If you looked at the meaning of the sentences that we use to express moral judgements, it seemed odd to think of this kind of sentence as used to express attitudes or emotions. Sentences that express moral judgements are not at all like the kind of expressions that are characteristically used to express emotions. A judgement that lying is morally wrong, for example, appeals to impersonal considerations for its justification. In uttering such a judgement, you are appealing to reasons for not lying which are intended to guide action independently of your own particular preferences and position, and the preferences and position of your hearers.

By contrast, MacIntyre wrote in *After Virtue*, in the case of purely emotive utterances, such as 'Boo to lying!', whether you are giving the hearer a reason not to lie *does* depend on your and his position—for example, if you are his superior and are in a position to punish him if you catch him lying, then by expressing your disapproval of lying you may have given him a reason not to lie. But you have given him no reason independently of such facts about your respective positions.

It does not follow from these differences in meaning between moral judgements and emotive utterances, however, that sentences expressing moral judgements cannot be used in a purely emotive way. As MacIntyre puts it:

> Of course, any sentence can be used to express emotions or attitudes—think of Gilbert Ryle's example of the angry schoolmaster saying to the child, 'Seven times seven equals *forty-nine!*' This certainly expresses irritation, but nobody would suggest that mathematical sentences should be given an emotivist construal on this account.

With this distinction between a sentence's meaning and its use in mind, it occurred to MacIntyre that the emotivists were right about something: given the nature of contemporary moral discourse, people often use moral language merely to express their moral preferences or emotions rather than to argue rationally for their views:

> It did seem to me that there was a case for saying that moral sentences were *used* to express emotions, that they were *used* *as if* emotivism was true. When I looked at the culture around me, at the way in which moral discussion was carried on, the case for an emotivist account of *use*, rather than an emotivist account of *meaning*, seemed important. So here, then, was the anomaly: how was it that meaning and use were discrepant in this way for a particular class of sentences?

In *After Virtue*, MacIntyre offers, roughly, the following answer. Contemporary moral discourse is made up of fragments of various moral traditions. Different participants in the debate use concepts such as 'virtue', 'the good life for man', 'rights', 'good consequences', and 'moral law' in different and often incommensurable senses, drawing on different historical thinkers' formulations of these concepts. Moreover, these concepts are used in ways that divorce them from the body of theory and practice in which they were originally at home; cut loose in this way, it is unclear, MacIntyre suggests, what their sense is. Part of the reason that we cannot reach rational agreement on morals is, therefore, that we formulate our views using concepts that we do not fully understand.

MacIntyre traces the origins of this condition to the rejection during the Enlightenment of a broadly Aristotelian conception of morality. For Aristotle, human beings have a specific nature that determines their proper goal, or *telos*, in life. This goal, which Aristotle called *eudaimonia* — which is alternatively translated as 'happiness', 'well-being', or 'flourishing' — gave content to moral judgements of personal virtue. For, on this account, virtues are excellences of character that are both instrumentally useful for attaining this goal and an essential part of its attainment, their possession being itself a constituent of the good life. To later scholars in the Aristotelian tradition, such as Aquinas, the human *telos* also provided a basis for the 'natural law' — a set of precepts that each agent must follow in order to participate in the social activities necessary to achieving his *telos*.

MacIntyre argues that with the Enlightenment came the rejection of a conception of human life as having a goal set by human nature. The history of moral philosophy from the Enlightenment onwards is, as MacIntyre paints it, a history of attempts to ground moral requirements in something other than the human *telos*, as, for example, Hume attempted to do by arguing that moral judgements are grounded in our capacity for fellow-feeling. (Hume saw our moral judgements as an educated extension of our natural tendency to feel pleasure when we contemplate dispositions of character and institutions that benefit people, and pain when we contemplate dispositions of character and institutions that harm them.) These attempts, MacIntyre argues, have all failed. He concludes that it is only by trying anew to formulate an end for human life in the Aristotelian tradition that we can hope to arrive at a standpoint from which we can rationally evaluate claims about what is morally required.

MacIntyre began this attempt in the later chapters of *After Virtue* and pursued it in subsequent work, including *Dependent Rational Animals*. We meet in his office at the University of Notre Dame in September 2006 to discuss this project. Among the clippings and pictures of favourite philosophers on his office door, MacIntyre points to a copy of a letter by the Dalai Lama which encourages his followers to read Aquinas. 'Good advice,' he says, smiling.

∽

ALEX VOORHOEVE: *How did you come to regard Aristotelian philosophy as basically right?*

ALASDAIR MACINTYRE: I can give you a retrospective account of my thought, but it will be what [the philosopher of science] Imre Lakatos called a 'rational reconstruction'. That is, it may not be history as it actually happened, though it is an attempt to be that.

As a graduate student, I was struck not just by the inability of moral theorists to resolve their fundamental differences — most notably the differences between Kantians and utilitarians — but also by the fact that these differences were about issues that were at stake in policy decisions in the latter days of World War II, decisions that resulted in the fire-bombings of Dresden and Tokyo. I was and am convinced that those are prime examples of actions that should never be done. The official case was that the end of the war would be hastened by so acting and that those fire-bombings could therefore be justified by appealing to the utilitarian aim of the maximization of aggregate well-being. Clearly, some kind of consequentialism ruled in public policy.[1] Yet the most compelling justification for going to war against the Nazis had derived from what seemed to be Kantian principles, according to which there are certain ways in which no one should

---

[1] Roughly, consequentialism is the view that an action is right if and only if it leads to the greatest expected balance of good over evil. Utilitarianism is a type of consequentialism.

ever be treated, whatever the consequences. So I asked myself, 'How is it that we have these two incompatible moral views, each of which provides a rational justification for its moral judgements, but neither of which appears to be able to come to terms with the other?' This led me to examine more closely the characteristics that made each view objectionable.

ALEX VOORHOEVE: *What is most objectionable in utilitarianism?*

ALASDAIR MACINTYRE: Utilitarianism appears to provide no place for genuinely unconditional commitments — yet such commitments play a crucial role in human life. Take, for example, the commitment of a parent to a child of the form: 'However things turn out, I will be there for you.' Such a parent is committed to caring for his or her child, even if the child is gravely retarded or delinquent. *This* parent accepts that *this* child is *her* or *his* responsibility, whatever the consequences of assuming that responsibility. It is essential for a child's development that the parental attitude should take this form, for only in a relationship structured by this commitment does the child enjoy the security and recognition it needs to develop. And this type of commitment — there are quite a number of others — is not compatible with a utilitarian calculation of the overall expected balance of good over bad consequences of devoting oneself to caring for the child.

ALEX VOORHOEVE: *And what is wrong with Kantianism?*

ALASDAIR MACINTYRE: For a start, I do not think that Kant's derivation of the categorical imperative succeeds, either in his own version or in any of the versions elaborated by his followers.[2] But, more importantly, Kant's conception of moral motivation is flawed.

---

[2] The categorical imperative is the command always to act on a maxim that one can will to be a law for all rational beings, which Kant took to be the supreme principle of morality.

On Kant's view, the basis of moral motivation lies not in one's desires, but in a recognition that some type of action is morally required or prohibited. But I was and am unable to understand how we could be motivated to act as we should by anything but our desires. The hard work of morality consists in the *transformation* of our desires, so that we aim at the good and respect the precepts of the natural law.

I therefore knew very early in my enquiries what I rejected, but I had at that stage no idea what I wanted to say instead. And then, partly under the influence of Marxism, it occurred to me that although philosophers present moral theories as if they were free-standing, those theories generally are articulations of concepts and presuppositions embodied in forms of social life. By articulating those concepts and presuppositions, moral theorists open them up to criticism and so make it possible to question what has hitherto been taken for granted in a culture. So the emergence of moral philosophy in a culture—indeed the emergence of philosophy in general—is a mark of that culture having reached a point at which it can become self-critical. (As an aside: one way to think about cultures is in terms of the degree to which they are self-critical; and they may fail to be self-critical, not because philosophy does not flourish in them, but because philosophy has become such that it can have little effect on the dominant modes of practical thinking—which is the case here and now in our own culture.)

If moral theories articulate the presuppositions and concepts that are embodied in our everyday judgements, then one interesting way to begin our enquiries in moral philosophy is to ask ourselves what it is to which we are already committed by our everyday life and our everyday judgements. This is often not an easy question to answer, especially if you inhabit the morally fragmented culture of modernity. But when I began to ask myself this question, I discovered quite soon that I was and had been—without knowing it—an Aristotelian. For when I identified more precisely the reasons why I had rejected both utilitarianism and Kantianism, it became clear that those reasons stemmed from Aristotelian attitudes. Aristotle's account of the virtues entails that there are certain types of action that one will never perform, whatever the consequences, unless one has already gone badly wrong—unless one has become the kind of human being who is unwittingly or perversely frustrating himself in developing those relationships needed to achieve his good or goods. Aristotle also enables us to understand how and why it is that our desires, as they develop through and from early childhood, need to be transformed so that we acquire the virtues. My initial reasons for rejecting utilitarianism and Kantianism had been inchoately and unconsciously Aristotelian. Now they became explicitly Aristotelian. And so I found myself at work within a particular philosophical tradition and committed to undertaking two kinds of philosophical work. First of all, I needed to ask why in the past history of our culture a broadly Aristotelian standpoint had been displaced by those heirs of the Enlightenment, utilitarianism and Kantianism. It was by pursuing an answer to this question that I came to write *After Virtue*. Secondly, I had to spell out further what was involved in Aristotelianism, not only the Aristotelianism of Aristotle, but also that of his greatest interpreters, especially Aquinas.

ALEX VOORHOEVE: *What was the source of your Aristotelian commitments?*

ALASDAIR MACINTYRE: Perhaps autobiography may get in the way here, but obviously this happened in part as a result of how I had been brought up, of how some older family members and friends had influenced me by passing on thoughts and judgements from a still older way of life. Yet to tell this story would not be particularly interesting philosophically. I should instead focus on how my thinking developed.

One concern was with the place of rules in ethics. Rules must be a constituent of any morality, but rules can never be formulated so that they can be brought to bear unproblematically on all the cases to which they are relevant. And there are always situations in which no rule will give us the guidance that we need. So we cannot do without a capacity for judgement that is not itself rule-governed, that capacity to which Aristotle gave the name *phronēsis*, or 'practical intelligence'. This is the capacity that enables us to identify in each particular situation which rules, if any, are relevant and then to frame our choices accordingly. And it became clear to me that the exercise of *phronēsis* is always informed by some conception both of a good at which we are aiming in these particular circumstances and of a further good at which we are aiming as our ultimate good. So I needed to elucidate both the concept of *a* good and the concept of *the* good.

Consider the range of evaluations that we make in calling something good. We may evaluate something as instrumentally good — good as a means to further ends — and we may also call 'good' a range of things worth pursuing for their own sake, including goods internal to particular activities, such as those goods that are to be achieved in the playing or the enjoyment of music, in scientific enquiry, or in the activities and relationships of the family. With respect to this range of goods, we need to judge which of them to pursue and in which combination. In thinking about this question, I made a characteristic Aristotelian thought my own: that when I am assessing how such goods should be ordered, I am considering what part they play in human flourishing, what contribution they might make to my flourishing as a human being. I took and take this to be a quasi-biological question, like the questions 'What is it to flourish as a wolf?' or 'What is it to flourish as a dolphin?' In each case — humans, wolves, dolphins — what an individual needs to flourish is to develop the distinctive powers that it possesses as a member of its species.

ALEX VOORHOEVE: *What are these distinctive powers for humans?*

ALASDAIR MACINTYRE: The crucial difference between human beings as rational animals and other animal species is that human beings are able to reflect on the norms that govern their lives, on the nature of the activities they engage in, and the experiences they have, and can ask: 'Is there a better way to live than the way I am living now?' Indeed, in all sorts of ways, each of us recurrently asks this question, even though we do not usually make it explicit. So any human life is going to be impoverished without the exercise of this reflective, critical, and constructive capacity for practical reasoning. To have this capacity is to be able to stand back from one's desires and to evaluate them in the light of one's knowledge of goods and of the good. It is to be able to evaluate the reasons for action that others propose to me and that I propose to others.

ALEX VOORHOEVE: *What, if anything, follows from recognizing that part of my good is to engage in practical reasoning?*

ALASDAIR MACINTYRE: One thing that follows is the importance of friendship. For rational deliberation is essentially social. To think constructively about my own good in practical terms in everyday life, I need to deliberate along with and in the company of others. This is not only because I will have to make shared decisions with people around me, but also because my own thinking is likely to be defective unless it is exposed to criticism by others who are, to some significant degree, concerned about my good in the same way that I am, and who know that I am concerned about their good in the same way that they are. What is the consequence of not having critical friends? It is that one becomes the victim of one's hopes and fears, of wishful thinking and fantasy. I have learned from psychoanalysis that, to an extraordinary but generally unrecognized extent, unless we are very careful, we tend not to see things as they are, but as our fantasies predispose us to see them. And we can only be rescued from this by a certain kind of friendship. One important type of such friendship is marriage. It is crucial that husband and wife know enough and care enough about each other to be able to make perceptive, even if harsh, judgements. It is therefore also crucial that marriage be an unconditional commitment, because otherwise one may not have the security to give and take such criticism. But one always needs critical friends to rescue one from a distorted view of oneself.

I should add that reasoning together with others about my and their good requires some significant measure of agreement on our goals — where there is no common ground concerning ends, there can be no useful common deliberation. Fortunately, the range of goods about which we and others are able to agree without much difficulty is impressive. They include, as I indicated earlier, the goods of community life and of the workplace, the goods of enquiry, and various kinds of artistic and athletic goods. All of these enrich a life, and a life lacking all of them would be unhappy and impoverished. And since it is as practical reasoners that we achieve those goods, it is undeniably a good to engage in practical reasoning and to reason well.

Now, what we share with others depends crucially on the social relationships in which we find ourselves. When Aristotle discussed human flourishing, he was talking about flourishing in the context of the relationships of a *polis* [a Greek city-state] when it is in good order. When *we* are thinking about virtues, norms, and ends, we always have to begin where *we* are, with our having been brought up in a particular way and in a particular set of social relationships with its own conception of virtues, norms, and ends.

When we are engaged in this type of enquiry, the following questions arise: Why should we continue to give to this particular conception of moral requirements the authority that hitherto it has enjoyed? Is it for our good to continue to live in these ways? How these questions are answered in particular social circumstances will be, in part, a matter of the extent to which there is a shared conception of their good that is available to members of that particular group.

ALEX VOORHOEVE: *Your way of phrasing the question about the authority of moral norms as one about whether we think they serve our good differs from the typical way of asking the question, which is: Does regarding certain moral norms as authoritative serve my good? That's the way the question is put by Glaucon in Plato's* Republic, *for example. Why don't you phrase it that way?*

ALASDAIR MACINTYRE: We need to distinguish two kinds of goal and two kinds of deliberation. Some goals are peculiarly mine, so that I take others into account as people with independent goals, whose cooperation I might need or who might stand in the way of achieving my goals. In such cases, I deliberate with others in order to coordinate our actions so that we can each best pursue our independent goals. But many of our important goals are not like this. For most of us, in such contexts as the family, the workplace, and many other areas of social life, the goods that we try to achieve are common: in the family, educating and nurturing our children well; in the workplace, doing one's work according to some standard of professional excellence; and so on. Such goods are common because each participant recognizes their achievement by others as well as by her- or himself as part of her or his overall good. They are also common because what the relevant goods are is not up to each participant independently of others; instead, we identify these common goods and our shared goals only in the course of our transactions with others in the family, the workplace, or elsewhere.

Each individual therefore has a variety of common as well as individual goods, and we have to be able to order the various goods that we acknowledge, finding the place of each good in a life aimed at achieving the overall good. There is therefore one more type of good that each of us has in common with others: that of creating and sustaining the larger communities within which such shared deliberations about the overall good of human life can take place. In sum, our lives are structured by asking 'What do *we* want?', not 'What do *I* want?'

ᔑ

Following these lines of thought, MacIntyre outlines three kinds of goods as part of human flourishing: becoming an independent practical reasoner; the goods generated in particular practices; and belonging to a community which supports participation in valuable practices and joint enquiry into the good. This conception of the goods that contribute to human flourishing leads him to the following account of the virtues. Virtues are dispositions of character to judge, feel and act in ways that promote each of these goods. Typically, they do so in two ways: by being instrumentally useful for the attainment of these goods and by being partly constitutive of them.

Two examples that MacIntyre discusses in *Dependent Rational Animals* are temperateness and trustworthiness. Temperateness — the virtue concerned with the pleasures and pains of eating, sex, exercise, etc. — involves knowing how to avoid both overindulgence and addiction on the one hand and unappreciative insensitivity on the other. It therefore enables one to stand back from some of one's immediately pressing desires, to evaluate them in terms of their tendency to lead to one's good, and follow them only when it really is good to do so. These capacities are part of what it is to be an independent practical reasoner. Trustworthiness — the virtue which renders its possessor someone who can be counted on to fulfil her responsibilities, keep confidential information to herself, disclose information that others are entitled to, etc. — is essential for securing the other two goods on MacIntyre's list: participation in a variety of practices and sustaining a community in which shared deliberation is possible.

Temperance and trustworthiness fit within Aristotle's original catalogue of the virtues. But MacIntyre also believes that Aristotle's account of the goods of human life and his corresponding list of the virtues are deficient in several respects. Among the most important of these, he believes, is a failure fully to appreciate our vulnerability to physical and mental illness and the nature of our dependence on others' assistance during early childhood, old age, and when we are afflicted by illness and other forms of deprivation. This failure, MacIntyre writes, is exemplified by Aristotle's account of the *megalopsychos* (literally the 'great-souled man', often translated as 'magnanimous man'), whom Aristotle regards as a paragon of the virtues. The *megalopsychos* takes pride in doing good to others because he thereby becomes a partial creator of his beneficiaries. He can take pride in his creation, Aristotle writes, in just the same way a potter can take pride in his pottery. However, the *megalopsychos* regards being a recipient of assistance as demeaning, because it makes him the product of others' activity. As a consequence, such people believe that 'doing good is proper to the superior person, but receiving is proper to the inferior' and prefer 'to remember the good they do, but not what they receive'. MacIntyre regards these attitudes as symptomatic of a forgetfulness of our vulnerability and consequent dependence. Such forgetfulness, he claims, leads to a wrong view of flourishing.

∽

ALASDAIR MACINTYRE: In order to flourish, we must receive the kind of care that we need when we are very young, ill, injured, disabled, or very old. Acknowledging this means not sharing, in certain respects, the attitudes of Aristotle's *megalopsychos*. It involves, as Aquinas knew, being able to ask for and graciously receive others' help. It also means acknowledging what we owe to others as a consequence of what we have received.

ALEX VOORHOEVE: *Your focus on dependence differs not just from Aristotle, but, as you say, from much of the tradition in Western moral philosophy. John Rawls is an example of a contemporary author who takes the central case for an account of justice to be the relationship between healthy adult citizens who can be fully cooperating members of society. The question of what we owe to adults who are barred from being fully cooperating members of society because of illness or disability is then meant to be dealt with by a supplementary account. Why can't we proceed in this way?*

ALASDAIR MACINTYRE: The kind of vulnerability that is experienced by children, the very old, and adults who are sick or injured is indeed absent from Rawls's discussion. What is wrong with this way of proceeding is that when one *does* consider this vulnerability, it becomes clear that Rawls's 'central case' is *not*, in fact, the central case for developing an account of justice. What's more, it is a *misleading* case. For the individual who has been made the focus of the enquiry is someone who has been a child and who will, if she lives long enough, become old and infirm.

It is interesting that Rawls begins his account of justice with *society* and not with families or schools. For all of us first encounter questions of justice in the family and at school, and it seems plausible that the questions of what justice is in the family and what it is at school are good places to start an enquiry into justice. Consider two things that are not given their due place in Rawls's account. First, family members' needs, particularly the needs of children, but also the needs of parents. And second, the contributions that each person makes to the common enterprise of the family and what, in consequence, each deserves. Both provide grounds for allocating goods.

Now, once we bring needs into view, we discover that justice in the family — and elsewhere — requires generosity: it requires that we give to those with whom we share common goods in an unstinting, non-calculating way. The kind of care that we need, and that others need from us, does not have the character of a *quid pro quo*. In order to become independent practical reasoners, we needed from our parents, teachers, and others a kind of care that was not conditional on the expectation that we would render them some service in return. Moreover, the people to whom we owe assistance when we have become independent adults may be people who never have done and never will do anything for us. So a certain generosity beyond justice is required if justice is to be done. And one needs to have this virtue of 'just generosity', as I call it, in order to participate in a community that achieves the common good of caring justly for those in need.

ALEX VOORHOEVE: *I don't fully understand this concept of just generosity. Can you give a further example?*

ALASDAIR MACINTYRE: Consider the United States penal system. The United States locks up a larger proportion of its residents than any society in history. Moreover, the conditions in most prisons are bad in all sorts of ways, and for many who deserve punishment it is bad to be in prison because the experience contributes to their moral decline. Just generosity therefore requires us to help people newly released from prison, so that they may find their way back into society. I have an admirable colleague who devotes a substantial part of his spare time to meeting people on their release from prison, footing the bill for a meal, taking them to the place where they will be staying, making sure that they have enough money in their pockets, and so on. This is the sort of thing that it is necessary that some people do without thinking of any return. Moreover, people who do not contribute to this kind of enterprise are not acting unjustly. But they *are* failing to *sustain* justice.

ALEX VOORHOEVE: *Isn't it the case that we need this kind of generosity only because the penal system is unjustly organized? So it would seem that this case doesn't show the need for a generosity beyond justice; it merely shows that when a society is unjust, it is a good thing that there are people who are willing to relieve some of the effects of that injustice.*

ALASDAIR MACINTYRE: If the penal system of the United States were justly organized, then there would be less need of generosity towards ex-prisoners. But, no matter how well organized, it could not dispense with the exercise of the virtues of justice and generosity. I would go so far as to say that there is no real justice where there is no generosity.

ALEX VOORHOEVE: *In* Dependent Rational Animals, *you claim that we must extend this type of generosity to those with severe mental disabilities. At the same time, you write that we do not need to show such generosity towards non-human animals with the same cognitive capacities. Moreover, on your view, we are permitted to do things to non-human animals that we are not permitted to do to humans with similar capacities. Peter Singer has famously challenged this type of thinking as a form of unjust discrimination against non-human animals, which he calls 'speciesism' in order to draw out the analogy with racism. He proposes that our tendency to view animals like chimpanzees as having lesser claims on us than those humans who have the same mental capacities stems from similar psychological tendencies as racism, such as that a person with a disability looks more like us, and that it is easier to sympathize with him. Now, by way of justification for the claim that we must care generously for and protect humans with severe mental*

disabilities in ways we need not care for and protect non-human animals
with similar capacities, you write that our attitude towards these humans
should be governed by the thought, 'That could have been me,' and that
no such thought applies in the case of non-human animals. Isn't this just
an expression of the type of unduly partial sympathy of which Singer
complains?

ALASDAIR MACINTYRE: If I come across a severely injured chimpanzee, I should certainly do something about it. What I do not have
to do is weigh its suffering on the same scale as human suffering.
It is never a matter, for example, of judging that this chimpanzee
is more severely injured than this human so that I should help the
chimpanzee if I cannot help both. I do not share a form of life
with chimpanzees in the same way that I share a form of life with
other humans. I do not have the same relationship to them. Here I
differ not only from Peter Singer, but also from some animal rights
campaigners. For I take it to be an important question what kind
of relationships we have with particular members of other species,
rather than with non-human animals in general. As a farm worker, I
may have particular relationships with this cow, that dog, this horse.
And so I will acquire responsibilities to those particular animals in the
course of working with them and living alongside them, of depending
on them and having them depend on me. These relationships are part
of our form of life, and someone involved in this form of life needs
to know how to behave in relation to the animals that live alongside
him. But I would not want to generalize from such cases to our duties
to all animals.

So I do not think that the tendencies that Singer refers to ground
our commitment to those who are severely disabled. The thought
is, rather, that this is one more example of human vulnerability and
that our form of life is such that coping with the vulnerabilities of
others, and of ourselves, is one of the central tasks that confront us.
In order to flourish, each of us needs to live in a community in which
we are committed to meeting others' needs. And this commitment
is, in certain respects, unconditional. I am *never* entitled to turn away

from someone in great need if the need is urgent, I am at hand, and no one else is going to fulfil it. This is something that Aquinas makes clear in his discussion of the virtue that he calls *misericordia*, which we imperfectly translate as 'taking pity'. Such immediate and urgent need trumps other obligations and duties, always. A person who cannot see and feel this cannot fully enter into the relationships of giving and receiving that characterize a community in which these commitments are accepted, and so cannot achieve the common goods of that community.

ALEX VOORHOEVE: *So for someone in such a community, the thought 'That could have been me' expresses his recognition of two facts. First, in becoming who he is, he depended on others being prepared to care for him if he had ended up with a severe disability. And second, in his everyday life, he still relies on others to care for him should he end up in that position.*

ALASDAIR MACINTYRE: Yes. And if somebody said, 'I need an argument that will show that from this it follows that I have special duties towards the disabled,' the response should be: 'This is not something for which there could be an argument. If you genuinely need an argument, you must be lacking in a kind of responsive sensibility that is crucial to human life.' Many people who *do* ask for an argument will, of course, not be so lacking. They will just be academic philosophers, whose professional training has misled them into asking for arguments in situations where arguments are not to the point. They are better people than their theories suggest. As indeed is Peter Singer, whom I regard as an admirable human being even if he is, in my view, a wrong-headed theorist.

ALEX VOORHOEVE: *In closing, I would like to turn to your discussion of Aquinas's concept of 'natural law', which adds an account of moral rules to the Aristotelian account of the virtues. Can you explain how, like the virtues, the rules of natural law can be derived from your account of human goods?*

ALASDAIR MACINTYRE: On Aquinas's view, the precepts of the natural law are justified as rules that agents must observe in order to be able to participate in those social activities and relationships without which they cannot achieve their goods and their good. In these activities and relationships, each rational agent must treat others as rational agents, acting together in order to achieve their common goods. But to treat someone else as a rational agent is to engage in shared deliberation, in which my or the other's reasons for belief and action are to be advanced and evaluated solely as better or worse reasons. If instead we are moved in our deliberations by fear of the other, or if we try to inculcate such fear, or if we are merely charmed and seduced by the other, or if we attempt merely to charm and seduce, we have ceased to treat the other as a rational agent. We have also ceased to treat our common goods — the goods of families, of schools, of political societies, and so on — as the goods of rational agents. So the precepts of the natural law prohibit those attitudes and activities that violate the relationships of rational agents in pursuit of such common goods.

ALEX VOORHOEVE: *I wonder whether this concept of natural law really provides a secure foundation for the kinds of prohibitions of deceit, manipulation, and harm that, intuitively, seem morally right. For it seems that basing these prohibitions on what is necessary for our pursuit of common goods will give us reason to follow the natural law only with regard to those people with whom we might productively deliberate or otherwise pursue common goals. It seems to give us no reason to accept these prohibitions as absolute vis-à-vis those from whom we have nothing to learn or to gain.*

ALASDAIR MACINTYRE: Yes, but we always potentially have something to learn and to gain from any other person.

ALEX VOORHOEVE: *Even if that's true, I might be able to deliberate and pursue various cooperatively generated goods more successfully, on balance, if I exclude certain people from consideration and adopt the relevant moral attitudes only towards those with whom I can engage especially productively.*

ALASDAIR MACINTYRE: Something that we badly need to learn is that that is false. We may start by writing off lots of people as those from whom we have nothing to learn, but then, if we are fortunate, we will discover that we were wrong. We are apt to find out that what we have to learn from and about others is unpredictable and surprising. And to act towards others in certain ways prevents us from learning this. So, for example, purely coercive relationships frustrate us and prevent us from learning what it is that we have to learn from those we coerce. And a great many people initially write off the disabled, not recognizing how much there is to be learnt only from them and with them. Only by learning from such others can we rid ourselves of illusions of self-sufficiency, illusions that stand in the way of our recognizing our need for some of the virtues that we need to flourish.

References and further reading

Alasdair MacIntyre has authored or edited a number of books. Of greatest relevance to the topics discussed in the interview are *After Virtue* (London: Duckworth, 2nd edn 1985), *Dependent Rational Animals* (London: Duckworth, 1999), and *Selected Essays. Volume 2: Ethics and Politics* (Cambridge: Cambridge University Press, 2006). *The MacIntyre Reader*, ed. Kelvin Knight (Notre Dame: University of Notre Dame Press, 1998), collects some of his most important work.

My commentary and questions are informed by David Solomon, 'MacIntyre and Modern Moral Philosophy', and Mark Murphy, 'MacIntyre's Political Philosophy', both in *Alasdair MacIntyre*, ed. Mark Murphy (Cambridge: Cambridge University Press, 2003): 114–51 and 152–75, respectively.

For the emotivist position, see C. L. Stevenson, *Ethics and Language* (New Haven: Yale University Press, 1944) and A. J. Ayer, 'Critique of Ethics and Theology', in *Language, Truth and Logic* (New York: Dover

Publications, 1952). An interesting account of the consequentialist reasoning at work in the decisions to fire-bomb Japanese cities in World War II is offered in Errol Morris's documentary *The Fog of War*.

I paraphrase and quote passages from Aristotle's *Nicomachean Ethics*, 1168a1–18 and 1124b10–12, tr. Terence Irwin (Indianapolis: Hackett, 2nd edn 1999). For Aquinas's account of natural law, see *Summa Theologiae*, first part of the second part (*prima secundae partis*), question 94. The *Summa Theologiae* is easily accessible online at <www.newadvent.org/summa>; a more recent, standard edition is the Latin text and English translation by the English Dominicans reissued by Cambridge University Press (2006).

Peter Singer discusses the comparative moral status of animals and humans in his *Practical Ethics* (Cambridge: Cambridge University Press, 2nd edn 1993).

III

ETHICS AND EVOLUTION

6
KEN BINMORE

THE ORIGIN OF FAIRNESS

Ken Binmore is best known as the 'ruthless, poker-playing economist' from University College London who, in 2000, netted the British government £22 billion (then around $US 35 billion) when he led the team that designed the third-generation (3G) telecommunications auctions. Binmore took up economics after a career in mathematics, during which he held the Chair of Mathematics at the London School of Economics. Since his switch to economics, he has been at the forefront of the development of what is known as 'game theory', the study of the logic of strategic interaction between 'players' — which is how game theorists refer to the entities engaged in strategic interaction. (These entities can be anything from governments, firms, and individuals to animals and even inanimate objects like genes.)

What makes Binmore of interest to philosophers is his attempt to bring game theory to bear on questions in moral philosophy. Binmore's work is part of a distinguished tradition. Since the early 1950s, leading economists and philosophers have drawn on game theory and the broader theory of rational decision-making in the development of their moral theories. Best known among them is John Rawls, who famously argued in *A Theory of Justice* that the terms of a just society are the terms that everyone would agree to if each of them were placed in an 'original position' and was charged with looking after her interests while being shielded by a 'veil of ignorance' from knowledge of her personal characteristics, such as her class, sex, race, abilities, and even her moral or religious outlook and life goals. The rules people would agree to in ignorance of these characteristics would be fair, Rawls held, because they would be impartial.

Which social rules would people agree to in the original position? Before we can answer this question, we need to know more about its inhabitants' *interests* and *beliefs*. Which conception of their interests will they have in mind when they evaluate different social arrangements? (After all, the veil has stripped them of all knowledge of their personal values; they must, however, have *some* values with which to assess possible social contracts — but which?) And what do they believe about the probability of ending up in the shoes of any given person once the veil is lifted?

Rawls answered these questions as follows. First, he endowed the inhabitants of the original position with an abstract view of the good life that, he argued, people from different walks of life would find acceptable as a shared basis for assessing the quality of a person's situation. This 'thin theory of the good', Rawls held, should represent our overriding interest in securing the conditions under which we can freely develop and pursue our aims, whatever these aims might be. Rawls concluded that people behind the veil would assess social positions on the basis of the access that these positions afforded to certain all-purpose goods, including basic liberties, jobs, and income.

Second, Rawls stipulated that the inhabitants of the original position would be completely ignorant of the probability of ending up in anyone's shoes after the lifting of the veil. In other words, they would not be told that they would be *equally likely* to be anyone when the veil was lifted; rather, they would be given *no information at all* about the chance of ending up in anyone's shoes. (By way of illustration: in a two-person society, someone in Rawls's original position must gamble on the toss of an utterly unfamiliar type of coin, without any idea of the probability that this coin will come up heads or tails; this is quite different from gambling on the toss of a coin that one knows is equally likely to come up heads or tails.)

Rawls argued that since the inhabitants of the original position faced a leap in the dark, they would be extremely concerned about ending up in the worst position. As a consequence, he thought, they would choose the social contract that maximized the prospects of the least well-off. This conclusion became known as the 'maximin conception of justice' (after the decision rule that tells one to maximize the minimum outcome when deciding under complete ignorance).

Rawls's work generated a wave of responses, most of them critical. Like many others, Binmore concluded that Rawls's argument was not valid. (To see why, consider that using the maximin rule involves caring exclusively about what would happen if one were to end up in the worst position once the veil is lifted; one is therefore deciding as if one is *certain* that one will end up in this position. But this seems entirely arbitrary: given their complete ignorance about the probability of ending up in any position, the inhabitants of Rawls's original position have no reason to assume with certainty that they will end up in any particular position.)

Nonetheless, Binmore thought that Rawls was on to something when he proposed using the original position as a device for coming up with fair rules. He also thought there was something attractive about Rawls's egalitarian conclusions. So he decided to investigate whether these conclusions might be derived from a different version of the original position.

Binmore long seemed an unlikely candidate to undertake such a task. As a boy, his interest in philosophy was confined to the philosophy of mathematics. During his time at the LSE, he attended lectures by Karl Popper, where, he recalls at the start of our conversation, he 'joined in the discussion in a rather timid way'. He adds:

> In those days, I would have been amazed if you had told me that I would get involved in moral philosophy. And it happened by chance. In 1984, I was invited to a conference on moral philosophy and economic theory. I had always thought

that Rawls didn't get his bargaining theory right, so I thought, 'I'll write a paper applying bargaining theory to the original position.' In the process of writing that paper, I got into more and more trouble trying to find out what Rawls meant when he wrote that he was 'operationalizing Kant's categorical imperative'. Before I knew it, I was into moral philosophy.

Binmore's search for the philosophical foundations of the original position took him to Kant's works, but he concluded a long struggle with Kant's obscure prose by trading him in for David Hume. Hume's *Treatise of Human Nature*, which tried to give a thoroughly naturalistic account of our moral sentiments, inspired Binmore to take a very different perspective on the original position than Rawls's: he came to believe that one should focus on the evolutionary origin and current function of our ideas of fairness, and he set out to uncover them.

The result of this enterprise is the massive, two-volume *Game Theory and the Social Contract*, which Binmore jokingly refers to as 'the Bible'. Binmore has cast aside his past timidity in philosophical discussion, and in addition to his own theory, the book contains a robust critique of leading contributions to philosophy. He displays the same combative (though good-natured) spirit during our conversation, which starts on a bright summer's day in 2001, in the garden of his farmhouse in the beautiful Monmouth Valley of Wales, and continues over dinner in a local restaurant. We start by discussing his criticism of non-naturalistic views.

∽

ALEX VOORHOEVE: *You argue that traditional moral philosophy goes wrong at the outset when it asks the question, 'How ought we to live?' Why is this a mistake?*

KEN BINMORE: 'How ought we to live?' seems to me to be a nonsensical question when asked in the usual way, with the expectation that the answer will be some categorical imperative that commands that we perform particular actions or have particular intentions irrespective of our actual preferences and plans. I think there is no such thing as a categorical imperative. I am a total thoroughgoing naturalist, reductionist, and relativist; all those naughty things. Asking 'How ought we to live?' is like asking 'What animals ought there to be?' Like the animals that exist, the moral rules that we have are shaped largely by evolutionary forces. If one wishes to study morality, it therefore makes no sense to ask how moral rules advance 'the Good' or preserve 'the Right'. One must ask instead *how and why these rules survive*.

Key to answering this question is the realization that in a lot of human interaction there is a potential for people to achieve gains by cooperating and by coordinating their behaviour. A simple example is the so-called 'Driving Game': each person can drive on the left or on the right, and it doesn't matter whether everyone drives on the left or on the right, but it *does* matter that everyone drives on the same side of the road. Game theory analyses this game in terms of what we call an equilibrium. Players' chosen strategies, like 'Drive on the left' or 'Drive on the right', are *in equilibrium* just in case each player's chosen strategy is an optimal response to the other player's chosen strategy.[1] Now, in the Driving Game, there are three possible equilibria: one in which everyone drives on the left; one in which everyone drives on the right; and one in which everyone randomizes over which side of the road to drive on, with a 50 per cent chance of being on either side.[2] Of course, the two equilibria that involve settling on one side of the road are better for everyone than the equilibrium

---

[1] A player's response is optimal if and only if he cannot gain by switching to a different strategy, given what he expects the other player's strategy to be.

[2] If the possibility of this last equilibrium is surprising, think of facing someone who flips a fair coin to choose the side of the road he will drive on. Employing the same strategy in return is a best reply to his strategy, since you can't improve your odds of avoiding a head-on collision by doing anything else. If you do so, *he* can't improve *his* odds of avoiding a collision by switching to a different strategy, so you are both playing a best reply to each other when each of you is randomizing in this way. When you both flip a fair coin to decide which side of the road to drive on, your strategies are therefore in equilibrium.

involving randomization. And depending on certain facts, like the side of the road that neighbouring communities drive on, one of these two equilibria may likewise be better than the other.

Game theory helps us to see that in human life in general, there are a lot of games with multiple equilibria, in which it is important to coordinate on one that is advantageous. I think morality is a device which evolved along with the human species for the purpose of solving such coordination games. Morality, thus conceived, has two aspects. It includes the rules for *sustaining* an equilibrium in a game, which specify those actions that are permitted and those actions that will be punished. It also involves rules for *selecting* an equilibrium on which we are going to coordinate.

ALEX VOORHOEVE: *I am puzzled by your conception of morality. When asked to give an example of a moral rule, few people would think of the rule: 'In the UK, drive on the left.' In addition, the coordination problems you refer to typically have solutions that are advantageous to both parties, at least in the long run. But many canonical examples of moral rules, like the principle of mutual aid, require that one give up a significant amount for people from whom one has no expectation of receiving anything in return. It follows that your understanding of morality regards as canonical elements that we don't normally regard as such, and excludes elements which many regard as canonical. Why should we accept your view of what morality is when it is so different from our everyday understanding of it?*

KEN BINMORE: My conception of morality is indeed both more and less inclusive than most people's. The full answer to the question why I see it this way has two parts. First, I think that we use fairness norms in everyday coordination problems without consciously attending to the fact that we are doing so. How much should each person move when they approach each other in a narrow corridor? Who washes the dishes tonight? These problems may seem picayune, but if conflict arose every time they needed to be solved, our societies would fall apart. In such situations, we are solving moral problems, but when interacting with people from our own culture we solve them so effortlessly that we do not even think of them as problems. Our fairness norms then run below the level of consciousness.

Second, the key thing to realize is that we become aware of our moral norms when they are *not* working so effortlessly. When we encounter new situations, we try to use fairness norms that were developed to handle situations that we or our ancestors encountered previously. The trouble is that these might not work in the new situation. Insofar as our fairness norms are biological, they were developed in the circumstances under which human beings evolved. In those days, hominids lived together in groups of at most 150. In such groups, everybody knew everyone else. The fairness norms which evolved in such groups, which evidence indicates were highly egalitarian, may to some degree be programmed into our genes. If so, our fairness norms, or 'moral intuitions', as philosophers like to call them, are adapted to this small scale. When we try to use them in situations to which they are ill adapted, we become aware of them because they don't work. We are then in the same position as the baby jackdaw that the biologist Konrad Lorenz observed going through the motions of taking a bath when placed on a marble-topped table, the shiny flat surface of which triggered the 'being in a pool of water' routine. Like the baby jackdaw's behaviour, our behaviour is pathological in such cases.

ALEX VOORHOEVE: *Are you suggesting that someone who acts in accordance with the principle of mutual aid, which requires us to help others in distress when we can do so without great cost to ourselves, is acting in a pathological manner unless he is in circumstances in which he can expect to receive some benefit (or avoid some sanction) in return for acting in accordance with this principle? That he is merely in the grip of a norm that is ill adapted to his situation?*

KEN BINMORE: This principle is a case in point! Why does this moral rule say that you should help someone when he is in distress? Going back to the small groups in which human beings evolved, we must first ask, 'Why did they live in groups?' The answer is, basically, that they had the opportunity to help each other and insure each other against misfortune. You then have to ask the question, 'Why is it an equilibrium for people to help each other?' And the answer is: reciprocity. The way reciprocity works is that I will do something for you and then you will do something for me. If you fail to do something for me in return, then, if we want the situation to be in equilibrium, something will happen to you which will make you worse off than you would have been if you had reciprocated. In such small groups, reciprocity, and the punishment of those who don't reciprocate, possibly by third parties, will be effective at ensuring behaviour in accordance with the norm of mutual aid. Now try to apply this commandment of mutual aid in a large, anonymous setting, where the person you might be prompted to help is a stranger who will never be in a position to reciprocate. In the absence of third-party enforcement, it will not work, except in the rare case where people have a taste for helping others. We call people saints or give them medals when they act selflessly or bravely in such situations because such behaviour is so rare. So you know that, in such settings, people usually don't behave altruistically towards complete strangers in a way that would require major sacrifice on their part, except once or twice. You might, for example, leap into a river to save a stranger from drowning if you only very rarely encountered this scene, but if there were a stranger struggling in the river every time you took the dog for a walk, and if you were like most people, you would soon find some reason why it was not your duty to risk your life for another in these circumstances.

ALEX VOORHOEVE: *Still, many would intuitively think that we have a duty to save someone in such a case, at least so long as the risk to ourselves was relatively small . . .*

KEN BINMORE: Philosophers who proclaim that we have certain rights and duties on the authority of their 'considered intuitions' are getting matters the wrong way around. Such philosophers think that it is somehow a given that we have rights or duties, and that it follows from our having such rights and duties that institutions should be arranged in a certain way. This way of thinking involves assigning some special binding force to rules that are mere conventions. 'Rights' are merely rules recognizing that certain actions will not be punished, and 'duties' are actions that must necessarily be taken to avoid punishment. These rules have a role only when they help sustain an equilibrium — when the actions they allow or prescribe are in the true interest of each individual when others follow the rules and everyone expects everyone else to follow the rules.[3] So it isn't because we have certain rights and duties that we should have certain institutions; it is because certain institutions are necessary for coordinating behaviour that we have certain rights and duties.

ALEX VOORHOEVE: *You believe that judgements of fairness have a special place in helping us coordinate our behaviour. What, precisely, is the role of these judgements?*

KEN BINMORE: There are many types of situations in which there are several possible equilibria on which we could coordinate, and in which it is important to coordinate on an equilibrium that is 'efficient', in the sense that it doesn't lead to waste.[4] While both players have an incentive to coordinate on an efficient equilibrium, there might be many efficient equilibria, and they might have opposing interests when they consider which efficient equilibrium to settle on. For

[3] Here, and elsewhere in the discussion, an individual's 'interests' are meant to encompass everything he cares about. Game theorists do not make the assumption that individuals care only for their own well-being, narrowly conceived; their view is that natural selection has shaped us to care about our kin and close friends, among others. The well-being of those close to us will therefore be part of our interests, so conceived.

[4] An efficient equilibrium is one in which there is no other possible equilibrium that is better for at least one of the players and worse for none. The 'Each tosses a fair coin to randomize over driving on the left or the right' equilibrium in the Driving Game discussed above is an example of an *in*efficient equilibrium, since both players could do better in a different equilibrium.

example, suppose that two friends are trying to decide where to meet for a night out. Both prefer that they meet up, but one of them most prefers meeting in the pub down the street from her house and least prefers a pub in the city centre, while the other most prefers a pub in the city centre and least prefers the first friend's local. Each of these meeting points is an efficient equilibrium — but which should they settle on? Now, we can't always bargain directly in such situations — it may be impossible or too costly. So we need some device to help us settle on an equilibrium. Although this is of course very speculative, I think the underlying mechanism by which we solve everyday coordination problems is similar to Rawls's original position — I think we use something like the original position to help us settle on the equilibrium that strikes us as fair. The thought is that mankind's notions of fairness share a deep structure that evolution has written into our genes, and that something akin to the original position is part of this deep structure. That is why the first time someone hears about the original position, her immediate reaction is, 'Oh yes, that sounds about right.'

ALEX VOORHOEVE: *Why might this particular coordination device have evolved?*

KEN BINMORE: I think it evolved from the need to handle contracts of mutual insurance. In a time before cooperative hunting had evolved, people would have foraged for food independently. On any given day, some might return from foraging with more than they needed and others with less. No one would know in advance who would be lucky and who would be unlucky. Everyone would therefore benefit from an insurance contract that would lead those with a surplus to share with those who came back empty-handed. Now, while bargaining about the terms of such insurance contracts, participants would be ignorant of whether they would be lucky or unlucky. They would therefore evaluate such contracts by assigning some probability of ending up in each position. This provides a first step in the direction of the original position, which substitutes not knowing whose shoes you will be in for not knowing in which situation you will find yourself.

~

Though he believes Rawls got close to characterizing the coordination device we have been hard-wired to use, Binmore believes there are four respects in which this device differs from Rawls's version. First, he believes Rawls was wearing rose-tinted glasses when he supposed that we can renegotiate the entire social contract from scratch. Instead, Binmore argues, when we use the original position as an everyday coordination device, we simply accept the *status quo* as our starting point and confine our attention to arrangements that can be reached through consensus, that is, arrangements that make everyone better off than the *status quo*. (Here, the *status quo* is understood as the arrangements that will remain the equilibrium settlement unless we agree to something new.) We do so because its use as a mechanism for establishing mutually advantageous coordination presupposes that both parties are seeking to realize gains from establishing a new equilibrium; this means its use excludes the consideration of alternatives that would be worse for some players than failing to coordinate on a new equilibrium.

Second, rather than assuming complete ignorance of the probability of ending up in anyone's shoes, Binmore thinks people in fact assume they have an equal probability of being anyone. By way of illustration, consider a two-person society of Adam and Eve. When Eve uses the original position to assess social contracts, she will assess each contract as a gamble that gives her a 50 per cent chance of ending up in Adam's shoes and a 50 per cent chance of ending up in her own shoes — and the same goes for Adam. From behind the veil, each person will therefore choose the feasible social contract that yields the most valuable of these outcomes.

But how will Adam and Eve assess how good (or bad) it would be to end up in each other's shoes? This question leads us to the third difference between Rawls's and Binmore's original position. As a naturalist, Binmore cannot rely on Rawls's argument that people *should* use a shareable 'thin theory of the good' for the purpose of assessing social contracts. Instead, he must explain the origins of the standard that people *actually* use when they compare the quality of each person's situation from behind the veil. Moreover, he must explain why the standard Adam uses will be the same as the one Eve uses — for it is only if they use the same standard that they will be able to use the original position as a device for coordinating on a social contract.

Binmore's explanation starts with a distinction between two types of preferences. What we might call 'personal preferences' range over various situations in which a person might find herself with her current tastes and aims. For example, if she values modesty, Eve might prefer a fig-leaf loincloth to an apple. Of course, people have different personal preferences: if Adam is a hungry naturist, he may well prefer an apple to a loincloth.

What we might call 'empathetic preferences', by contrast, involve imaginatively placing oneself in a person's situation *with his personal preferences*. Eve, for example, could consider what it would be like to be in Adam's shoes with Adam's personal preferences, eating an apple. She could then ask herself whether if, hypothetically, she had the choice, she would rather be Adam eating an apple than Eve wearing a fig-leaf loincloth. She could also ask herself whether, if there was an apple to distribute between them, this apple would do Adam more good than it would do her. Her empathetic preferences are expressed in these kinds of judgements.

Binmore thinks that while the veil denies Adam and Eve knowledge of their identities and personal preferences, it allows them knowledge of their empathetic preferences. This is all they need to assess social contracts. For example, if Eve thinks that an apple would do Adam more good than it would do her, then from behind the veil, she will prefer the social contract in which the apple is given to Adam, since this contract will do most to improve the expected quality of her situation, given that she believes there is a 50 per cent chance of ending up as Adam and a 50 per cent chance of ending up as Eve.

Binmore thinks that while the capacity for such empathetic preferences is written into our genes, the particular content of these preferences is not. Instead, he speculates that this content is determined by the following process of cultural evolution. In the course of trying to settle on equilibria they consider fair, people start out using different standards for assessing the quality of each person's situation (i.e. they have different empathetic preferences). Some will be more successful in settling on an advantageous equilibrium than others, simply because of the standard they are using. Onlookers will seek to emulate the people with the more useful standard — and this leads individuals within the same group to converge on shared empathetic preferences.

The final revision to Rawls's original position is that its inhabitants should take seriously the question whether, in the absence of outside powers that can enforce a deal, people might baulk at fulfilling their part once the veil is lifted and they see that they are disadvantaged by the social contract. (Rawls had also highlighted this problem when he wrote that the parties behind the veil should take account of the 'strains of commitment' that real people might feel if the social contract left them worst off.) After all, although when she is behind the veil, Eve would be happy if Adam got the entire apple when the apple would do him more good, in the real world, she may refuse to play her part in a social contract that gives Adam the whole apple. Binmore believes that the solution to this difficulty is radical: to ensure the willing cooperation of the person who gains least under a new social contract, the parties behind the veil choose the contract that makes the *smallest* gain *as large as possible*. The person who gains least will then have no incentive to baulk at the agreement — since there is no way in which she can achieve a larger gain. Moreover, if, as Binmore believes is typically the case, all gains from social interaction are divisible, then the smallest gain will be as large as possible precisely when the gains are divided equally. In sum, in the absence of outside enforcement, the need to secure everyone's cooperation leads us to agree to an equal division of gains.

All this may sound unduly complex. After all, it doesn't seem that we work through a process of this kind when we make everyday fairness judgements. However, Binmore believes that these judgements don't result from consciously thinking through the aforementioned process. Rather, we judge agreements fair in the same way we judge a sentence in our mother tongue grammatical: the complex rules generating the judgement run below the level of consciousness. Moreover, the upshot is simple: social contracts are perceived as fair just in case they lead to equal gains over the *status quo*. This result is recognizable: it would lead, for example, to what we regard as a fair (i.e., equal) division of the gains of cooperation in many small-scale problems, like how to divide an apple or which pub to meet our friend at tonight. Nonetheless, it is questionable whether it fits all the facts.

ى

ALEX VOORHOEVE: *You argue that we commonly use the original position to decide on fair improvements over the status quo. When considering the small-scale problems to which we apply our everyday concept of fairness, this seems to make sense: typically, we focus on the fair solution to the limited coordination problem at hand, and don't analyse the overall fairness of our situation vis-à-vis the situation of the other person. Nonetheless, we don't always so confine our evaluative judgements; we can 'stand back' and evaluate the fairness of the status quo itself, especially when dealing with larger aspects of the social contract. You seem to think that this is a mistake — a misapplication of a device that evolved to help us find equilibrium improvements over the status quo to cases in which the judgements that this device generates have no useful purpose. But are we really making a mistake when we judge the current social contract unjust? For example, if the status quo is a slaveholding society, doesn't it make perfect sense to judge it unjust?*

KEN BINMORE: It is a mistake to think that we can somehow start anew or that the alternative to complete reform is a Hobbesian war of all against all. If we don't agree on a new social contract, it seems to me we would just remain stuck where we are. The best that we can hope for is to say, 'Here is where we are now. Are there enough of us who want to change it?'

You know, there is no such thing as slavery being absolutely wrong, in the sense of being forbidden by every social contract. Aristotle was quite enthusiastic about slavery. It is only because I was brought up in this society that I share its abhorrence of slavery. But if enough people find slavery abhorrent, then they will put slaveholders under pressure to cooperate in dismantling the institution. These slaveholders will then be better off than the status quo if they cooperate, since the status quo carries the risk of their being forced to do so.

ALEX VOORHOEVE: *One might think that if, throughout human history, people had used the original position every time they had to coordinate on an improved social contract, we would have ended up with a sequence of quite egalitarian social contracts. But it seems that we have not. If you are right about the way we use the original position, how is it that our actual societies are so inegalitarian?*

KEN BINMORE: Egalitarianism fits the anthropological literature on the kinds of societies in which we evolved. Two things stand out about these societies. First, they have no bosses. Though, of course, every individual would like to be the boss, they have social mechanisms that take bossy types down a peg. In extreme cases, they expel them from the group. Second, the sharing is very egalitarian — astonishingly so. This is universal, from Greenland Eskimos to Australian Aborigines. This tells me that it must be biological. It couldn't be so similar everywhere unless there was some biological basis for this sharing mechanism.

ALEX VOORHOEVE: *However egalitarian the Eskimos and Aborigines may be, modern societies are not. Why should evidence from hunter-gatherer societies outweigh the evidence from other social forms?*

KEN BINMORE: The standard anthropological explanation is that as the population increased, hunter-gatherers were driven by necessity to move to agriculture. But the anthropological data show that when the economic means of production change, the social contract changes as well. Private property appears — and so do bosses to organize things. Fairness as a coordinating device gives way to leadership. These new hierarchical forms of social organization can't be biologically determined, for the time is too short for a new set of genetic adaptations to have occurred. They are cultural adaptations that overlay our basic genetic character. The sociologists Alexandra Maryanski and Jonathan Turner point out in their book *The Social Cage* that we have a social contract that is at odds with our biology. They think that this explains why there is so much unhappiness in the world. I think they are right. We are programmed to live in an egalitarian society in which nobody tells us what to do, but economic necessity forces us to tolerate an unequal society in which even the bosses complain that they can find no satisfaction.

ALEX VOORHOEVE: *Suppose that your descriptive theory of morality captures the rules and procedures people actually employ, at least in small-scale situations. Why should this constrain our view of right and wrong? After all, a descriptive science of morals is separate from normative moral philosophy. Why should one impinge on the other?*

KEN BINMORE: You can invent a moral philosophy if you want, a system of categorical imperatives, but there is no reason that I should pay attention to it. For you have to give me reasons to do what you say is right and to refrain from what you say is wrong, and that means that we have to have certain judgements in common. Maybe you will be proposing something I like, but you won't convince me that there are categorical imperatives. Naturalists like me think that only hypothetical imperatives make any sense, such as, 'If you care about starving children, you should give your money to good causes instead of spending it on the expensive Margaux you just ordered to accompany our dinner.'

ALEX VOORHOEVE: *So how do you see the relationship between a descriptive science of morals and moral advocacy?*

KEN BINMORE: What a science of morals can do for you is tell you what will work and what will not work. Do-gooders who are convinced of the truth of their moral principles are often dangerous because what they propose will not work. Our attempts at social reform will be more successful if we understand human interaction and moral psychology.

∽

Binmore's view is therefore not unlike the opinion Hume expressed in a letter to Francis Hutcheson, professor of moral philosophy at Glasgow, who had criticised Hume's *Treatise* for being exclusively devoted to the study of human nature, while 'wanting a Certain Warmth in the Cause of Virtue'. Hume responded with an analogy, writing that 'one may consider the Mind as well as the Body either as an Anatomist or as a Painter; either to discover its most secret Springs & Principles or to describe the Grace & Beauty of its Actions'. He admitted that '[w]here you pull off the Skin, & display all the minute Parts' this does not make for a pretty picture, but he pointed out that an anatomist can give good advice to a painter. 'In like manner', he wrote, 'I am perswaded, that a Metaphysician [by which Hume meant someone who gave a naturalistic account of our moral sentiments] may be very helpful to a Moralist'.

The particular way in which Binmore believes a science of morals can aid the reform-minded is by identifying the equilibrium selection device people are attuned to use, so that they can effectively appeal to people's sense of fairness.

∽

KEN BINMORE: There is no way I could say to anyone, 'You ought, categorically, to use the original position to make decisions.' All I can say to people is: 'I don't like to live in the world as it is and I don't like my children living in the world as it is. If you would like to change the world, then here is a way we can proceed. People are accustomed to this device; their intuitions are keened to this device. Currently, we don't use it on a large scale, but we could.'

ALEX VOORHOEVE: *What would using it on a large scale involve?*

KEN BINMORE: Though a large society cannot avoid hierarchy, we can revise the authoritarian nature of many of our institutions in order to lessen the distress caused by living in an inegalitarian society. If we set up incentives properly, we can allow people greater scope to determine the conditions of their everyday interactions in accordance with their egalitarian sense of fairness.

ALEX VOORHOEVE: *This sounds surprisingly idealistic for a self-confessed anti-Utopian thinker . . .*

KEN BINMORE: Unlike Utopian thinkers, I am not relying on individuals' love of justice. The fundamental reason why people use the original position is not that they have a taste for fairness. Rather, they have a desire to coordinate their actions and reap the consequent benefits. Of course, when one asks the question, 'Why do people behave fairly?' it is tempting to answer, 'Because they have a taste for fairness; because they like fair outcomes.' I think this is fundamentally wrong, in the way it would be wrong to answer the question 'Why do the French drive on the right?' with 'French people like driving on the right.' The actual motivation is: these players don't want to be involved in an accident, and they drive on the right only because, given their belief that the other person will drive on the right, this is the best way to avoid an accident. There is no need to invoke a special taste for driving on the right to explain their behaviour. In the same way, if people believe that others will aim to settle on a fair equilibrium, they, too, will want to settle on that equilibrium, because they want to coordinate their behaviour with them; there is no need to invoke a further special 'taste for fairness' to explain how they wish to act.

ALEX VOORHOEVE: *But it seems that many people won't recognize themselves in your description of what they are 'really' doing when they are engaged in thinking about what is fair and acting accordingly. Rather than simply trying to coordinate with others in a mutually advantageous way, they think that they are engaged in something higher-minded; and this thought motivates them to act fairly. If they came to believe your view of morality, wouldn't this undermine their attachment to the 'fairness device' you suggest they use?*

KEN BINMORE: This is a similar question to, 'Won't society fall apart if people stop believing in God?' Hume, in part 12 of his *Dialogues Concerning Natural Religion*, has the character Philo give the right answer to this question. Philo says something like, 'Ask any person what he holds most certain, and he will tell you his belief in God. Look at his behaviour, and you wouldn't think he believed in God.' Philo is pointing to the fact that people who are otherwise very good at looking after their interests appear to be very bad at looking after what, given their professed beliefs, they should regard as an interest of overriding importance: avoiding divine punishment. This indicates, Philo suggests, that these people do not really believe in God — their behaviour speaks more loudly and accurately of their beliefs than their professions of faith. I think the same applies in the case of people's professed moral beliefs. People talk about noble principles all the time, but look at their behaviour! Generally speaking, they don't act on these principles unless doing so is in their interests, given how they think others will act. I remember one particular occasion in a philosopher's sitting room where there was a carpet I supposed was made by child labour, with people sitting around talking about their moral principles. If they diverted only 10 per cent of their income to good causes, they would do a lot more good. Only once when I said this at a seminar was I taken aback. A young man stood up, and the light shining behind him made his hair look like a halo — it turned out that he gave 40 per cent of his income to good works! When I hear of moral philosophers giving such amounts to charity, I will believe that what they claim to be true really influences their behaviour. But I predict that nothing will happen if we say to people, 'Just carry on as you were, but see morality for what it is.'

References and further reading

The best place to start for Ken Binmore's account of justice is his *Natural Justice* (Oxford: Oxford University Press, 2005), which summarizes his more detailed account in the two-volume *Game Theory and the Social Contract* (Cambridge, Mass.: MIT Press, 1994, 1998). Binmore is also the author of the accessible *Game Theory: A Very Short Introduction* (Oxford: Oxford University Press, 2008) and the more demanding *Rational Decisions* (Princeton: Princeton University Press, forthcoming).

For the original position, see John Rawls, *A Theory of Justice* (Oxford: Oxford University Press, 2nd edn 1999), ch. 3. The economist John Harsanyi proposed a different version of the original position before Rawls: see 'Cardinal Utility in Welfare Economics and the Theory of Risk-Taking', *Journal of Political Economy* 61 (1953): 434–5 and *Rational Behaviour and Bargaining Equilibrium in Games and Social Situations* (Cambridge: Cambridge University Press, 1977), ch. 4.

Konrad Lorenz's studies of jackdaws are reported in *King Solomon's Ring*, trans. Marjorie Kerr Wilson (London: Methuen, 1961).

Hume's remarks to Francis Hutcheson are quoted from his letter to Hutcheson of 17 September 1739, in *The Letters of David Hume*, ed. J. Y. T. Greig (Oxford: Oxford University Press, 1932). The other works of Hume referred to are *A Treatise on Human Nature*, ed. P. H. Nidditch (Oxford: Oxford University Press, 2nd edition, 1978) and *Dialogues Concerning Natural Religion*, ed. J. C. A. Gaskin (Oxford: Oxford University Press, 2008). Binmore also refers to Alexandra Maryanski and Jonathan Turner, *The Social Cage: Human Nature and the Evolution of Society* (Stanford: Stanford University Press, 1992).

7
ALLAN GIBBARD

A PRAGMATIC JUSTIFICATION OF MORALITY

Woody Allen's film *Crimes and Misdemeanors* tells the story of Judah Rosenthal, a pillar of the community and loving family man who has his ex-mistress murdered when she threatens to expose his infidelity and financial misdeeds. Tormented by guilt and a fear of punishment that has its origins in his religious upbringing, Judah returns in imagination to a boyhood Passover dinner at which his father Sal and Aunt May are arguing about whether there is a God-given 'moral structure' to the world. Judah asks the company about his case: what will happen to a man who commits murder to further his own ends? His father declares that only a life lived in obedience to God's commands can be a good life; God, he claims, has ordered the universe so that whether or not an evildoer is caught, 'that which originates from a black deed will blossom in a foul manner'. Aunt May, by contrast, argues that it is up to us whether to give moral commands any force in our lives. She concludes that 'if [the murderer] can get away with it and chooses not to be bothered by the ethics, he is home free'. Several guests weigh in, asking why they should accept Sal's point of view, since it rests on unreasoning faith. (One opines: 'Sal's kind of faith is a gift . . . . He believes, and you can use logic on him all day long and he *still* believes.') Sal counters that it is Aunt May's judgement, not his own, which is clouded — her unhappy life, he suggests, has made her bitter and unwilling to acknowledge the world's 'moral structure'. In spite of the evident goodwill among the family members, the tension created by this disagreement is palpable. Dinner only resumes with a semblance of peace when Sal ends the discussion by declaring that arguments are irrelevant, because he 'will always prefer God to the truth'.

Few dinner-table conversations are as intense as this. Nonetheless, from the fireside discussions about appropriate gift-giving that anthropologists report among the hunter-gatherer !Kung to a Western family's TV-dinner debates about the behaviour of guests on a talk show, normative discussion is an ineliminable part of human life. What does it make sense to do in a certain situation? How does it make sense to feel? When the situation concerns us, we ponder these questions alone and with others; we trade opinions and try to persuade. We also judge situations that do not concern us directly: we gossip about our neighbours and discuss the behaviour of film characters. Usually, we consider particular circumstances, such as whether it made sense for Judah to have his ex-lover killed, and whether he was right to feel guilty afterwards. Less often, we mull over general questions, such as whether it ever makes sense to feel guilty for what one has done, or whether it would be better not to be susceptible to this painful emotion.

Typically, we engage in normative discussion to arrive at a more considered point of view. To this end, we exchange information and enlist others' help to draw out the implications of our positions. Often, we also aim to reach agreement by persuading others of our point of view. This latter aim raises a number of questions, however. Why do we think it is important to arrive at agreement? When we think others are wrong and demand that they see things our way, what kind of authority are we claiming for ourselves — and are we entitled to claim it?

Questions of this kind occupy the philosopher Allan Gibbard. Much of Gibbard's early training was in mathematics and physics, and he is well known in economics and political science for his proof of a fundamental result in voting theory. (Known as the Gibbard–Satterthwaite theorem after the two scholars who proved it independently, it establishes how difficult it is to create an attractive voting system that gives voters an incentive to vote for the candidates they truly prefer rather than to vote tactically.) As a consequence, Gibbard brings a scientific mindset to these questions about normative discussion and judgement. In order to answer them, he proposes, we should draw on what psychology, anthropology, and game theory (the theory of strategic interaction) tell us about our capacity for normative judgement and its role in guiding our behaviour. Moreover, he urges, we should try to understand this capacity as part of our evolved nature. Gibbard knows that what the sciences can tell us about these matters is partial and often tentative. Nonetheless, he believes that we know enough to make such speculation fruitful.

We meet in May 2006 to discuss Gibbard's theory of normative judgement and the conclusions he draws from it on two topics: our search for consensus in normative discussion and the appropriateness of guilt. On my way to Gibbard's office at the University of Michigan, Ann Arbor, I come upon a large mural of Woody Allen, that icon of guilt-prone conversationalists. I decide to take it as a good omen, even though Allen's mournful countenance doesn't hold out the promise that the conclusions we reach will be heartening.

⟨∽⟩

ALEX VOORHOEVE: *How did you become interested in philosophy?*

ALLAN GIBBARD: My parents told me that it would be something that I would find interesting, so when I went to college at Swarthmore I took a philosophy course taught by Jerry Shaffer, who was a brilliant teacher. I became really enchanted with it, and though I took a math major and a physics minor, I decided to take a philosophy minor also.

One of the things that really interested me was the status of morality. I had become quite disturbed by emotivism.[1] I thought: 'Isn't there more to moral judgements?' — though I was somewhat reconciled to emotivism after reading Sartre's *Existentialism is a*

---

[1] Roughly, emotivism is the view that moral judgements simply express and are intended to arouse emotions. For example, according to emotivism, saying that betraying one's friends is wrong is akin to saying 'Boo to betraying one's friends!'

Humanism, in which he talked about having to choose one's moral commitments freely.

In the fall of 1962, my senior year, I took a seminar on contemporary philosophical problems with Shaffer and a moral philosophy seminar with Richard Brandt, who was a marvellous teacher. I was trying to decide whether to go to graduate school in philosophy or mathematics. I thought I would end up teaching either way, and teaching philosophy looked like a lot more fun than teaching mathematics. But then I decided I would go into the Peace Corps first. I got an assignment to teach math and physics in Ghana for two years — a fascinating job. On my return, I went to graduate school at Harvard. It was a marvellous time to be there, with Quine, Putnam, and Rawls on the faculty, among others.

ALEX VOORHOEVE: *So this was just before Rawls's* A Theory of Justice *came out? That must have been inspiring!*

ALLAN GIBBARD: Yes, it was. When I took a social philosophy course with Rawls in my first term there, he handed out sections of the draft of his book. In his seminars, we argued about whether there was genuine bargaining in the original position.[2] I argued that since everyone would be identical behind the veil, it did not involve bargaining; instead, it involved just a one-person decision problem. I managed to convince him, which was exciting; Rawls was very generous in acknowledging students' contributions.

ALEX VOORHOEVE: *Who else influenced you at the time?*

ALLAN GIBBARD: Well, I first came across Kenneth Arrow's book *Social Choice and Individual Values*. And then I learned that Arrow

---

[2] This is the position from which Rawls believed that individuals should decide on the terms of a fair social contract. In the original position, people are shielded by a 'veil of ignorance' from knowledge of their particular social circumstances, idiosyncratic characteristics, and personal values.

and Rawls were going to teach a joint seminar along with a young Indian economist, Amartya Sen, whom I'd never heard of.[3] The famous decision theorist Howard Raiffa attended, as did Franklin Fisher, who was editor of *Econometrica*, the leading economics journal. And Richard Zeckhauser, a young man who, it was whispered, was national bridge champion. I wondered whether there had ever been so much intelligence in one room at one time! This course focused my mind on problems in social choice, as did my first job at the University of Chicago, where they asked me to teach a course on social choice theory. This provided me the impetus to try to work out the conditions under which voting systems could be manipulated. It turned out to be no easy thing to figure out, although I did eventually.

ALEX VOORHOEVE: *Why did you turn to questions about the nature of normative enquiry?*

ALLAN GIBBARD: Well, as I said, as a student, I had been quite disturbed by emotivism. Then when I came to work at Ann Arbor, Richard Brandt, who had moved here, was working on rationality. So I began to look at the question of rationality — what it is and what it means to call something rational. And this seemed to me to be a major part of the question of normative enquiry. Because it struck me that the questions: 'What would it make sense to do?', 'What would be valid reasons to do things?', 'Is a feeling apt in this situation, or it is inappropriate?', all relate to how it would be rational to act, to judge, and to feel.

　　Then it occurred to me that to call something rational is to endorse it. But endorse it in what way? Basically, my answer is that to think something is rational is to accept a norm that permits you to do it. (Isaac Levi proposed this way of putting what I was saying.) Someone who calls something 'rational' is therefore expressing his state of

---

[3] Both Arrow and Sen were awarded Nobel Prizes in Economics, in 1972 and 1998 respectively, in part for their work in welfare economics and 'social choice' — the branches of economics that deal with the evaluation of social states.

mind; he is expressing his acceptance of a norm that permits that thing.

ALEX VOORHOEVE: *What is involved in accepting a norm?*

ALLAN GIBBARD: This is where I believe we have to look to biology and psychology. I think we have a system of motivation and control that involves a special capacity to consider and decide which norms to accept, and to be guided by one's acceptance. I also think that this system is an adaptation.[4] We are, in a sense, 'designed' by evolution for living together in complex social groups. A primitive human's prospects for survival and reproduction depended crucially on the bonds he could cultivate, on his ability to coordinate his actions with others and to cooperate with them. We developed language, in part, because it enables us to coordinate in this way. Language allows us to consider not only the present situation, but also past, future, and fictional circumstances. It allows us to discuss these situations with others and to consider how to act in them and how to feel about them. It also enables us to persuade and pressure others to judge in a certain way about what to do and feel in these situations. So language allows for the development of shared evaluations of situations that might arise; it enables us to put our heads together and engage in joint planning.

Now, this normative discussion must influence what we actually do if it is to serve the function of coordinating our behaviour. There must, therefore, be some connection between the views one would tend to avow in unconstrained discussion and one's tendencies to action and feeling; there must be a propensity to be governed by a norm to which one would express adherence in such discussion. Accepting a norm is the psychic state we are in when we have these tendencies to avow a norm and be governed by it.

---

[4] Roughly, an adaptation is a feature whose existence is explained by its being favoured by evolutionary pressures because it contributed to the reproductive success of those among our ancestors who possessed it.

ALEX VOORHOEVE: *On your account, normative deliberation helps us coordinate our behaviour in advantageous ways by enabling us to reach agreement on how to act and how to feel. But does discussion really tend towards agreement? We are all familiar with discussions that simply end up sharpening our disagreements.*

ALLAN GIBBARD: Well, we have been shaped by evolutionary forces to be persuadable — to gravitate towards accepting the norms of others around us. The reason we are so shaped is, presumably, that if we didn't have these tendencies, others would find it hard to coordinate their actions with us. (There are, of course, opposing forces; it could be very costly to always give in to someone whose norms differ from yours.) Another force moving us toward consensus is that we feel some pressure to be consistent in our positions.

ALEX VOORHOEVE: *I can see how our psychology drives us towards accepting the views of those around us. I guess the history of immigrant groups offers examples of this. I remember reading about the Pilgrims, some of whom fled England early in the seventeenth century to take up residence in Holland because of that country's religious tolerance. Their leaders soon discovered that regular and easy interaction with people who practised 'ungodly faiths' (as the Pilgrims saw it) had the effect of corrupting and dissipating their close-knit community, which is why they decided to sail for America, where they could live in isolation. (Indeed, they were corrupted quite rapidly by the experience of living among the Dutch — when the first group of forty sailed for Cape Cod in 1620, they left behind several hundred more, many of whom eventually blended into Dutch society.) But I do not yet understand how consistency alone can push us towards agreement. Take a case in which two people discover that they disagree fundamentally about a normative issue. Suppose, for example, that I think that anyone who was raised lovingly is obligated to take care of his ailing parents. Suppose further that someone else denies that parents have such a special claim on their children; instead, he believes that such obligations to care for one's parents obtain only if one* *has freely assumed them as an adult. Each of us might be fully coherent and possess all relevant factual knowledge, so that the disagreement arises only because we see certain basic things differently. We have arrived at a point where each of us claims that the other's perception is wrong. How does consistency push us towards agreement?*

ALLAN GIBBARD: What is going on here is that each person is claiming a certain authority on this matter. And one can ask to whom one should give such authority. I approach this question by asking what would follow if I thought I had to *deny* such authority to everybody else. Then I would have to ask: 'Why stop there? Why trust *my own* judgements?'

Now, for some judgements this question doesn't really arise. Some norms appear to me wholly self-evident; I am not moved to doubt them by questioning, and I find that I need no arguments to accept them.[5] Accepting these norms does not involve self-trust. But accepting other judgements does — conclusions that rely on long chains of reasoning, for example, or that I arrived at in the past and want to rely on now. Self-trust is also involved in the things that I accept from others because I think that if I had their knowledge, then I would agree with them. If I did not trust myself in these matters, I would have to relinquish almost all my opinions; I could rely only on the things that appeared to me self-evident. I would also have to see any further enquiry into what to do as pointless — for I wouldn't trust my own deliberative judgements. A reason to trust my own judgements to at least some degree is, therefore, that the alternative is bleak scepticism.

The same type of argument for *self*-trust establishes that I must also accord *others* some authority. After all, others' opinions have so thoroughly shaped my views that completely distrusting *their* views would force me to relinquish almost all my beliefs. To avoid such scepticism, I must accord some limited authority to others. That is, I

---

[5] In *Wise Choices, Apt Feelings*, Gibbard mentions as an example the judgement that 'the fact that I would enjoy something speaks in favour of it' (177).

must think that under some favourable conditions, others' espousing a view counted in favour of my accepting it. And if I am consistent, whatever made these people good judges will make others who have the same characteristics good judges. So I will have to grant some fundamental authority to all people who are, in relevant respects, like the people whose judgements I think legitimately shaped my judgements.

ALEX VOORHOEVE: *Why can't I just stop regarding myself as an authority on norms for action and feelings in the same way I might already do with some cases of aesthetic appreciation? Such as when I say: 'I like that painting, but I don't think I should like it or that I shouldn't like it—I just happen to like it.'*

ALLAN GIBBARD: Well, you might just *react* to something, but when you try to *think* about what to do, you have to rely on conclusions that you reached a few moments ago, which is something you don't have to do with aesthetic taste. When you ask yourself which principles to accept, you must accord yourself some authority, since the fact that you would accept a principle if you thought about it means that you are according authority to yourself as you would be after deliberation.

ALEX VOORHOEVE: *And you are saying that, on the same grounds that I accord authority to myself, I must accord some authority to others? So, in my example of an argument about our duties to our parents, I might try to undermine my opponent's claim to authority by arguing that the resentment he feels at his unhappy upbringing is clouding his judgement. For his part, my opponent might claim that my judgement that we have special obligations to our parents is unreliable because it is merely the result of my failure to resist emotional pressure put on me by my parents—pressure that he believes I should resist in order to form reliable judgements. But if neither of us can provide some story of this kind, then each of us has to accept that there is some reason to see things the way the other sees them . . .*

ALLAN GIBBARD: Well, each of you faces an epistemological challenge: what makes you think that you are a better judge? You would be embarrassed in discussion if you had no reply to this question. Of course, even if you didn't have a reply, you could still stick to your views and think that the other should accept them because there is a story that could be told to justify your claim, even though you don't have this story ready. But taking this stance would involve opting out of full discussion, at least for the time being.

ᔐ

In sum, Gibbard concludes, the logic of normative discussion contains some pressures towards consensus: if we disagree with someone who lacks none of the things we think make for a good normative judge, then consistency requires that we weigh the mere fact that he sees things the way he does as a reason that counts in favour of his point of view.

This conclusion leaves us open to the influence of everyone we regard as a good judge. A lot hangs, then, on what we think makes for a good judge. Some of the first things that come to mind are familiar: being open-minded, empathetic, and capable of grasping the implications of the norms one accepts. Gibbard refers to such characteristics as 'content-neutral', because they make no reference to the content of the norms a judge should accept. Still, these content-neutral criteria will render certain judgements unlikely. An example Gibbard mentions is the judgement that gratuitous cruelty is to be admired. We can think it very unlikely that someone who possessed the ability to empathize with someone who is cruelly treated could endorse this norm — and we could then mistrust a claim to be a competent judge advanced by anyone who admires gratuitous cruelty.

Nonetheless, Gibbard argues, we cannot limit our definition of what makes for a good judge to content-neutral criteria, because we will find some views so abhorrent that we would simply refuse to give them any weight, even if the person advancing them met all these criteria. Suppose that we become convinced that Caligula possesses vivid, empathetic understanding of the consequences of cruel acts, and has all the other content-neutral characteristics of a competent judge. Nonetheless, Caligula believes that gratuitous cruelty is to be admired. We would probably think that we should not see Caligula's judgement as giving us a reason to admire gratuitous cruelty; we will, in other words, employ some 'content-fixed' criteria for determining which judges to whom we should accord authority. We must do so, Gibbard argues, to avoid being pushed by the demands of consistency towards accepting views we simply cannot allow ourselves to accept.

At this point, however, we may wonder whether Gibbard's initial argument — that consistency in according authority pushes us towards agreement — really has much force. For if we can simply classify as incompetent those whose views we find unappealing, it seems that consistency alone will do little to move us towards the position of those we disagree with.

∽

ALEX VOORHOEVE: *What is there to stop us from simply dismissing those we disagree with on the grounds that the content of their judgements disqualifies them?*

ALLAN GIBBARD: Such dogmatism is costly, because it normally ends discussion. And unless the person you are disagreeing with is unusually influenceable or can be browbeaten into accepting your point of view, once you proclaim that his judgement is not to be trusted simply because of the content of his views, you have to give up on any possibility of discussing matters with him. But we need to engage in discussion with others. Shared norms enable us to live together. Moreover, we easily lose our balance if we don't talk to others — isolated thinking is disorienting. So it is costly to give up on normative discussion.

ALEX VOORHOEVE: *I can see that it is damaging to our interests to cut ourselves off from all joint deliberation. But it might not be so damaging to dismiss people we have little to do with anyway. So there would seem to be a balance of costs here, which will cause us to allow those around us* *to have some influence on us, because the price of excluding them would be too great, while not really pressuring us to accord much weight to the views of others with whom we hardly interact, since it is rarely more costly to allow them to influence us than to dismiss them.*

ALLAN GIBBARD: It's hard to make general pronouncements, but I think we can say this much. Each of us lives in various overlapping communities. We choose our communities, to some extent, on the basis of what we can share with the people in them. According other people authority is not an all-or-nothing matter: we can trust their judgement in some things and not in others; and we can be open to discussing some things with them but not other things. Agreement is not required on everything: in some communities, we can make do with very minimal shared norms and limit our discussion to those. But, typically, we also need to be part of smaller communities of people whose normative judgements we trust on a range of important matters, so that we can put our heads together and figure out how to live.

ALEX VOORHOEVE: *Among the norms we discuss with others are, of course, moral norms. You define morality, narrowly conceived, as involving norms for feeling guilt and anger. On this account, an action is morally wrong if and only if the norms one accepts hold that it is rational to feel guilty about doing it and rational to feel a form of anger—like resentment or indignation—if someone else does it. But you also acknowledge a wider range of moral emotions—pride, shame, compassion, and idealistic inspiration, to name a few. So why focus on guilt and anger?*

ALLAN GIBBARD: Well, I was interested in Bernard Williams's and Nietzsche's attacks on morality, and especially on guilt and resentment. And then I thought of John Stuart Mill's point that self-regarding actions, no matter how deleterious, aren't matters of morality, even though some people say they are. Mill wrote of morality in the narrow sense that it pertained to what was wrong or not wrong and that 'to say that an act is wrong is to say that there ought to be a sanction against it—a sanction of law, of public opinion, or of conscience'. Now, it seemed to me that whether there ought to be a sanction of *law* is not the real issue. For example, we might think that people should be fined for overparking at parking meters while thinking that overparking is not morally wrong. So I think that morality in the narrow sense is simply about whether there ought to be a sanction of opinion and conscience.

ALEX VOORHOEVE: *So what is guilt, precisely?*

ALLAN GIBBARD: I think we should define guilt as the emotional state that involves the following syndrome of tendencies. We feel that guilt is warranted when we believe that others would rightly feel angry—resentful or outraged—at us for our actions. So guilt meshes with the resentment or outrage of others. We think that it makes sense to feel guilty when it would make sense to be angry with others if they had done what we have done. In other words, guilt involves the thought that anger would be warranted. So it arises primarily in circumstances when our place in cooperative arrangements is threatened by others' responses to our actions. Guilt leads us to take steps that, typically, avert this threat. When we feel guilty, we regret and feel bad about our actions, and we are moved to display this regret and pain. We are also moved to act in ways that bring about reconciliation. So guilt tends to actions that placate anger.

Of course, one might think that 'guilt' is simply a concept we use to refer to a whole set of negative feelings about ourselves. But it does seem to be distinct from other negative self-regarding feelings, like shame. Unlike guilt, shame doesn't seem to be narrowly focused on the fact that one's actions were faulty. Rather, shame seems to me focused on other things—one's skills and possessions, for example. While at the University of Wisconsin, the psychologist Dacher Keltner did a study in which he asked people to describe 'guilt scenarios' and 'shame scenarios'. And people gave different answers for each emotion. For example, in describing situations in which they felt shame, people typically mentioned scenarios that involved 'a failure to meet others' expectations' and 'poor performance'; typical guilt scenarios were a 'failure at duties' and 'neglecting another'. Moreover, the guilt scenarios described by people from Wisconsin matched the kind of situations that I would find guilt-provoking. So it looks as if in Wisconsin they feel the same way I do. Of course, I am from Michigan, and the two states are close.

ALEX VOORHOEVE: *I am not sure your view of guilt matches everything we refer to as 'guilt'. What about survivor guilt, which might be better understood as a response to the realization that one is liable to others' envy rather than to their anger?*

ALLAN GIBBARD: I think the emotional response to the realization that one is liable to being envied is not to feel guilt, but rather to feel abashed. Survivor guilt is, I think, a response to the belief that one is open to others' resentment. It seems to me that successful people from an unsuccessful community are the objects of resentment, and react with an emotion that responds to the fact that they are exposed to this form of anger. Now, I think neither survivor guilt nor survivor resentment is warranted. But they mesh. We have to distinguish the question whether these feelings are warranted from the question whether it is understandable that people feel them. The same thing goes for feelings about other cases, like breaking a promise with adequate justification. One might feel guilty over doing so, but one can tell oneself this guilt is unwarranted and then, usually, it will die down.

ALEX VOORHOEVE: *In your view, if someone violates a moral norm he accepts, he will feel that guilt is warranted, and this will typically lead him to feel guilty. This raises questions about how your account deals with people who appear to accept a moral norm but feel no guilt at breaking it, and do not think they should feel guilty. For example, in Truman Capote's In Cold Blood, one of the main characters, Dick Hickock, who is a murderer, a paedophile, and probably a rapist, says: 'I know what I do is wrong. But at the same time I never give any thought to whether it is*

right or wrong.' Moreover, he shows no signs of guilt and doesn't appear
to think that he should feel guilty. Would you say that he doesn't really
accept moral norms?

ALLAN GIBBARD: Well, he is speaking in a public language, so one
possibility is that he has picked up the language but he doesn't have
the responses that the rest of us do. I think that, in the population
as a whole, there may be many people who don't have the normal
emotional reaction to moral judgements. In the case of a sociopath,
the uptake of moral language is abnormal. We then have to ask
ourselves whether we should interpret such a person as someone who
doesn't understand the concept but knows how to use the term, or
as someone who understands the concept but doesn't care. It doesn't
seem to matter much which way we interpret the behaviour. If we
say, 'Well, he has the concept but just doesn't care,' then the sense in
which he has the concept *is* just that he is capable of using the public
language, not that he has the kind of mentality that most people in
the population have when they use the language. You know, my son
once told me that when he was very young he thought 'exercise' was
some kind of fluid which flowed into you when you did things like
running, and which would then seep away, so you would then have
to get some more—which is when people would say that they would
have to get some exercise! In a similar way, Hickock probably picked
out some of the features that are generally attributed to 'morally
wrong', such as that murder and rape count as wrong.

ALEX VOORHOEVE: *Take a less unusual case. Suppose I am persuaded*
by Peter Singer's arguments that we have very demanding duties to aid,
but I nonetheless do not have strong feelings of guilt when I fail to direct
most of my resources to aiding distant strangers in need. Would you say
that I don't really accept the moral norm that I avow?

ALLAN GIBBARD: Well, I think it is an interesting datum that we
are pulled both ways on this. It seems to me that it is difficult to
know whether you really think an action is wrong when you have

no tendency to avoid it. The question, in my view, is whether you think that guilt and anger are *warranted*. You can think that guilt is warranted and not feel guilty, but, on my account of it, you do need to have a mechanism engaged that normally would make you feel guilty. That is, to think that a feeling is warranted is to have a psychic mechanism engaged that normally generates the feeling in question.

ALEX VOORHOEVE: *You say that in order to think that guilt is warranted, one must regret doing the action. But mightn't there be cases in which we can coherently feel guilty for what we've done, even though we think we should do the same thing in similar circumstances? For example, in* Crimes and Misdemeanors, *Judah has his ex-mistress killed when she threatens to expose their affair and his financial improprieties. It seems coherent for him to feel guilty over this — to think his action would properly elicit outrage on the part of others — and to think that so much was at stake for him that he does not regret doing what he did. Indeed, for a time, Judah is wracked by guilt, even though it seems that he never really regrets his action.*

ALLAN GIBBARD: It is puzzling what is involved in finding an emotion incoherent. I certainly think that guilt is *possible* conjoined with the thought: 'In a similar situation, let me do the same again.' Nonetheless, I am pulled towards the thought that it *is* incoherent for someone to feel guilt when he does not regret his action. If he is thinking, 'How reprehensible of me!' and also 'Let me do it again!', that does seem incoherent. Think of the story of David and Bathsheba in the second book of Samuel. David has an affair with Uriah's wife, Bathsheba. Bathsheba becomes pregnant with David's child, and in order to cover this up, David arranges for Uriah to be killed. After the deed is done, God sends the prophet Nathan to tell David of a case in which a rich man steals a poor man's only lamb in order to kill it, because he's too mean to kill one from his own huge flock for a dinner-guest. The text reads: 'Then David's anger burned greatly against the rich man, and he said to Nathan, "As the LORD lives, surely the man who has done this deserves to die!" Nathan then said to David: "You are the man!" ' As Nathan in effect says to David: 'How can you think it is right for the rich man in this case to die, and therefore think this about yourself, and yet think "Let me do it again?" '

ALEX VOORHOEVE: *Can't David think that personal reasons outweigh moral reasons in this case? He could then feel guilt without regret. In* Crimes and Misdemeanors, *Judah is thinking: 'I shouldn't have to give up my whole life on account of this woman!' So he imagines himself to have self-interested reasons that outweigh moral reasons. But it would seem coherent for him to think, at the same time, that an observer could rightly be outraged at his behaviour.*

ALLAN GIBBARD: What if this observer thought: 'If I were in the same situation, I would do the same thing'? Would this observer then be justified in feeling outrage?

ALEX VOORHOEVE: *[pauses] I guess I see your point. This is hard to imagine . . .*

ALLAN GIBBARD: Of course, a third party *should* feel outrage in this case. So I would conclude that guilt is warranted on the part of the killer and that he should regret what he has done. You know, what we have just discussed goes to the heart of the question: can it ever make sense to do things that are morally wrong? This question is about what it makes sense to aim at in life, all things considered. To judge that it makes sense to do something, all things considered, is to not rule out doing it in similar circumstances. But guilt seems incoherent when combined with the thought, 'In similar circumstances it would be okay for me to act the same way.' It follows that if one thinks that guilt is warranted — if one thinks the action is morally wrong — then one should think that one should not do the action. So it would seem that one cannot coherently judge that, all things considered, it makes sense to act in ways that one thinks are morally wrong.

ALEX VOORHOEVE: *Guilt involves imposing a pain on ourselves. Wouldn't we be better off without being prone to such self-flagellation?*

ALLAN GIBBARD: The characteristics of guilt—that it focuses on voluntary action and that it meshes with anger—mean that, though painful, it is a useful emotion. For if the norms for guilt prescribe it when one violates norms for cooperative action, then people have an incentive to avoid behaviour that threatens cooperative arrangements. It also prompts reconciliation when people have acted so as to jeopardize these arrangements. So it aids cooperation. I am very interested in the hypothesis that guilt is a biological adaptation—a psychological mechanism adapted to aid in coordination. That would mean that guilt is universal. Evidence from anthropology, however, is mixed. It seems that though anger at people who violate norms is universal, guilt may not be. But the ways in which guilt is useful give us reasons to favour a guilt-based morality.

ᔐ

From the standpoint of people who are trying to settle on norms for the joint regulation of behaviour and feelings, Gibbard concludes, a morality of guilt and anger is attractive because it polices shared norms. But couldn't we do without this police force? Given human nature, Gibbard writes, it seems unlikely that coordination could be assured without anger at the violation of shared norms. Moreover, the anthropological record indicates that it is simply in our nature to feel such anger. And while we might be able to accept norms that prescribed other self-directed feelings in response to the possibility or reality of such anger, it is hard to find another emotion that does the job of pre-empting and defusing anger as efficiently as guilt. Shame, for example, typically applies not just to actions that make one a poor candidate for cooperation, but also to things one can't necessarily control, such as one's looks, possessions, and skills. Moreover, shame seems to prompt withdrawal rather than making up with others. So, Gibbard concludes, as an alternative to a guilt/anger morality, a shame/anger morality would seem to be less cost-effective: it would direct negative feelings at a broader target than necessary, and wouldn't be as effective at restoring good relations. Given the alternatives, guilt is good.

In sum, Gibbard's evolutionary perspective on morality yields what he calls 'a pragmatic justification' of the morality of guilt and anger. It also depicts our ordinary practices of moral enquiry as a natural part of the social life of our species. But what, if anything, does it say about moral philosophy?

↷

ALEX VOORHOEVE: *Moral philosophy can seem a strange and even dangerously disorienting enterprise, as it did to the Athenians who sentenced Socrates to death for corrupting their youth by his incessant questioning of prevalent moral beliefs. On your account, moral philosophy is simply an extension of our common practices of normative discussion, albeit one that takes elements of this ordinary practice—a search for consistency, consideration of different points of view, and demands for a justification for one's claims to authority—and pushes them to extraordinary lengths. Seen in this light, philosophy hardly seems odd or threatening. Do you think nonetheless that there is something to the worry that philosophy pushes questioning to a point at which it becomes useless or even destructive?*

ALLAN GIBBARD: Philosophy typically aspires to several aims. One is consistency. This is attractive, since it helps us avoid patterns of action that are self-defeating or incoherent. It also aspires to objectivity—to advance views that one can consistently demand that others accept. This, too, can be good, since the attempt to enter into discussion with others and address oneself to them can foster consensus. Finally, philosophy tries to find a deep rationale for moral norms: it searches for a point that underlies these norms, so that we don't regard them simply as taboos. Still, pursuing these aims through critical, systematic enquiry can leave us more uncertain than before we started. It can also leave us alienated from impulses from which we were not alienated before we questioned them so thoroughly. So in terms of its overall effects, there is no guarantee that engaging in moral philosophy will have good results. But I hope that it will; and I don't think that we should shy away from it. I do think that it is a good thing; otherwise I wouldn't be devoting my life to critical enquiry into morality and rationality. But it is a matter of judgement.

References and further reading

Allan Gibbard is the author of *Wise Choices, Apt Feelings: A Theory of Normative Judgement* (Oxford: Clarendon Press, 1990), *Thinking How to Live* (Cambridge, Mass.: Harvard University Press, 2003), and *Reconciling Our Aims: In Search of Bases for Ethics* (New York: Oxford University Press, 2008). Gibbard's well-known article on voting theory is 'Manipulation of Voting Schemes: A General Result', *Econometrica* 41 (1973): 587–601.

The Pilgrims' experience in Holland is recounted in Russell Shorto, *The Island at the Center of the World* (New York: Vintage, 2005): 95–6. Nietzsche attacks resentment and guilt in *On the Genealogy of Morals*, trans. Walter Kaufman and R. J. Hollingdale (New York: Vintage Books, 1967); Williams does so in *Ethics and the Limits of Philosophy* (Cambridge, Mass.: Harvard University Press, 1985), esp. ch. 10. For another interesting plea for a guilt-free morality, see Gilbert Harman, 'Guilt-free Morality' (2008), available at <www.princeton.edu/~harman/Papers/Guilt.pdf>. The quotation from Mill on the nature of wrongness is from *Utilitarianism*, ed. Roger Crisp (Oxford: Oxford University Press, 1998): ch. 5. Truman Capote's *In Cold Blood* is published by Vintage (New York, 1994); the quoted passage from Hickock's psychological self-assessment appears on p. 270.

Gibbard also refers to Jean-Paul Sartre, *Existentialism is a Humanism*, trans. Carol Macomber (New Haven: Yale University Press, 2007), Kenneth Arrow, *Social Choice and Individual Values* (New York: Wiley, 1951), and Dacher Keltner and Brenda Buswell, 'Evidence for the Distinctness of Embarrassment, Shame, and Guilt: A Study of Recalled Antecedents and Facial Expressions of Emotion', *Cognition and Emotion* 10 (1996): 155–71.

IV

UNITY AND DISSENT

8
T. M. SCANLON

THE KINGDOM OF ENDS ON THE CHEAP

Thomas Scanlon is a philosopher's moral philosopher. His writing is like the Carpenter Centre by Le Corbusier that he points out as we walk across the Harvard campus: both are without ornamentation and constructed with their purpose always in mind. In this measured style, Scanlon addresses the basic questions of moral philosophy: When we call an action morally right or wrong, what kind of judgement are we making? What kind of reasoning do we employ to arrive at such judgements? Further, when we consider an action wrong, this gives us an important reason not to perform it, and to condemn ourselves if we do. But why should moral considerations carry such weight in our lives?

As a student at Princeton in the late 1950s and early 1960s, such questions held no attraction for Scanlon. In contrast with logic and the philosophy of mathematics, moral philosophy seemed hopelessly vague, an area in which there were no definite answers, and in which there was nothing to discover. However, having been told that he must take such a course in order to graduate, he enrolled in a moral philosophy course taught by J. Howard Sobel, and found the subject fascinating. At first, his interest was in technical approaches to ethics based on game theory and decision theory. Then, during a year in Oxford, 'more or less by accident', he bought Kant's *Grounding for the Metaphysics of Morals*, a 'perplexing and difficult' book, which he came to love. He continued work in logic, however, and it wasn't until the early 1970s that moral and political philosophy became his leading occupation.

Since that time, he has been motivated by two central questions. First, how do we assess the moral rightness of an action? Second, why should we give moral considerations priority in guiding our actions? As he puts it early on in our conversation:

> Long before I started studying philosophy, I discussed legal issues with my father, who was a lawyer. And I had been stopped dead by the question, 'If you could promote a better state of affairs by interfering with people's rights to freedom of expression, then why not do so?' I thought, 'Well, you shouldn't do it, but why not?' So, from early on, I have been occupied with the tensions between consequentialism — which judges an action morally right just in case it brings about a better state of affairs — and rights-based or deontological theories. The second question that motivates me is foundational. How do moral considerations get their distinctive importance? How do they differ from other considerations?

Scanlon answers these questions in *What We Owe to Each Other*, a book begun in the late 1970s and completed in 1998. In it, Scanlon gives an account of the moral wrongness and rightness of our actions in terms of their justifiability to others. For Scanlon, an action is permissible if and only if it conforms to a set of principles for the general regulation of behaviour that no one motivated to achieve agreement could reasonably reject, and wrong if and only if someone could reasonably reject every principle that allowed it. He calls this view of morality 'contractualist' because of the central role it assigns to a notion of agreement. Of course, the scope of morality is broader than what is permissible from the perspective of other people. Moral criticism and human values extend to such things as personal development and the preservation of nature, which do not always involve our duties to others. Nevertheless, Scanlon sees the morality of 'what we owe to each other' as being the core. We discuss his views in the summer of 2000, in the grand, wood-panelled Bechtel Room of the Harvard Philosophy Department, which is hung with portraits of Harvard philosophers. Scanlon takes a seat in a corner, and during our conversation, William James, wearing a red and black gown and gripping several loose-leaf pages, looks sternly over his shoulder.

ⸯ

ALEX VOORHOEVE: *Why do you focus on the idea of what others could not reasonably reject rather than what they could reasonably accept?*

THOMAS SCANLON: Well, lots of things might be reasonable to accept. It wouldn't be unreasonable to accept a very demanding set of principles if you were so inclined. But though it might be reasonable for you to accept a principle that assigned you greater burdens than others, it might still be wrong for others to regulate their actions by such a principle. 'Principles that it would not be reasonable to reject' therefore seems to capture more adequately what it means to justify your actions to other people.

ALEX VOORHOEVE: *You argue that each person wields a veto in the imaginary gathering in which principles for conduct are agreed upon, and that this means we cannot straightforwardly trade off one individual's well-being against the well-being of many others. Why do you place such stress on what it would be reasonable for a single individual to reject?*

THOMAS SCANLON: The way I understand the idea of justifiability to others has an individualistic bias. I speak of the grounds of rejection considered from the perspective of each individual, because that seems to be the way to explain the authority of deontological or rights-based principles. Why would it be wrong to violate one person's rights for the benefit of others by, for example, using him harmfully and against his will for important medical research? Well, the answer is: it is not justifiable to him.

ⸯ

Still, each action-guiding principle will lead to a distribution of burdens and benefits to people, and some weighing of separate people's interests is necessary. The requirement of unanimity, Scanlon argues, blocks simple solutions to this problem, such as maximizing the sum of well-being, as utilitarianism demands. Rather, it directs our attention to the people most severely burdened by the principle we are considering, allowing tradeoffs only between people who face burdens of comparable seriousness. For example, if a serious accident occurs to someone in the control tower of a television station and aiding him requires ending the broadcast of a World Cup football match that millions of fans are watching, we must, Scanlon claims, attend to the wounded person, since missing a football match is not comparable to severe pain or death. (By contrast, utilitarianism would require us to stay on air if enough people would be sufficiently upset by the termination of the broadcast.) In sum, Scanlon offers us a test with which to determine the rightness of our actions. But how useful is this test?

ᔑ

ALEX VOORHOEVE: *It seems that to get some determinate answers to questions of right and wrong, we must first decide which things count as valid grounds for rejecting a principle. But this would appear to leave the procedure devoid of content: any moral principle you pull out of the contractualist hat is put there at the outset, when you decide which things count as grounds for rejecting a principle.*

THOMAS SCANLON: The very structure of the test is already a moral principle that constrains the kind of norms that can pass it. It is already a moral principle that everybody counts — that we should be able to justify our norms to everyone. The reason is that we are all reasonable creatures, to whom it makes sense to want to justify one's actions.

　　Still, one can ask what has to be presupposed to give this framework further content. Of course, someone could say, 'Well, I reject this principle because I wouldn't like to do what it makes me do.' We could say to such a person, 'This alone is not enough, for other people, too, might have to bear certain burdens.' Given that all of us have to search for principles that we can all agree on, this simply doesn't count, in itself, as a reason to reject a principle. We have to compare the reasons that someone has to reject a principle with other people's grounds for rejecting it. We have to compare, for example, whether it is a more serious objection that someone would be inconvenienced in a certain way or that someone else would lose the opportunity to engage in some valuable activity. We have to make substantive judgements about which of these claims is more important.

So we can't avoid questions of judgement, and this could lead to the charge that the contractualist reaches conclusions only because he has helped himself to lots of substantive ideas along the way, and that the theory itself therefore doesn't really yield new answers. It may be that this criticism is justified. There are different desiderata of a moral theory. I am inclined to think that providing a way of cranking out novel principles is overrated. I do not think many theories do this. Some theories do, of course, but in those cases, I do not necessarily find the principles generated the most enlightening aspects of the theory. Take Rawls's so-called 'Difference Principle'.[1] I doubt whether Rawls's theory stands or falls with the Difference Principle. Rather, his theory offers us a way of thinking about what the question of justice is. What I mean to do is offer a way of understanding what moral thinking is. This is a more important theoretical objective, in my view, than any specific answers to moral questions.

ALEX VOORHOEVE: *Still, the scope for actual disagreement between people with different ideas about what count as good reasons for rejecting a principle seems large. Is this a problem for contractualism?*

THOMAS SCANLON: This problem is not particular to contractualism. Take utilitarianism: we can have different ideas about what will

---

[1] The Difference Principle requires that social and economic institutions should maximally benefit the occupants of the least advantaged social position.

maximize utility, or about the relative importance of the different components of utility. This does not in itself invalidate utilitarianism as a theory.

On the other hand, you might say, 'Well, even though it isn't a problem for your view alone, it hits you harder, because, after all, yours is a theory of hypothetical agreement. If people aren't going to agree, that is more of a problem for you than for a utilitarian, who doesn't have anything to say about agreement or disagreement.' This objection is based on a natural but mistaken reading of the theory. To describe it as a 'hypothetical agreement' is already mistaken. It isn't about what people would agree to under certain conditions. Rather, what matters is what it would be *reasonable* for them to reject under certain conditions, that is, if they, too, were trying to find principles that others could not reasonably reject.

ALEX VOORHOEVE: *So is what's required an act of the imagination?*

THOMAS SCANLON: Not quite. That would involve imagining what people *would* or *would not* reject under certain conditions. Rather, what's involved is an act of *judgement* about what it would and would not be *reasonable* for them to reject under those circumstances. So the idea does not really involve actual or imagined agreement.

Now, I can see what you are going to say here: since my theory of moral motivation depends on being able to justify oneself to others, then of course, ideally, I will want to be able to reach *actual* agreement, to be able to justify myself to others in a way that they will accept. But everybody knows we aren't always going to get that. What we try for is justification that can't reasonably be rejected. We hope that they'll not actually reject it; but if they do — if they are unreasonable — then getting their agreement is an extra distance we can't expect to go.

There is something further to be said on the issue of disagreement. If two people find the arguments on both sides equally compelling, maybe that renders indeterminate the answer to the question of what is right and what is wrong. You might think that morality admits of such unclear areas, particularly where the cases involve a gradation, such as abortion. But again, whether any given case is unclear depends on a substantive judgement about the balance of reasons in that case. This is another thing about which people may disagree.

ALEX VOORHOEVE: *Is justifiability really fundamental to morality? It seems that the fact that an act is not justifiable to others is something that follows from a deeper, prior fact about the action: that it causes pain, or betrays someone's trust. That is why an action is wrong, and you cannot justify it to others because it is wrong. Aren't actions wrong to begin with, and therefore unjustifiable?*

THOMAS SCANLON: Of course, you could say: 'The idea of justifiability is really derivative — it is downstream from the fundamental idea that something is wrong. If something is wrong, then of course you could not justify it to others, because justifying it to others is a matter of showing that it is not wrong! So you need a prior notion of wrongness in order to explain what justifiability is.' That is certainly a common criticism, but I don't accept it. What I want to say is this. The notion of wrongness has a grip on us because it is connected to the notion of justifiability. They go together. I find it hard to accept a notion of wrongness that is prior to or independent of justification, because such a notion doesn't explain the distinctive force with which wrongness motivates us.

∽

Seeing moral rightness and wrongness as essentially tied to justification, Scanlon argues, gives us a handle on the problem of moral motivation. The reason to act morally, and what can motivate us to act in this way, is not just the good our action would bring about or the evil it would prevent. Rather, all wrong actions have an unappealing aspect: performing them estranges us from others, since we cannot reasonably justify ourselves to them. Thus, according to Scanlon, we shrink from acting in a way that is unjustifiable independently from shrinking from doing something cruel or unkind, or whatever other characteristic makes the action unjustifiable.

∽

THOMAS SCANLON: Why be moral? You answer this question by thinking about how your relationship with others is altered if you are behaving in ways that you could not reasonably expect them to accept. This puts you on a footing of revealed or concealed antagonism towards them. You are, in a way, contending parties. The reason not to have our relationships be on this footing is the reason why we can be motivated to be moral.

ALEX VOORHOEVE: *So, as you point out, you share Mill's view that a 'desire to be in unity with our fellow creatures' gives us reason to be moral. On this account, the experience of moral guilt is one of estrangement from others, of having violated the requirements of a valuable relationship with them. But this feeling of estrangement relates only to the demands that others could reasonably place on you, and this may be very different from people's actual demands. In situations where you are acting on principles that you believe others could not reasonably reject, but which they do, in fact, reject, how can this motivation still be operative?*

THOMAS SCANLON: Let us examine such cases. Suppose that you are dealing with people who have low self-esteem and you are treating them in ways you believe they could reasonably reject. However, their self-esteem is so low that they do not demand much of you and are, in fact, quite happy that you are not treating them even worse. So you might have very warm relations with them, even though you know that you are not treating them correctly. I think there is something very undesirable about relating to people in this way.

The opposite case is where you believe that, morally, you must demand more of others than they are willing to do. If you did so, you might become estranged from them because they'll regard you as a moralistic prig or something like that. Nonetheless, there would be something false about your relations with them if, for the sake of getting along with them, you simply pretended that their behaviour was all right.

So sometimes you can get good relations on the cheap and sometimes you can get them only by being morally concessive and self-effacing. But consciously acting towards others in a way you believe to be wrong creates a tension, and so does accepting others' actions when you know that they are not acting correctly towards you. Even though you are preserving good relations on the surface, there is something flawed in your relations with them. So, although it may seem that both actual and ideal agreement appeal to the same desire to not feel estranged from others, it is *not* the same desire in both cases.

ALEX VOORHOEVE: *The kind of moral motivation you propose strikes me as particular to a society like ours, in which citizens are educated into a sense of civility and are concerned that their conduct not be objectionable. But could a hunter-gatherer, for example, with an ethic of allegiance to his family and his tribe, and who prizes qualities like bravery and ruthlessness in exploits against outsiders, appreciate this abstract view of right and wrong?*

THOMAS SCANLON: I think this kind of relationship to others is something that people in all cultures and all times have reason to care about. Whether people have implicitly recognized it in all places and all times is another matter. Nevertheless, we find it in many places. The Golden Rule, for example, is advanced by many religions in some form or another. One way of understanding this rule is to think of it as an attempt to capture the idea of justifiability to others. Insofar as something like it is put forward as a theorem or a lemma in various religions, then it is recognized as a non-fundamental value. I am saying it is really *the* fundamental value.

Moreover, I am inclined to think that human beings in general are capable of understanding the kind of justifiability I am talking about. This ability is almost always evidenced in some of their interactions with other people, especially with the people to whom they are close and with whom they interact on a daily basis. That shows that people can understand the concept of justifiability, although they may not apply it as widely as I propose. Historically, all of us have been selective in submitting to the demands of justifiability. This is not entirely attributable to a lack of understanding; it is also, in part, a failure to live up to what we realize is required of us.

More generally, I am suspicious of this pressure towards a more relativistic stance, that is, a stance that involves reining in categories of appraisal that we apply to ourselves when we confront inhabitants of other cultures. There is a common idea that to apply to them our categories of moral thought shows a lack of respect, because it doesn't take into account how different they really are. I am not inclined to take this charge seriously, for two reasons. First, I think it shows a lack of respect to assume that they may not be the kind of creatures who can understand this way of thinking about morality. Second, we must show respect not only towards those we are judging as perpetrators, whom we might argue with and to whom we might say 'You shouldn't do this!', but also towards the victims. And refraining from criticism implies that we disallow the complaints of the victims against the perpetrators. Of course, this doesn't mean that we cannot see that there are circumstances in which people's wrongdoing is understandable, or even excusable. But such extenuating circumstances do not make their actions right, or shield them from moral criticism.

There is one further thing to say on the issue of respecting others. Contractualism respects people by taking seriously the most fundamental aspect of human life: each individual's capacity to select and assess various ways he may want to live, and to evaluate reasons and justifications. Recognizing the value of a rational creature is recognizing the importance of its ability to respond to reasons for believing something or acting in a certain way. And I think that behaving towards people in a way that would be allowed by principles that they could not reasonably reject is the way of relating to them that is most appropriate to their status as rational creatures. It is a way of responding to the value of humanity.

ALEX VOORHOEVE: *This fits well with a philosophical tradition that considers people's rational capacities the fundamental source of what is valuable about being human. But why should this capacity for reason be privileged over other human capacities, such as to play, to love, or to make great discoveries?*

THOMAS SCANLON: Well, partly because it governs these other capacities. It is more general. I think we relate to others in many ways: as people who respond to poetry, who play soccer, or who do mathematics. Such relations with others are based on the recognition of the value of these pursuits. Now, some people say, 'When these diverse values come into conflict with the requirements of treating others in accordance with principles that they could not reasonably reject, why shouldn't the value of poetry, soccer, or mathematical discovery trump these requirements?' I would answer: interacting with others *qua* poets, soccer players, or mathematicians is an instance of interacting with them *qua* rational creatures. If we didn't think of them as having the status of rational creatures, we wouldn't be able to relate to them in the way that we do. Therefore, I would say that a relationship to others that brings the moral requirements of what we owe to each other in train is presupposed by these more specific relationships. That's one of the reasons why moral requirements take precedence over other relationships.

ॐ

Just as the capacity to assess and act on reasons is foundational for all valuable human pursuits, so, Scanlon argues, caring about justifying oneself to others is fundamental to all valuable human relations. At the root of our relationships with others as colleagues, lovers, or friends lies our recognition of these others as people with separate moral standing, to whom justification is owed in their own right, not merely in virtue of the ties of work, love, or friendship that bind us to them. There would, remarks Scanlon, be something unnerving about a friend who would steal a kidney for you if you needed one, or, we might add, about a friend like the main character in Dominic Moll's thriller *Harry, un ami qui vous veut du bien* (*Harry: He's Here to Help*), who cares so much about another character's well-being that he rids him of his parents because they make him miserable. The attitude of such a 'friend' implies that the only reason you are not harmed is that he happens to like you.

This foundational place of morality explains its importance and its priority over other concerns and attachments in our lives. But beyond the everyday relationships that a moral attitude makes possible, Scanlon sees it as creating a community in which people live by principles to which all could reasonably agree. This ideal is similar to the moral community that Kant described as the 'kingdom of ends, the systematic union of different rational beings through common laws'.

ᔥ

ALEX VOORHOEVE: *What is the relationship between your work and Kant's kingdom of ends?*

THOMAS SCANLON: You can see Kant's work as being about an ideal of a moral community. That is what is really appealing about it. He describes acting on the categorical imperative (which tells you to act only on principles that you can will to be a universal law) as the only way of standing in a very appealing relation to other people. I have no doubt Kant was moved by that, and I think that many of his readers, myself included, are moved by that.

However, for Kant, this is not what is fundamental, which is an idea of human agency and freedom. As rational agents, says Kant, we cannot conceive of ourselves as heteronomous — as determined by outside considerations, which for Kant include all our desires. The question is then, 'Well, how can we think of ourselves as autonomous — as free from outside determination?' and Kant's answer is: 'By accepting the categorical imperative as our ultimate practical principle.'

Now, I don't find Kant's analysis of freedom convincing. In addition, I do not think that one can get much of substance out of the categorical imperative and the associated tests for whether you can coherently will your principle of action to be a law for everybody. In order to determine what kinds of principles conform to the categorical imperative, there are the so-called 'contradiction in conception' and 'contradiction in the will' tests.[2] My own way of understanding it is that the contradiction in conception test is not really a viable independent standard. This throws you back on the contradiction in the will test. And I think that in order to interpret that test in a way that actually fits with our view of morality, we have to understand it in a way that doesn't really involve a *contradiction* at all. My 'could not reasonably reject' test is an attempt to provide an alternative to these ideas of a contradiction in conception or in the will.

So to me, neither Kant's idea of freedom nor his idea of a contradiction seem to really work, and when you give up these two ideas you've relinquished a lot of Kant. However, I do find his idea of moral community very appealing. So I try to develop a notion of morality which simply takes as basic that notion of moral community. When you ask, 'Why be moral?', I think we can simply describe the appeal of that kind of community and the disappeal of its alternative. Now, in Kant's view, acting morally because one is motivated by the appeal of this kind of community is heteronomy. But not being a great believer in Kant's particular notion of autonomy, I do not see this as a problem. In a way, my view is Kant's without the really fundamental bit (for him), without the difficult part. So you could say I offer the kingdom of ends on the cheap! [*laughs*]

---

[2] The contradiction-in-conception test asks whether you can *think of* your proposed principle of action as a universal law without contradiction; the contradiction-in-the-will test asks whether you can *will* your principle of action to be a universal law without contradiction. For further discussion of these tests, see John Rawls's second lecture on Kant in his *Lectures on the History of Moral Philosophy*, ed. Barbara Herman (Cambridge, Mass.: Harvard University Press, 2000) and the sections on Kant's Formula of Universal Law in Derek Parfit, *On What Matters* (Oxford: Oxford University Press, forthcoming).

References and further reading

Thomas Scanlon is the author of *What We Owe to Each Other* (Cambridge., Mass.: Harvard University Press, 1998), *The Difficulty of Tolerance: Essays in Political Philosophy* (Cambridge: Cambridge University Press, 2003), and *Moral Dimensions: Permissibility, Meaning, Blame* (Cambridge, Mass.: Harvard University Press, 2008). The quotation from Mill is from *Utilitarianism*, edited by Roger Crisp (Oxford: Oxford University Press, 1998): ch. 3, para. 10. The quotation from Kant on the kingdom of ends is from *Grounding for the Metaphysics of Morals*, trans. James W. Ellington (Indianapolis: Hackett, 1994), Akademie page 433. For a critical analysis of Scanlon's work, see *On What We Owe to Each Other*, edited by Philip Stratton-Lake (Oxford: Blackwell, 2004).

9
BERNARD WILLIAMS

A MISTRUSTFUL ANIMAL

Bernard Williams (1929–2003) was a Fellow of All Souls College, Oxford, and taught at University College London, Cambridge University, and the University of California at Berkeley. He is the author of, among other works, *Morality, Utilitarianism: For and Against* (with J. J. C. Smart), *Ethics and the Limits of Philosophy*, *Truth and Truthfulness*, and several volumes of essays, including the famous collection *Moral Luck*.

'Philosophy,' Williams says at the beginning of our conversation, 'starts from the realization that we don't fully understand our activities and thoughts; its task is to suggest and open up ways in which we might better understand them.' Especially in the case of ethics, with which most of his work is concerned, he is sceptical of the idea that philosophers can do this through advancing theories, seeing philosophical theories instead as barriers to increased self-understanding. (He famously responded to his one-time tutor R. M. Hare's question: 'You pull everything down, but what do you put it its place?,' with 'Well, in *that* place, I don't put anything. That isn't a place anything should be!')

We meet at his home in Oxford on a cold, dark afternoon in December 2002. Having heard of Williams's love of opera, I have brought him a recent recording of Jean-Jacques Rousseau's *Le devin du village*. He seems pleased with the addition to his collection, even though he must be well acquainted with the opera, since he hums the peasant girl Collet's catchy opening aria while he makes us a cup of tea. A power failure in part of the house leaves the living room illuminated by a single lamp, and we talk and sip our tea in semi-darkness.

ᔕ

ALEX VOORHOEVE: *How did you become interested in philosophy?*

BERNARD WILLIAMS: It was the old story of getting interested in the subject before I knew that there was such a subject. When I was at school, some friends and I started talking about a set of issues which I would now call 'philosophical'. Some of these issues were political. At that time, we were at war and allied with the Soviet Union, so discussions about Communism occupied us. Also, I was already much occupied with questions having to do with art and morality and the autonomy of the artist. As it happened, my headmaster, who was a fervent Oxford man, sent me in for a scholarship in Classics at Oxford. Only after I got there did I discover that the course I had enrolled in, the so-called Greats Course, included philosophy. That was rather nice, since it meant that I was going to be studying the kind of things that already interested me. However, it wasn't that I wanted to do philosophy and just did some Classics along the way; I was always very interested in Classics. This shows in my philosophical work, on which Classical thought has had an important influence.

ALEX VOORHOEVE: *Who among your teachers and contemporaries most influenced you?*

BERNARD WILLIAMS: Though I did not agree with his views, I admired many of Gilbert Ryle's attitudes to philosophy. I particularly learned from his criticism of dividing philosophy into what he called 'isms'. He believed there were many philosophical questions and ways of arguing about them, but that attaching labels like 'physicalism' or 'idealism' to any particular way of answering philosophical questions was extremely mechanical and misleading. In general, Ryle was an extremely sensible, open-minded, and fair-minded teacher. I was also very impressed and influenced by my friend David Pears. In the 1950s, when I was a young don, David and I gave classes together, and I very much admired his methods. Another person who had *one* kind of influence on me—though, I am glad to say, I think she didn't influence me in other ways!—was Elisabeth Anscombe. One thing that she did, which she got from Wittgenstein, was to impress upon one that being clever wasn't enough. Oxford philosophy had a great tendency to be clever. It was very eristic: there was a lot of competitive dialectical exchange and showing other people were wrong. I was quite good at all that. But Elisabeth conveyed a strong sense of the seriousness of the subject and how the subject was difficult in ways that simply being clever wasn't going to get round.

ALEX VOORHOEVE: *What is required in addition to being clever?*

BERNARD WILLIAMS: A good appreciation of what is *not* there in the argument or on the page, and also some imagination. Many philosophers pursue a line of argument in a very linear fashion, in which one proof caps another proof, or a refutation refutes some other supposed proof, instead of thinking laterally about what it all might mean. There is a tendency to forget the main issues. An example is that people used to go on about what the difference is between a moral and a non-moral this, that, and the other. 'What is a moral consideration as opposed to a non-moral consideration?' 'What is a moral judgement as opposed to a non-moral judgement?' They belaboured these questions without ever asking why the distinction was supposed to be so important in the first place.

ALEX VOORHOEVE: *What are your motives in doing philosophy?*

BERNARD WILLIAMS: Stuart Hampshire used to say that historically, there have been two motives for philosophy. One was curiosity and the other was salvation. Plato, as he managed to combine almost everything else, combined the two. I think that Wittgenstein was very much on the side of salvation. So was Kierkegaard—though he was so clever that his curiosity was always catching him out!

Now, I am not into salvation. I suppose my interest in philosophy is primarily a curiosity that stems from puzzlement. It is the old philosophical motive of *simply not seeing* how various ideas, which are supposed to be central to human life or human activities, hang together: the notion of the self, obviously, the notion of moral and aesthetic value, and the place that certain kinds of valuable things, such as works of art, have in our lives. Yes—some of it is just puzzlement.

But I suppose there are two other emphases in my work. First, given my temperament, my curiosity was always aligned with suspicion. What Ricœur has called the 'hermeneutic of suspicion', which was so characteristic in Nietzsche, Marx, and Freud, came rather naturally to me, with the result that the pretensions of certain kinds of value always aroused my suspicion.

The other development in my work, which has been more gradual, is the realization that if you are puzzled by any idea that matters in human affairs, it is almost certain that you won't actually resolve your puzzlement merely by philosophical analysis. You almost certainly need to know the history of the term you are dealing with. This historicist turn has become more prominent in my work in the last ten or fifteen years.

ALEX VOORHOEVE: *Can you say more about the role of historical understanding in ethics and political philosophy?*

BERNARD WILLIAMS: History, in a broad sense, is important in various ways. First, it may present us with a problem about our views. When we ask why we came to use some concepts rather than others that were prevalent at an earlier time, we typically come to see that this history is not vindicatory. That is, we might like to see our ideas, like liberal ideas of equality and equal rights, as having won an argument against earlier conceptions, like those of the *ancien régime*. History, however, shows that though these ideas 'won', they didn't win *an argument*. For the standards or aims of the argument practised by the proponents of liberal ideas were not shared by the defenders of the *ancien régime*. This brings home to us the historical contingency of our ideas and outlook.

Now, this contingency need not be a problem for us, in the sense that it might not undermine our confidence in our outlook. For the idea that a vindicatory history — one that showed that our ideas were better by standards that could have been accepted by their historical opponents — is what is required looks like the idea that we should search for a system of ethical and political ideas that is best from a point of view that is as free as possible from contingent historical perspective. And I believe it is an illusion to think that that is our task. But although it may not lead us to reject our outlook, the fact that there is no vindicatory history of it does matter for our attitude towards the outlooks of others, among other things.

Second, history can help us understand particular ways in which our ideas seem incoherent to us. For instance, I believe liberalism has problems with ideas of autonomy that have their roots in Enlightenment conceptions of the individual, because these conceptions do not make sense to us.

Third, the content of ethical and political ideas that are useful for us will be determined in part by an understanding of the necessities of our way of life. The question 'What is possible for us now?' is, I believe, really a relevant consideration in political and moral philosophy. This question demands empirical social understanding and insight. I would claim that you are not going to get such insight except by historical methods. That is, I don't believe that there is, for instance, a substantive enough, or interesting enough, sociology that could tell you what is possible for us.

ALEX VOORHOEVE: *Can you give an example of these ways in which history is important for a political concept?*

BERNARD WILLIAMS: Take liberty. I think that, like other political concepts, we need to construct a concept of liberty that is historically self-conscious and suitable for a modern society. I distinguish between 'primitive freedom', which I understand as being unobstructed in doing what you want by some form of humanly imposed coercion, and liberty. Since liberty is a political value, to determine which losses of primitive freedom can count as a loss of liberty, and especially when considering what counts as 'humanly imposed coercion', we have to consider what someone could reasonably resent as a loss. Here, the question of the form of society that is possible for us becomes relevant. From this perspective, a practice is not a limitation of liberty if it is necessary for there to be any state at all. But it is also not a loss of liberty if it is necessary for the functioning of society as we can reasonably imagine it working and still being 'our' society. Thus, while some force and threats of force, and some institutional structures which impose disadvantage on people, will count as limiting people's liberty, being prevented from getting what I want through economic competition will not, except in exceptional cases. That is because competition is central to modern commercial society's functioning.

Understanding our historical condition also helps us understand the value that liberty has for us. The concept of modernity I have in mind here is the concept that is the foundation of modern social science. It is akin to Weber's concept of modernity. This notion involves the disenchantment of the world, and a retreat from believing that the order of how people should treat one another is somehow inscribed either in them or in the universal realm. It also involves an associated tendency to hold up various traditional sources of authority to question — it is a notable feature of modernity that we do not believe the traditional legitimation stories of hierarchy and inequality.

Now, the link between modernity and the value of liberty is as follows. It is because our legitimation stories start with less than other outlooks that liberty is more important to us. Because of our doubts about authority, we allow each citizen a strong presumption in favour of pursuing the fulfilment of his or her desires.

This — admittedly rough — account of liberty also illustrates how a historical explanation of the value that a concept has for us need not undermine it. For we can regard our current mistrust of the legitimation stories of the past as a good thing, because this mistrust is a consequence of the fact that, under the conditions of modernity, we have a better grasp on the truth.

ALEX VOORHOEVE: *I'd like to turn to the question what modernity, and the reflective consciousness it implies, means for our view of ethics. Much of your work focuses on the virtues. Consider someone who doesn't possess these virtues, and who is thinking about acquiring them. As you discuss in* Ethics and the Limits of Philosophy, *Aristotle had an answer for such a person (even though, if he was a bad person, he might not be able to appreciate the answer's truth). He believed that each kind of thing has a perfect form of functioning, towards which it naturally strives. This ideal form of functioning for human beings consists of a state of well-being, a state that requires the possession of the virtues. But we no longer believe Aristotle's assumptions about the natural striving of each kind of thing towards its perfection. So do we have an answer for this person?*

BERNARD WILLIAMS: Yes, good. I think this is like a lot of features of modernity. There is an increase in insight, in knowledge, in irony, and a decrease in all-round satisfaction about the world all fitting together. Actually, although I don't think I've made this as clear as I could have in *Ethics and the Limits of Philosophy*, I believe that Aristotle's own account, which from the *Nicomachean Ethics* emerges as a pretty satisfied account of the virtues, is an astonishing piece of cultural wish-fulfilment. Because that absolutely cannot have been what Athens in the fourth century BC was all about. If you consider the Athens of which Plato gave a far more honest and realistic, though also jaundiced, picture and you consider that it was, after all, on its way to the collapse of democracy, then the idea that all these people were swimming around in this state of huge self-satisfaction and in harmony with the universe, the polity, and their own desires is completely ridiculous! Aristotle was a provincial who became exceedingly impressed by a conservative view of a certain kind.

ALEX VOORHOEVE: *In* Ethics and the Limits of Philosophy, *you present our disbelief of Aristotle's assumptions as undermining our ethical confidence. But is this really true? If acquiring the virtues is, as Aristotle thought, a matter of being brought up in a certain way, rather than a conscious undertaking, and if we accept that these virtues are going to be attractive to us when we have some of the dispositions that they require, then why should the falling away of an external justification for the virtues affect our view of their value?*

BERNARD WILLIAMS: These are extremely good questions. I think you have to take what I was saying in the context of a discussion in which it is assumed that an external justification of the ethical will make some difference to our attachment to it. Rather early in the book, in the second chapter, I do question this assumption. I say that it seems rather odd that it should be true, and ask, 'What does the professor's argument do when they come to take him away?' But on the assumption that the philosophical justification of the ethical will make some difference, this is the place at which it will do so.

Now, I don't think Aristotle delivers on his promise to show how all the virtues hang together in an attractive package. But since I don't believe that the question about the philosophical justification of the objectivity of ethics has quite the foundational or all-changing role which was assumed in that discussion, you are quite right that this external perspective doesn't seem to make quite so much difference. But I do think that there is a point to be made, as so often in moral philosophy, which consists of turning the same point around. The trouble is that if you get a story which presents an idealized account of the ethical in the virtue repertoire by stressing the unity of the virtues and their unity with happiness and all that, then this can encourage its dialectical opposite. When the news gets out that for the vast majority of human beings the virtues don't necessarily go together and that some of them are a great disadvantage (actually, this isn't news — that the virtues can do you harm was extremely well known to Socrates, for instance), there is a strong tendency to say,

'The whole of the ethical is bogus!' The business of defending *some* of the ethical becomes much harder. So we come to a point where most of my efforts have been concentrated: to make *some* sense of the ethical as opposed to throwing out the whole thing because you can't have an idealized version of it.

ALEX VOORHOEVE: *Throughout Ethics and the Limits of Philosophy, there is a theme that self-consciousness, intellectual criticism, and knowledge destroy both Greek and Enlightenment ideals. Still, the Greek way of thinking about morality seems to emerge less damaged than modern ways of thinking . . .*

BERNARD WILLIAMS: You are right that, up to a point, there are quite a few Greek ideas that are more robust, that have more material to give us, than more recent ideas. The reason is that they are less indebted to ideas of free will of an over-ambitious kind. I think that the more exposed parts of modern ideas — the parts that are in the worst shape — are the bits that have to do with Christianity. Nonetheless, one must add heavy qualifications to the claim that Greek ideas better withstand scrutiny. The problem with Greek thought is that a set of ideas that arose from a totally different period, over two thousand years ago, will be completely out of place in the modern world. Some conceptions, particularly of rights, have emerged that we simply can't do without. The idea that we could would be ridiculous. Once we realize this, we must try to get these ideas that we can't do without into a shape where they need less metaphysical fuel than they do in the form given to them by philosophers like Kant.

ALEX VOORHOEVE: *One current set of ideas that is less dependent on metaphysics is contractualism, as expounded by Thomas Scanlon, for example. This doesn't seem to be susceptible to the same criticisms you level at some other Enlightenment ideas. Scanlon even jokingly characterizes his account of morality as offering 'Kant's kingdom of ends on the cheap' . . .*

BERNARD WILLIAMS: [*laughs*] I think he's selling himself short!

ALEX VOORHOEVE: *Scanlon has an interesting idea about characterizing moral motivation as originating in the desire to be able to justify ourselves to others. As he puts it, the reason to act morally is the reason we have to not place ourselves in a position of revealed or concealed antagonism to others. In* Truth and Truthfulness, *when you examine the origins and value of the virtue of sincerity, you place a lot of emphasis on a similar idea. You give an example of an old woman to whom we lie for her own benefit, and you say that although much of what Kant says about lying is mistaken, what is right about the Kantian account is that it focuses on how our relationship to her changes when we lie to her. As you write:*

> It is a violation of trust. I lead the hearer to rely on what I say, when she has good reason to do so, and in abusing this I abuse the relationship which is based on it. Even if it is for good reasons of concern for her, I do not give her a chance, in this particular respect, to form her own reactions to the facts . . . I put her, to that extent, in my power and so take away or limit her freedom.

And you conclude that the value of sincerity lies in the value of the relationships of trust that it makes possible.

BERNARD WILLIAMS: As they say, it is no accident, comrade, that in *Truth and Truthfulness* I write in the chapter about lying that I am very much in agreement with, and indebted to, Scanlon's book. I also think Scanlon's book has been misunderstood and unfairly treated. You will remember the criterion which holds that an action is permissible if and only if it conforms to a set of rules that no one could reasonably reject. Some have complained that Scanlon does not offer a criterion for what someone can't reasonably reject. But I take it that the point is, simply, that *that* is the question we should be asking — that what goes into reasonable rejection is just what we should be thinking about.

So I am quite sympathetic to this formulation. Certainly, it doesn't require all the metaphysical baggage [that Kant required], and it also has the right shape to be a formula for moral consideration, since equality of some kind is a core moral idea for us. We have to understand the precondition for membership in the kingdom of ends — that is, for membership in the set of persons whose behaviour is regulated by the contractual test and towards whom we must act in ways that pass this test — on the basis of equality. By contrast, if you think of the outlooks of the *ancien régime*, or indeed of the Greeks, then the idea that the core of morality has to do with what *anybody* could not reasonably reject is simply a non-starter. In these outlooks, the fact that our acts and institutions could reasonably be rejected by some classes of persons is not an issue. No doubt, the lower orders wouldn't want to accept some of the principles by which the higher orders live, but from the perspective of the higher orders, that is of no consequence: members of the lower orders don't count (or don't count as much). Of course, the question is how far our notion of equality, which is itself a moral notion, is constitutive, or 'factual', as it were, and how far it is an aspiration that is expressed by this way of treating people.

ALEX VOORHOEVE: *What would it be for it to be 'factual'?*

BERNARD WILLIAMS: Well, I think that does have some bite. For when you get people to reflect on the bases of discrimination, then you get into the area of the factual. Here is one way of putting it. In the past, people have discriminated against other people, not treated them equally in a Scanlonian or Kantian sense, because they were people of colour or because they were women. Yet, it is not that 'Because she is a woman' or 'Because he is black' was really much of a reason. It wasn't articulated in this way at all, it was simply inherent in their institutions. But when someone questioned why they were so discriminated against, they had to offer a justification, such as 'Blacks are stupid,' or 'Women don't have the requisite skills and character for certain jobs.' But these were just rationalizations, false consciousness really, to support the institutions in question. Now, it is very important that these claims are false and known, in a sense, to be false. Take the case of the slave owners who drafted the Bill of Rights. There was a great deal of false consciousness there, since when these slave owners took advantage of their women slaves, they didn't think they were engaged in bestiality. They were well aware that they were having sex with a human being!

ALEX VOORHOEVE: *I expected you to be more critical of contractualism . . .*

BERNARD WILLIAMS: Well, I think that it does raise a whole class of problems about one's relations to other people, although it is probably not a criticism of contractualism that it raises these problems, since they are probably problems anyway. Contractualism is likely to give rise to what I call the 'one thought too many' problem — because, no doubt, other people could not reasonably reject the rule that a man should save his wife from a shipwreck, but it is not *that* thought, one would hope, that motivates the man who saves his wife from the wreck. So, there is always the question about the relationship between moral considerations and considerations of a non-reflective or non-morally mediated kind. But then I think you could say that problem exists anyway.

ALEX VOORHOEVE: *I don't understand this purported 'one thought too many' problem. Aren't there simply two different questions here? The first is, 'How are people acting in such a situation; what's going through their heads?', and the second is the reflective question about our habits of acting. It seems to make perfect sense to ask the reflective question, since we can't always follow the demands of friendship or love, and we need some perspective from which we evaluate how far it is morally permissible to act from these motives . . .*

BERNARD WILLIAMS: Well, up to a point. What you say is perfectly sensible, but if you go too far in that direction, you get into the false

disjunction between justification and motivation of which Henry
Sidgwick and other higher-order utilitarians make a great deal,
namely that such-and-such is the justification for acting in a certain
way doesn't mean that it should enter into the motivations of the
people who are so acting. I think that leads to an absurd alienation
problem. I mean, up to a point there is a possibility there, but, in the
end, one needs unity between the language and thought of action,
and the language and thought of reflection.

ALEX VOORHOEVE: *There seems to be a further point at which your
views are in conflict with contractualism. In* Moral Luck, *you discuss
an ideal of ethical consistency that appears to figure in contractualism,
according to which 'an action being morally justified implies that no one
can justifiably complain from the moral point of view'. You argue that this
ideal is too demanding, partly by referring to political cases, where, you
claim, a political leader can be justified in an action that harms innocent
people, even though these people could reasonably reject this action on
account of its cost to them . . .*

BERNARD WILLIAMS: Indeed. In the political case, I think you cannot
always say that the people who have to bear the burden of a decision
have no justified complaint — that they haven't been wronged because
they should take the perspective of the *raison d'état*.

ALEX VOORHOEVE: *What about a case of personal morality, in which it
seems conceivable that someone does what is morally right, but still wrongs
someone else in the process? For example, a man might break a solemn
promise in order to pursue some good end that is important enough to
justify breaking the promise — and nonetheless it might seem that the
recipient of the promise can sensibly feel wronged. Do you think that such
cases render implausible Scanlon's contractualism, which doesn't seem to
allow for them?*

BERNARD WILLIAMS: I was glancing at that when I made the earlier
point. The difficulty is the usual 'level of description' problem.

Nobody could reasonably reject, in the Scanlonian sense, there being such an institution as promising. And moreover, they can't reasonably reject the idea that there are certain kinds of circumstances in which it is justified to break a promise. But how far down should you go here? For instance, if I have broken a promise, does that mean I should recompense or apologize to the parties I have disadvantaged? If so, if there is an 'ought' here, as there seems to be, then that seems to imply that nobody could reasonably reject a rule that requires that I give compensation, an apology, etc. But I must say I think it is clearer that recompense is appropriate than that it is a principle that no one could reasonably reject that one should offer recompense in such situations. We are reading back from the intuition into the formula. Now, does it mean that the recipient of the apology ought to accept it? That is very unclear. Or does it mean that the recipient of the apology either ought to accept it or ought to disagree that the principle on which I was acting was not reasonably rejectable by him?

ALEX VOORHOEVE: *I think it does have that implication.*

BERNARD WILLIAMS: Well, it looks to me that when you get too far down here, you get to the idea that everybody's responses would be harmonized in a way that would suit the kingdom of ends (which would be better named the republic of ends, if you ask me!). So we come to the usual problem with contractualism, that it requires too much harmonization of people's moral sentiments. We all know of situations in which people would, perfectly intelligibly, refuse to play this game of giving reasons for and against general principles.[1]

---

[1] The case of Paul Gauguin, which Williams discusses in *Moral Luck*, can perhaps serve as the basis for an example here. Imagine that Gauguin knew that he would produce his exceptional paintings if and only if he abandoned his wife and children and moved to Tahiti. Also suppose that from an impartial perspective, the value of his art is such that no one, not even his family, could reasonably reject this course of action. Given these assumptions, it seems contractualism would have to hold that Gauguin's wife should not resent him for leaving. But it would seem perfectly sensible for her to refuse to regulate her moral sentiments by this test.

ALEX VOORHOEVE: *I'd like to end with some questions on your work on truthfulness and modern culture. Nietzsche wrote that 'man is a venerating animal, but also a mistrustful one; and that the world is not worth what we thought is about the most certain thing our mistrust has finally gotten hold of.' He also wrote: 'The more mistrust, the more philosophy.' Do you think mistrust (rather than veneration) is characteristic of modern society—and does it make for 'more philosophy'?*

BERNARD WILLIAMS: Yes and yes. But there is a heavy qualification coming: modern entertainment, modern communication, and modern saturation with 'information' may make effective criticism and effective reflection impossible. Just as the tabloid newspapers get obsessed with the day's scandal and the Internet becomes dominated by the same kind of 'news', it is possible that our self-examination and questioning become merely superficial phenomena, and that there are simply a lot of unquestioned assumptions about how life is being led that are really quite unsatisfactory. If expressed, I don't think people would really believe in them, but they have no option but to go along with them. So I think that if one means *effective* criticism and self-examination, there is a very big question mark over it. Of course, a lot of what one has in mind when one thinks about social critics—I mean conservative social critics on the one hand and defenders of liberalism on the other—is a very intense and serious form of criticism which was the product of modernity, when the thinker was still protected by the institutions of an earlier time. Now that these institutions have devolved into one gigantic market, it is very unclear whether anyone will have thoughts of this highly directed kind at all. So the idea of a space in which philosophy and related kinds of critical and questioning activity can go on may itself be under threat.

ALEX VOORHOEVE: *In* Truth and Truthfulness, *you also suggest that our culture of suspicion threatens to undermine our faith in truth. You* *begin with Nietzsche's discussion of the ideal of truthfulness. Nietzsche comes to the conclusion that truthfulness is the last metaphysical concept, and that the investigation that is driven by truthfulness ends up undermining itself.*

BERNARD WILLIAMS: In *The Gay Science* and *The Genealogy of Morals*, when Nietzsche says that this fire that burns in our enquiries is the selfsame fire that burns in Plato, his aim is to upset the liberals who have been very happily nodding along with him while he was being rude to the Church. I think he certainly wanted an adequately naturalized account of the value of truthfulness. I hope my book, to some extent, offers that by constructing a genealogy of truth. A genealogy is a narrative that tries to explain an outlook or value by describing how it came about, or could have come about, or could be imagined to come about. An interesting question one can ask of such genealogies is whether they are vindicatory, that is, whether the genealogical account of a value, when it is understood, strengthens or weakens one's confidence in that value. A vindicatory genealogy makes sense of a particular value, although it doesn't quite make sense of it in the elevated terms in which others have described it. The basis then doesn't have to be metaphysical.

I hope I've offered, to some extent, such a vindicatory genealogy of truth and truthfulness. The further question is, of course, whether our commitment to truthfulness leads to tragedy or to everybody being happier. Nietzsche was occupied with this question, and rightly so. My book is optimistic about the possibility of naturalizing truthfulness, but I leave you to judge the last pages to find out whether I am optimistic or pessimistic about this further question.

ALEX VOORHOEVE: *I thought your book ended with a pious hope about the value of truth and truthfulness . . .*

BERNARD WILLIAMS: It certainly isn't a *pious* hope! The last writer I quote is Conrad in *Heart of Darkness*. As they say in New York, 'Think about it.'[2]

References and further reading

Bernard Williams's reply to R. M. Hare's question is quoted from J. Baggini, 'Beating the Systems', *Philosophers' Magazine* 21 (2003): 29. Williams draws the distinction between what he calls 'primitive freedom' and 'liberty' in 'From Freedom to Liberty: The Construction of a Political Value', *Philosophy and Public Affairs* 30 (2001): 3 – 26. The 'one thought too many problem' is introduced in his 'Persons, Character, and Morality', in *Moral Luck* (Cambridge: Cambridge University Press, 1981): 1 – 19. Sidgwick argues that the moral justification for people's actions need not be reflected in their motives for action in his *The Methods of Ethics* (Indianapolis: Hackett, 1981), book 4, ch. 5, sect. 3.

My quotations from Nietzsche are from *The Gay Science*, ed. Bernard Williams, trans. Josefine Nauckhoff (Cambridge: Cambridge University Press, 2000): remark 346. Williams ends *Truth and Truthfulness* with a passage from *Heart of Darkness* (London: J. M. Dent and Sons, 1946) in which the narrator says about Kurtz and his dying words:

> This is the reason why I affirm that Kurtz was a remarkable man. He had something to say. He said it . . . he had summed up — he had judged. 'The horror!' He was a remarkable man. After all, this was the expression of some sort of belief; it had candour, it had conviction, it had a vibrating note of revolt in its whisper; it had the appalling face of a glimpsed truth. (151)

---

[2] To my great regret, Bernard Williams did not have an opportunity to correct the transcript of this interview.

The following are Williams's principal works on ethics: *Utilitarianism: For and Against*, co-authored with J. J. C. Smart (Cambridge: Cambridge University Press, 1973); *Morality* (Cambridge: Cambridge University Press, 2nd edn 1993); *Moral Luck* (Cambridge: Cambridge University Press, 1981); *Utilitarianism and Beyond*, co-edited with Amartya Sen (Cambridge: Cambridge University Press, 1982); *Ethics and the Limits of Philosophy* (Cambridge, Mass.: Harvard University Press, 1985); *Shame and Necessity* (Cambridge: Cambridge University Press, 1993); and *Truth and Truthfulness* (Princeton: Princeton University Press, 2002).

For a critical assessment of Williams's work on ethics, see Thomas Nagel, 'The View from Here and Now', *London Review of Books* 28, 9 (May 2006), and Timothy Chappell, 'Bernard Williams', *Stanford Encyclopedia of Philosophy* (online at <http://plato.stanford.edu/entries/williams-bernard>).

V

LOVE AND MORALITY

10
HARRY FRANKFURT

THE NECESSITY OF LOVE

I n 'Rules for the Direction of our Native Intelligence', René Descartes sums up his method for gaining secure knowledge as follows:

> The whole method consists entirely in the ordering and arranging of the objects on which we must concentrate our mind's eye if we are to discover some truth. We shall be following this method exactly if we first reduce complicated and obscure propositions step by step to simpler ones, and then, starting with the intuition of the simplest ones of all, try to ascend through the same steps to knowledge of all the rest.

The work of the Princeton University philosopher Harry Frankfurt is a present-day exemplar of this method. Attracted by the clarity and rigour of Descartes' writing, Frankfurt began his career studying his work. Since the early 1960s, Frankfurt has written on, among other topics, moral responsibility, personal identity, freedom of the will, and autonomy. In each case, Frankfurt has proceeded by identifying a few simple ideas that he believes lie at the heart of these obscure and puzzling notions, and then using these ideas to arrive at a more accurate understanding of them. Often, the result is that established ways of thinking are shown to be mistaken. Thus, famously, Frankfurt has argued against the common view that a person is morally responsible for an action only if she could have acted otherwise than she did. He has also argued that constraints upon the will are in some cases necessary for, rather than contrary to, autonomy.

Frankfurt has also directed his attention to the problem of practical normativity, the area of philosophy concerned with the question 'How should one live?' We met to discuss this topic during Frankfurt's visit to University College London, where he was lecturing in the autumn of 2001.

∽

ALEX VOORHOEVE: *What brought you to study philosophy?*

HARRY FRANKFURT: You are asking me about something that happened a long time ago . . . I think it was a difficulty in deciding what else to do, and the thought that philosophy didn't require me to give up anything — that no matter what I was interested in, it was legitimate to focus my attention on it.

ALEX VOORHOEVE: *How did you become interested in Descartes' work?*

HARRY FRANKFURT: He seemed like a very clear-headed, rigorous thinker. Also, he declared that he wanted to find a way to distinguish between the true and the false, and between the right and the wrong course of action. That was what I was interested in too at the time. Finally, the fact that his books were short made it possible for me to think of coming to master his writing. Then, the more I studied Descartes, the more appealing I found it. In fact, think I learned more about philosophy studying Descartes than I did in any other way.

ALEX VOORHOEVE: *What was it about his work that taught you so much?*

HARRY FRANKFURT: The commitment to rationality and what reason entails. For me, the most important things about Descartes were his commitment to rigour and his desire to find beliefs that could be held in the face of any effort to undermine them — that could withstand any scepticism, however intense. I don't know if I still think that is a feasible or plausible ideal, but it was one I found very compelling at the time.

∽

Philosophy is said to have started with wonder at natural phenomena and puzzlement at certain logical or conceptual problems. Frankfurt observes, however, that the question 'How should one live?' doesn't arise from such wonder or puzzlement. Rather, it springs from a feeling of uncertainty about what one wants to do and what one stands for. Frankfurt believes that philosophers have commonly taken the wrong approach to addressing this question by focusing on what is required or endorsed by moral principles. One reason he thinks moral considerations provide an inadequate answer to this question is that they are impartial. The considerations that help us answer the question 'How should one live?' are, by contrast, personal. But is Frankfurt right to claim that morality is relentlessly impartial?

∽

ALEX VOORHOEVE: *You started your second lecture by drawing a contrast between the demands of 'strictly universal [moral] principles' and favour-itism towards friends, close relations, and ourselves. Is this contrast as stark as you make it out to be? We can come up with impartial reasons for allowing partiality. For example, it is clear that the close affective relations we have with friends and family are generally of great importance to us. If we had to respond to each person's demands equally, then we would lose these valuable relationships. Similarly, we generally want space to pursue our own projects. So there is an impartial argument for allowing us a space to pursue what we regard as important.*

HARRY FRANKFURT: These reasons you mention are impartial only if we all have similar goals. In this case, they seem to support the rule 'Live and let live.' You want to be able to lead your life, and I want to be able to lead mine, so we agree to respect each other's interests in these matters. But we have an impartial reason in this case only if each of us wants to be left in peace. And I might not want peace. I might be less interested in your forbearance than you are in mine. I might think that I can get away with murder. I might be like Callicles in Plato's *Gorgias*. It seems that Socrates' answer to Callicles' challenge on this issue was that even thieves have to respect one another's interests, because otherwise they couldn't work together in order to carry out their thievery. Now, perhaps it is true that I need the cooperation of other people to pursue the life I want to lead. But I certainly don't need *everyone's* cooperation. So the impartial reasons that you mention are contingent — they are not written in the heavens, nor are they eternal truths that come to us through reason. They are merely practical arrangements, and the need for them may vary from person to person.

ALEX VOORHOEVE: *Still, might we not say that whether or not they recognize it, all people have a reason to act morally, since doing so places them in a particular kind of relationship with others: of living on terms that they believe they can justify to them? Mill referred to this idea as 'being in unity with our fellow creatures'.*

HARRY FRANKFURT: I have no idea what this mystical phrase is supposed to mean. I would say that our motive to act morally is that we do not want to be abandoned. We are enormously dependent at birth, and we continue to be dependent, to one degree or another, as we mature. And that sense of dependency is very powerful. So we are made very anxious if it seems that we can't count on anybody and are left alone. Here, I am referring not only to physical dependency, but also to psychological dependency. Loneliness is a very painful condition — for many people, it threatens their sense of their own reality. The extent to which we feel real depends on the ways in which people react to us. We see ourselves in them, in their reactions to us, in their responses to us. If we don't get such responses, our sense of our own reality becomes very shaky. So loneliness is a very disequilibrilizing condition.

ALEX VOORHOEVE: *This fear of loneliness gives us reason to have loved ones around us, and friendships, and to have good relations with those people with whom we interact. But it seems to have little to do with morality, which regulates our behaviour towards everyone, not just towards people who are close to us.*

HARRY FRANKFURT: Well, I think that, to a considerable extent, this motivation is indeed much stronger at the level of personal or close relations. The universalistic, impartial sense of morality one encounters in philosophy . . . I don't know how widespread it is outside the circles that we move in. But I think what moves us in the direction of a universalistic morality is that we don't like to think of ourselves as having hostile relationships with anybody. And this takes on a life of its own. It becomes institutionalized; we make up general principles because it is easier to rely on such rules than to approach each person wondering whether it would be a good idea to be on good terms with him.

ALEX VOORHOEVE: *You seem to be suggesting that all we care about is being on good terms with others. But being on good terms might be consistent with having an exploitative relationship.*

HARRY FRANKFURT: That's true in individual cases, but it's not generally true. So the easiest thing is to follow some general principles of good behaviour which can reasonably be expected to lead to orderly, peaceful, and amicable relationships.

ALEX VOORHOEVE: *I would like to question your view of the conflict between morality and personal goals in one other respect. In* What We Owe to Each Other, *Thomas Scanlon has argued that many valuable pursuits and relationships need not conflict with what morality*

demands, since they have a built-in sensitivity to these demands. For
example, Scanlon argues that we have an ideal of friendship that involves
recognizing the moral claims of friends qua *persons, that is, as people*
whose moral claims on us are independent of our particular relationship
with them. This ideal of friendship will never demand that we violate
others' entitlements for the sake of friendship. Other personal values might
be similarly reconciled with the demands of morality . . .

HARRY FRANKFURT: I don't understand the view that moral considerations are always overriding. Scanlon, and others, hold that morality
has to do with the way we treat other people. Why should that be the
most important thing in our lives? Why should *that* take precedence
over everything else? It may, but I don't see what there is about my
relationships with other people that implies as a matter of necessity
that those considerations override considerations of any other kind.
After all, most people don't enter into my life in a significant way
at all.

ఌ

In sum, Frankfurt argues that philosophers should recognize that
morality cannot provide an adequate answer to the problem of practical
normativity. In addition, he believes we should abandon the rationalistic
ideal which holds that the answer to the question of how to live should
be found by discovering some command of reason. Instead, he proposes
we begin our enquiry with the will.

As Frankfurt understands it, a person's will is the desire by which he
is motivated in action. An essential characteristic of persons, Frankfurt
argues, is that they care about what kinds of desires they have. He refers
to such desires that take other desires as their object as 'second-order
desires'. A special kind of second-order desire is one which pertains
to the kind of desire a person wants to constitute his will. Frankfurt
calls desires of this kind 'second-order *volitions*'. Having such volitions
is, he argues, a consequence of a person's ability to reflect on the
springs of his actions and ask himself what he wants his motives
to be.

Starting with these simple ideas about the will, Frankfurt attempts to ascend to an understanding of the complex topics of personal identity, moral responsibility, freedom of the will, and practical normativity. An important part of our identity, Frankfurt claims, is constituted by the second-order desires we endorse. Suppose I have a desire to do well in my academic career and also a desire to lead a relaxed student lifestyle. Suppose, further, that I have a second-order desire for my desire to pursue my academic career to be my will — for it to be the desire I act on. If I wholeheartedly endorse this second-order volition, Frankfurt writes, I am saying that I want to be driven by my desire for academic success. I am thereby, he claims, identifying myself with this volition and committing myself to being a certain kind of person.

Commitments of this kind do more than shape our identity. They are also, Frankfurt argues, key to our attributions of moral responsibility. When someone commits himself to acting from particular motives, the motives in question become entirely his — they are not alien to him like compulsions or unwelcome cravings, but rather represent what, on reflection, he regards as the right things to desire and pursue. Because actions that spring from such reflectively endorsed motives can uncontroversially be attributed to a person, Frankfurt believes he can be held fully accountable for them.

There is something immediately appealing about Frankfurt's analyses of personal identity and moral responsibility. After all, one important way in which we describe who we are is by referring to the things we stand for and the motives we want to act on. It also seems right to say that we must take responsibility for the motives on which we wish to act. Nonetheless, his account of these concepts raises some questions.

◈

ALEX VOORHOEVE: *You take our identity to be defined by the desires we endorse. But I can characterize myself as someone with desires I would rather be without. For example, I might have a desire to be benevolent, but see this desire frustrated by my selfish impulses and say, 'Well, isn't that just typically me!'*

HARRY FRANKFURT: Well, I think that's right. The whole notion of identity is a very loose one. There are several ways in which you can talk about what you really are, and one of the ways is just to describe certain characteristics that you have. Now, part of the problem is that when I described this process of identifying with and taking responsibility for one's desires, I unfortunately used the word 'endorsement' when I should have used a different term. The term 'endorsement' suggests approval, or some positive attitude towards the object of endorsement. I never meant that. What I meant was something like acceptance of what I really am. I may identify myself as having certain characteristics and give up trying to fight against them, because I understand that they are my characteristics, even though I wish that they weren't. So although I don't endorse them in the sense of approving of them, I do endorse them in the sense of recognizing or accepting them as my own — like a cheque that I endorse by putting my name on it. It is that 'taking possession of', or 'committing oneself to', or 'identifying oneself with' that I really had and have in mind, rather than any form of approval. Now approval often comes into it, of course, since often we like to identify ourselves with things that we approve of. But that doesn't always happen; I can recognize that I am weak-willed, for example, and identify myself with my weakness of will, in the sense that I don't regard it as alien to me. It is what I really am, and I don't fight against it.

ALEX VOORHOEVE: *What if I do fight against it?*

HARRY FRANKFURT: Well, then I haven't really identified myself with it. It is not what I really am — I am trying to show that I am not really weak-willed. It is true that I still have that tendency to give into things, but I regard it as something I am trying to rid myself of. It is what I am, in some sense, but it is not a part of me that I identify with.

ALEX VOORHOEVE: *You argue that a person is morally responsible only for those motives that he identifies with. But one can easily imagine a* *person who has certain characteristics that he is struggling against who nonetheless feels that these characteristics are appropriate objects of moral condemnation. For example, someone could feel guilty about the kind of person he is, even though he doesn't want to be that kind of person and hasn't yet accepted that he will always be that kind of person. So moral responsibility doesn't seem to be confined to cases where someone has accepted the desires that constitute his will as his own.*

HARRY FRANKFURT: Of course, we have a lot of characteristics that we are not particularly responsible for, but that are attractive or odious, and that are the basis for how people treat us and of how we think of ourselves. The question of moral responsibility is very murky, and I am not really sure what it's all about. Often, blaming someone for what he has done is just a way of being angry with him—just as guilt is a way of being angry with yourself and of punishing yourself. Blaming somebody for something—unleashing moral insults—is a way of hurting him.

Now, I am not really sure what the point of blaming is. Maybe it doesn't really have any point; maybe it is just something that we are naturally inclined to do. We don't blame animals for vicious behaviour. Maybe we just assume that people ought to be able to control themselves. But I suppose that if we believe that a person can't control himself, we tend not to be angry. Instead, we tend to treat him in the way that we treat animals: defend ourselves against him, and maybe incarcerate him. Moral opprobrium would be missing in such a case.

I also think we have different attitudes towards a person who identifies himself with a particular harmful tendency than we have towards someone who does not identify himself with this tendency, because insofar as a person renounces the part of him causing this behaviour, he is on 'our' side rather than on the 'opposing' side. The fact that he is on our side mitigates our sense of him as an enemy. So, if a person isn't really wholehearted about the bad thing that he has done, if he wishes he hadn't done it and didn't want to do it, but found himself moved against his will, then our attitude towards him is less harsh, because he is, in a way, an ally of ours. After all, he was trying to prevent what happened.

✍

Besides its role in moral responsibility, the concept of second-order volitions also plays a central role in Frankfurt's conception of freedom of the will. Just as a person enjoys freedom of *action* if and only if she is free to do what she wants to do, on Frankfurt's account a person possesses freedom of the *will* if and only if she is free to have the will she wants to have. In other words, a person enjoys freedom of the will when she is free to bring her will into conformity with her second-order volitions. Conversely, a person's will is not free when she is incapable of having the will she wants to have.

By way of illustration: a person who wants to be benevolently inclined but whose actions are motivated by selfish desires does not possess freedom of the will. By contrast, a person who acts on benevolent motives because she wants to be benevolently inclined possesses freedom of the will. Here, it is important that she has the will she wants *because* she wants it. To see why, consider someone who always brings her second-order volitions into line with whatever she knows her will is inevitably going to be. A person who did this and claimed to possess freedom of the will would labour under the same illusion as the self-proclaimed King of the Universe in Antoine de Saint-Exupéry's book *The Little Prince*. When asked by the Little Prince to use his power to make the sun set, the King consults his solar calendar and replies, 'I will issue my command at 7:40 pm, and you'll see how well I am obeyed.' The King has no real power if the sun's setting isn't a response to his command. Similarly, someone enjoys freedom of the will only when her will is responsive to her second-order volitions.

Thus conceived, freedom of the will is consistent with binding constraints upon our second-order volitions. A person may, for example, be incapable of wanting anything else than to act on benevolent motives. Such a person's second-order volition is completely determined in this respect. But if her actual motivation is benevolent, she may still enjoy freedom of the will. For it is consistent with this constraint that her actual motivation is responsive to her second-order volition, so that if she wanted to act on different motives, she could do so.

Someone who has freedom of the will together with freedom of action (the ability to act as one wants to act), Frankfurt claims, enjoys 'the most extensive freedom it is possible to conceive'. But can we really not conceive of a more extensive freedom?

∽

ALEX VOORHOEVE: *Freedom of the will, as you define it, can come about through brainwashing—by someone shaping another person's desires in such a manner that this person comes to endorse the very desires he has been induced to have. Doesn't that strike you as counterintuitive?*

HARRY FRANKFURT: I am not sure what you mean by 'brainwashing'. Brainwashing, if such a thing exists, is simply an uncommonly deliberate attempt to shape the structure and content of somebody's mind. But something or somebody always happens to do just this. We come into the world malleable, and various forces and influences work to shape our minds and make us the kind of people we are. We don't speak of 'brainwashing' unless this process is managed by a person who has a specific goal in mind. But it is the same thing structurally—somebody's character is formed by external forces.

ALEX VOORHOEVE: *But consider the case of someone who, due to mal-treatment and intense psychological pressure, comes to have such low self-esteem that he believes he should have a servile disposition. Suppose, moreover, that he acquires the disposition he wants to have and is given the opportunity to act on his wholehearted desire to serve his master. You would say he is as free as it is possible to be. But this conflicts with a common idea of freedom that places certain demands on the conditions under which we form our aims and desires.*

HARRY FRANKFURT: I have a simple answer to that, although I don't know if anyone but me finds it convincing. Examples of this type simply show that there are other values besides freedom. All I am saying is that someone who does what he wants to do and wants what he wants to want has as much freedom as it is possible to understand. His life may be bad in several respects: he may be stupid or limited, and, as a consequence, he may not be leading a good life. But he is not lacking freedom. There is, in general, a sloganistic desire to cram everything that we think is good into the concept of freedom. But this is just a way to cash in on the rhetorical force of the word. It seems to me that it is a good idea to make some distinctions and to see that freedom is not the only good thing.

∽

Frankfurt extracts one more striking conclusion from his analysis of the structure of our desires: he argues that the answer to the vexing question 'How are we to live?' lies, simply, in the desires that we have and want most fervently to maintain and act on. Frankfurt refers to the mode of the will involved in having such desires as 'caring': when we care about something, he writes, we value it and wholeheartedly approve of our tendency to value it. As a consequence, when we care about something, we are free from troubling ambivalence towards it. It is what we care about, then, that provides us with guidance on what to aim at and what type of person to become. But it seems peculiar that we should end a normative enquiry with an appeal to a brute fact: that we should pursue what we most care about pursuing. Can't we ask whether we *should* care about what we care about?

∽

ALEX VOORHOEVE: *You remarked in your lectures that the question 'Should I care about what I care about?' induces a kind of dizziness. But the question does have an everyday sense, when we ask ourselves, 'Should I really care about this thing that I have devoted myself to? Should I really devote myself so wholeheartedly to it?'*

HARRY FRANKFURT: I can, of course, evaluate one potential object of care in terms of another object that is somehow more fundamental or that I care about more. So the question makes perfectly good sense if I mean, 'Given that I want to lead a certain kind of life, is this a good thing for me to care about and devote myself to?'

The question can also make sense if I mean 'Do I *really* care about it?' For example, if I ask myself 'Should I care about staying alive?', then except insofar as I see my life merely as an instrument in the service of other goals (like my children's well-being), I must mean 'Is it something I really do care about?' And, in this case, the only affirmative answer I can get is: 'I can't help caring about it.' The question 'Should I care about it?' then simply has no application, since I have no alternative.

In any case, it is impossible to ask 'Should I care about what I care about?' without making reference to something I *do* care about. For I need standards to determine which way of life is most worth living. I need such standards, for example, to evaluate whether living in a way that is pleasurable but in conflict with moral precepts is better than leading a different kind of life. And having such standards simply *is* knowing what I care about.

ALEX VOORHOEVE: *Sartre famously illustrated the idea of 'radical choice' (in which someone has to choose his most fundamental values) with a case in which a young man must decide whether to join the resistance against the German occupation or stay with his mother, who needs him close by. Are you saying that this idea of radical choice is mistaken?*

HARRY FRANKFURT: Well, the young man cannot be creating his values *ex nihilo*. So if that is what the idea of 'radical choice' means, then it is confused. As for the young man's decision: all he can do is try to find out which means more to him. If he can't find out that either of them means more to him than the other, then maybe what he should do is flip a coin. Otherwise he will just sit there like Buridan's ass and be unable to move in either direction. What we ordinarily do in such a situation is try to find out which option makes our heart leap up more. And we may be wrong to do so. For we are not interested in a momentary impulse, but in a prediction of what life will be like — we are trying to picture whether we want this or that kind of life. And we might easily make mistakes in this matter.

ALEX VOORHOEVE: *So is self-knowledge the central thing you recommend when we are conflicted about what we care about?*

HARRY FRANKFURT: Yes, that's right. Self-knowledge plays a very fundamental role because it is in knowing myself that I discover what I really care about. The rest is working out the details: being reasonable in pursuing the things that I care about and trying to avoid conflict between them whenever possible.

ALEX VOORHOEVE: *We also need confidence in the goals to which we have committed ourselves in order to eliminate doubt and internal discord. You argue that this confidence can't come from gathering rationally compelling evidence for the validity of our attitudes. Instead, you say it derives from love, which you define as a mode of caring that is insensitive to any such arguments, and that is even altogether beyond our voluntary control. As you said in your lectures: 'The source of our confidence in caring about our children and our lives is that we love our children and we love life. We love these things even when they disappoint us, and even when we may think it unreasonable of us to love them.' But doesn't coming to love things involve seeing reasons to love them?*

HARRY FRANKFURT: Well, understanding what it is about this object that I am responding to does require rational enquiry. Sometimes it is obvious, and sometimes it is unclear what it is about an object of love that makes us love it. So I might look into it to improve my self-understanding. But once I understand what I am responding to, the fact that I am drawn to it is not something that I can explain.

ALEX VOORHOEVE: *Love of our children and of life may indeed be instinctual and, for many people, inescapable. But surely when we pick a friend, a lover, or some goal as an object of love, we are responding to the value of the person or goal we decide to love.*

HARRY FRANKFURT: Love is a natural phenomenon; it is something that happens to us. And like other events in the natural world, it has its causes. There is nothing in my account that rules out the possibility that love will be caused by responding to the value of the object. I am merely insisting that this is not an essential condition, since it may be caused by lots of things.

ALEX VOORHOEVE: *So, on your view, it is possible for us to love someone or something without antecedently perceiving any value in the object of our love. Indeed, you turn around the idea of love being based on the recognition of value and argue that the objects of our love are valuable to us because we love them—the reason being that our wholehearted commitments to care about them give us confidence in our aims, thereby giving our lives direction and meaning. As an example, you mention children, whose value to their parents, you claim, derives from the parents' love of them.*

This raises a question about the possibility of loving unwisely. We can say of someone that she is unwise to love who or what she loves, or to use an old-fashioned expression, that she has 'invested herself unwisely'. However, in your account, it seems that expression doesn't make any sense. If the fact that someone loves a particular person has made the person valuable to her, how can it be said that it is unwise for her to love him?

HARRY FRANKFURT: Well, her love entails that she cares about what happens to this person — she wants him to flourish. But some people are very bad at flourishing — they are always getting themselves into trouble. Some mothers, I am told, advise their daughters that it is not a good idea to marry for money, but that it *is* a good idea to go where money is, since this increases the chances that they will spontaneously fall in love with someone rich. That's where wisdom comes in.

ALEX VOORHOEVE: *What about the idea that someone or something might be unworthy of my love? For example, I might judge that my* *children are unworthy of my love if I find that their behaviour or character so conflicts with other things I care about that I judge my love to be wrong.*

HARRY FRANKFURT: If my loving one thing conflicts with my love of other things that are even more important to me, that in itself would not warrant saying that the former is unworthy of my love. It might merely warrant saying that it would be imprudent, or too costly, for me to love it. I don't deny that some sense might be given to the notion of something being unworthy of my love, if loving it were somehow demeaning. But, as you suggest, the fact that it is demeaning would be a function of my loving other things.

ᔎ

In sum, for Frankfurt, the sources of practical normativity lie in the volitional necessities of love. Luther, for example, was not troubled by the question of how to live when he said, 'Here I stand; I can do no other.' As Frankfurt puts it, one way of understanding Luther's case is that he found it impossible not only to act differently than he did, but also to *want* to act differently than he did—in other words, Luther loved standing for and disseminating religious truth (as he saw it).

The demands of love, on Frankfurt's view, constrain the movements of our will. But these constraints are not external to us—they don't feel like an onslaught of passions or compulsions. Rather, as with Luther, they operate from within us and are based in our deepest commitments. The search for an answer to questions about how to live, then, comes to an end when we recognize things we *must* want to do. There is an echo here of Frankfurt's characterization of Descartes' project as finding 'beliefs that could be held in the face of any effort to undermine them—that could withstand any scepticism, however intense'.

ᔎ

ALEX VOORHOEVE: *Is Descartes' search for beliefs that one can hold in the face of all attempts to doubt them paralleled in your work on the will?*

HARRY FRANKFURT: It is in this respect: Descartes was looking for things that one cannot help believing, and he thought that one cannot help believing what one is in the midst of clearly and distinctly perceiving—that assent is constrained by clear and distinct perception. And I have become interested in what one cannot help being moved to do—in what constrains the will in action, rather than what constrains the will in belief.

References and further reading

Harry Frankfurt's book on Descartes is *Demons, Dreamers, and Madmen: The Defense of Reason in Descartes' Meditations* (Indianapolis: Bobbs-Merrill, 1970). Frankfurt's essays are collected in *The Importance of What We Care About* (Cambridge: Cambridge University Press, 1988) and *Necessity, Volition, and Love* (Cambridge: Cambridge University Press, 1999). The lectures referred to have since been published as *The Reasons of Love* (Princeton: Princeton University Press, 2004).

The quotation from Descartes' 'Rules for the Direction of Our Native Intelligence' is from *Selected Philosophical Writings*, trans. and ed. John Cottingham, Robert Stoothof, and Dugald Murdoch (Cambridge: Cambridge University Press, 1988): 5. The quotation from John Stuart Mill is from *Utilitarianism*, ed. Roger Crisp (Oxford: Oxford University Press, 1998), ch. 3, para. 10. The Little Prince's adventures are recounted in Antoine de Saint-Exupéry, *The Little Prince*, trans. T. V. F. Cuffe (London: Penguin, 1995). Jean-Paul Sartre discusses the moral dilemma of the young man in his lecture *Existentialism is a Humanism*, trans. Carol Macomber (New Haven: Yale University Press, 2007).

11
DAVID VELLEMAN

REALLY SEEING ANOTHER

L ove is a puzzling emotion. We want to be loved and, in being loved, we want to be treasured for who we are and regarded as irreplaceable. But a puzzle arises when we ask what the basis for such love is. People who want us to feel loved say they love us because 'we're special' and because 'there is no one quite like us'; they also say they love us for particular characteristics: for our red hair, for our quirky sense of humour, for 'being the baby of the family', and so on. It might seem natural to conclude that others' love of us is based on our uniquely valuable personal characteristics.

On reflection, however, this doesn't seem right. First, the same people who say that there is no one like us also typically acknowledge that *everyone* is unique. This makes it difficult to see how mere uniqueness could make us especially valuable to them when there are countless others who are no less unique than we are.

Second, if the value our lover places on us is based on our characteristics, it would seem to follow that someone with 'better' characteristics — someone funnier, for example, or possessed of more vibrantly red hair — would be more worthy of his love. But the existence of someone superior to us in these respects doesn't make us any less worthy of being loved; if he really loves us, our lover is not looking to 'trade up'.

Third, love should be independent, to some significant extent, of our traits. Parents are expected to love their children 'no matter how they turn out', and someone loved for 'being the baby of the family' would have been loved — he would hope! — if his parents had subsequently had another child. This independence is also reflected in the presumption that love will be constant in the face of a change in the beloved's characteristics and even in the face of an unwelcome discovery about the beloved. For example, in Roman Polanski's film *Tess* (after Thomas Hardy's *Tess of the D'Urbervilles*), when Tess's husband deserts her upon finding out that she has had a baby out of wedlock, we come to doubt whether he ever truly loved her. By contrast, in Neil Jordan's film *The Crying Game*, the purity of the love between Fergus and Dil is evinced by its persistence even after the strictly heterosexual Fergus discovers that Dil is a transsexual and Dil finds out about Fergus's involvement in the death of her former lover.

Fourth, the traits for which others claim to love us can seem relatively unimportant to who we really are. Someone who valued us only on the basis of our red hair and our sense of humour, for example, would be focusing his attention in the wrong place. (The same can be said of someone whose love for us is threatened by his discovery of what we regard as a trivial trait. As Dil says to Fergus when Fergus's initial response to his discovery that she's 'not a girl' is to withdraw his love: 'Details, baby, details . . .')

Finally, the idea that a person is treasured because his characteristics make him uniquely valuable doesn't fit the experience of loving someone. For one can love one's friend without thinking that she is a better 'fit' as a friend than others who are not one's friends but who could be; and one can treasure one's children above all others but still think they are not more worthy of being loved than other children are.

One puzzle about love, then, is this: what, if not particular characteristics, is the basis for others' love of us?

Another puzzle about love concerns the relationship between love and morality. Impartial moral views demand that a moral agent regard all persons as equally significant. Being loved, however, appears to involve being valued over others. It may therefore seem that a truly moral agent is incapable of wholeheartedly loving someone, because his partiality to his beloved will be at odds with his commitment to thinking and acting from the impartial, moral point of view. Bernard Williams famously illustrated this difficulty with a case of a man who can save only one of several people in peril and chooses to save his wife, but only because he thinks that 'it is permissible in situations of this kind to save one's wife'. As Williams put it, from his wife's perspective, such a person would seem to entertain 'one thought too many'.

Notwithstanding this apparent conflict in spirit between love and morality, it seems that love plays an essential part in our moral education. We are inducted into morality by our childhood experience of loving and being loved; later in life, loving relationships with partners and friends give us a deeper awareness of and responsiveness to the concerns of others, including those outside this circle of relationships. Our second puzzle, then, is this: how can an emotion that appears to be so at odds with the impartial spirit of morality perform this role?

David Velleman, who is a professor of philosophy at New York University, tackles these puzzles about love in several essays in his collection *Self to Self*. The collection as a whole addresses the selves we have in our sights in different contexts: the context of autobiographical memory and anticipation, in which we appear continuous with past and future selves; the context of our self-image, in which we come to regard certain motives as part of 'who we are' or 'what we stand for'; the context of autonomous agency, in which we consider our actions as governed by ourselves; and the context of emotions like shame and love, in which we feel ashamed of ourselves and want to be loved for ourselves. The nature of these various selves excites Velleman's theoretical interest, and he uses questions about them as proving grounds for ideas drawn from Kant's moral philosophy, psychoanalytic theory, and social psychology. But the topics he addresses also strike at the heart of what we care about and what we take ourselves to be, and although Velleman writes with professional detachment and dry wit, it is clear that he often has a personal stake in getting the answers right. This is true, for example, of

his work on love, as he explains at the start of our conversation in his
office in May 2006:

> In my work on love, I was mainly concerned with under-
> standing what we want in wanting to be loved. Somewhat
> autobiographically, it is an attempt to understand sibling
> rivalry. I am the middle of three boys, and sibling rivalry is
> often strongest for the middle child. The issue of sibling rivalry
> is: 'How can Mother and Father love me the way I want to be
> loved and love these two other guys as well? Given that I want
> to be treasured as special, how can it be that there are two sons
> besides me who are valued in the same way?' These questions
> lead to rivalry because you think that what you want is some
> kind of favourable comparison *vis-à-vis* your siblings, and then
> you all compete for such evaluation.
>
> Now, it seems to me that this is just like the problem of the
> supposed conflict in spirit between love and Kantian morality.
> Philosophers who think there is a conflict pose the following
> question from the perspective of someone who wants to be
> loved: 'How can it be that someone equally respects all persons
> in the way that Kantian morality requires and still treasures
> me as special?' This is just the problem of sibling rivalry writ
> large! For if someone fears that morality will prevent him from
> being loved in the way he wants, what really upsets him is the
> thought that something comparative is going on here—that
> the comparison of all persons as morally equal will threaten
> his being valued as special.
>
> So unless we can figure out the question of sibling rivalry,
> there is a very deep problem in the human condition. Now,
> insofar as the problem of sibling rivalry has a solution, it
> has to lie in seeing why no comparison is being made—why
> your parents' love is not based on seeing you as better or
> more precious than your siblings. This means that we are
> dealing with questions about value: What in you renders you
> as valuable as others, but at the same time ensures that you

are precious and not replaceable by these others? What kind of value demands appreciation in itself, shunning comparison to others? To answer these questions, I believe we need to understand Kant's idea that persons, as ends in themselves, have a value that is incommensurable with other values and, indeed, incomparable with the value of other persons.

To understand Kant's view of the value of persons, we first need to understand Kant's idea of personhood. For Kant, being a person consists in being a rational creature, both cognitively and in action. In *Self to Self*, Velleman offers the following interpretation of this idea. Part of what makes someone a rational agent is that she can stand back from her impulses and reflect on what to do. So, for example, when she is torn between her desire to stay in bed and her desire to stick to her exercise regimen, a rational agent is able to ask whether, in these circumstances, feeling like having a lie-in is a good enough reason for not exercising. That is not just a question about this particular occasion; after all, the reasons that lead her to a decision will apply on all similar occasions. Moreover, for this to be a decision of any moment, she must view matters as settled until she has reason to reconsider. Once she becomes aware of her ability to take up this kind of constant perspective on her desires, Velleman writes, she will be inescapably motivated to do so and act on what she believes she has most reason to do. In other words, she will be ineluctably drawn to being autonomous.

But, Velleman explains, Kant's idea of personhood involves something more than just an ability and a willingness to take up a steady individual perspective on what one has reason to do. Rational creatures have access to a more inclusive perspective from which they can see certain things, and see that these things are visible to *all* rational creatures. For example, anyone who is doing arithmetic sees not just that the sum of 2 and 2 is 4, but also that anyone who added 2 and 2 would see that it is 4, and that *that* person would see it too. Kant thought that just as all rational creatures have a shared perspective on arithmetic, all rational agents can have a shared perspective on what can count as reasons for action for any rational agent. They can take up such a perspective, Kant claims, by asking whether their principles for action are universalizable. Roughly, this means asking whether their reasons for action are of a type that they could consistently allow everyone to regard as valid in similar circumstances.

Acting for reasons that are universally shareable in this sense is what Kant took to be the moral law, or categorical imperative: 'Act only on a maxim that you can at the same time will to be a universal law.' Kant also believed that once someone becomes aware of the possibility of acting on the moral law, she will be drawn to do so. Kant had several reasons for thinking this. One of them is, roughly, that acting only for reasons that can be accepted by all rational beings is attractive because it is a way of being fully autonomous, in the sense that one's judgement of what counts as a reason for action becomes the sole force controlling one's actions. (In fact, Kant thought that this was *the only* way of being fully autonomous; unfortunately, it would take us too far afield to discuss this aspect of his views.) Another is, again roughly, that by acting for reasons that all others can rationally accept, one is doing one's part in establishing a harmonious relationship with them, since they can then endorse the ways in which one regards them and acts towards them. A striking upshot of Kant's definition of personhood is, then, that it necessarily involves an aspiration to act morally.

ى

DAVID VELLEMAN: It is part of the Kantian view, and it is part of my view, that personhood is, in some sense, potentially good; that there is in it a force for good, so that when you are seeing someone as a person, you are seeing something good in them. Now, what you are seeing is not fully realized perfection. It is, rather, rational agency, which involves having the springs of respect for the ideal that is expressed in the moral law. So while rational agency is less than acting in full conformity with the moral law, it is more than just the capacity to aspire to that ideal; the aspiration itself must be present — at least to some degree. And so, when we see someone as a person, we see them as having in them this aspiration. Perhaps it is hidden under a bushel. Perhaps it is overlaid with other motivations. But it has to be there.

ALEX VOORHOEVE: *Kant claims the proper attitude towards a rational creature is to regard it as an 'end in itself' and, as such, as an 'object of respect'. These are mysterious phrases. What is involved in regarding someone as an end, and how is this related to regarding him with respect?*

DAVID VELLEMAN: The notion of an end is hard to understand because it is closely associated with 'desired result' and with 'means – end reasoning'. Many people think of an *end* as equivalent to an *aim*, so that regarding something as an end is to regard it as something to aim at bringing about. But the two are not equivalent. An aim is something we act *in order to* achieve; an end is something *for the sake of which* we act. To see the difference between the two, consider the idea of acting for someone's sake. When you do so, you regard him as an end, but you obviously don't act in order to bring about this person! Rather, you act with him in view.

Kant makes clear that he has this sense of 'end' in mind when he calls a person a 'self-existent end'. Its value is not something that needs to be realized. Instead, its value affects the perspective we take on it, the things we allow ourselves to consider in thinking about it, and the ways we allow ourselves to consider acting towards it.

ALEX VOORHOEVE: *So the thought is that when I regard someone as an end, this involves an appreciation of his value that affects how I think about him and what I take to be good things to happen, and good ways to act? For example, suppose I could get a laugh by telling a deeply embarrassing story about a decent person. If I regard him as an end, I would not think that getting a laugh at his expense was in any way a good thing. In my mind, it is not just that the 'good consequence' of amusing people and being appreciated for my wit is outweighed by the possible 'bad consequences' associated with others knowing this embarrassing fact about him; it is, rather, that appreciating him as an end rules out thinking that amusing others in this way is a good thing at all.*

DAVID VELLEMAN: Exactly. Regarding someone as an end, respecting them, rules out certain considerations; they simply no longer count. The idea is that respect for the person expels certain thoughts from your mind; it makes these thoughts appear alien to you. That is what it means to take a person as an end: to take him as the object of an attitude that has motivational consequences for how you behave towards him.

In other words, on the Kantian view, when you respect a person, there are certain ways you think about the person and there are certain attitudes that you forbid yourself to take towards the person. There are also certain things that respect for a person prohibits you from doing. But there is this important aspect to it: in the first instance, it does not incline you to bring anything about, to achieve any result concerning the person. Rather, respect involves a kind of standing back, taking your hands off, appreciating the person for who he is.

ALEX VOORHOEVE: *How does what you just said help us understand Kant's view that persons have incomparable value?*

DAVID VELLEMAN: There is an important point about value here that I learned from Liz Anderson [a professor of philosophy at the University of Michigan, Ann Arbor]: to be valued is to be the object of an appreciative attitude, and each valuable object has an appreciative attitude that is appropriate to it.

Now, some objects should be appreciated in a comparative way: as things that can be more or less preferable to have, like a holiday or a car. We can compare the value of such things and choose to substitute one for another without loss in overall value. But it is also possible that part of the appreciative attitude that is appropriate to something is to focus on the thing as it is in itself, without thinking of alternatives or making comparisons. What Kant calls 'self-existent ends' (persons) should be appreciated in this way. And then you can see what it is to have an incomparable value. It is *not* to have a value that *cannot* be compared; it is, instead, to have a value the proper appreciation of which is an attitude that focuses attention on the thing as it is in itself, shunning all comparisons and all consideration of alternatives.

This, I think, enables you to make sense of incommensurable values in the following way: things have incommensurable value when they demand appreciation for themselves alone. And this is where most people's attempts to understand incommensurable value go wrong. Because most people's concept of value is of something that is potentially comparable. And when you start with this conception of value, you assume that for something to have incommensurable value is for it to have a value that is incommensurably *greater* than other values. But it can't be the case that each person has a value incommensurably greater than the values of other *persons*! So how can each person have an incommensurable value? The answer is that each person has a value the proper response to which is to regard her as she is in herself, shunning comparisons with others. This is an attitude that we can have towards more than one person.

ALEX VOORHOEVE: *I find it hard to understand the thought that it is inappropriate to compare the value of one person with the value of another. Suppose you are in a lifeboat, and you can save either a single person or two other people from death by drowning (you cannot save all three). In this case, it seems you should save the two; and you arrive at this judgement by comparing the value of one person's life with the value of two people's lives, and judging that two lives are more valuable than one.*

DAVID VELLEMAN: Of course, in the lifeboat case, you are forced to make a choice. But since the appropriate attitude towards people is to appreciate them as they are in themselves, you are being forced by the situation to do something that is inappropriate. Such situations are tragic or absurd because they force us to treat people in a way that violates their real value. We come to understand the essence of morality, not when we see how to make these decisions, but rather when we see why, in having to make these decisions, we are forced to violate people's real value. A morality that simply tells us how to choose in such situations without revealing why the situations are tragic or absurd would be inadequate.

ALEX VOORHOEVE: *I am surprised that you think that the essence of morality is not at stake when we determine how we should make such choices. I mean, much of ethical theory is devoted to analysing lifeboat cases, in which we must choose whom to save, or so-called 'trolley cases', in which we must choose whether to kill some people in order to save others from a mortal threat posed by a runaway trolley.*

DAVID VELLEMAN: Look, what we are trying to do is develop an ethics for the world we live in. Lifeboat cases and trolley cases usually rely on highly unrealistic assumptions. Very rarely do people find themselves in a lifeboat. No one ever finds him- or herself in the circumstances of these trolley cases. I am perfectly happy to say that this is a kind of situation in which life would be absurd. As it stands, our everyday life is structured by relationships with others whom it makes sense to appreciate for themselves alone. But if history placed us in radically different circumstances in which the mainstay of our life involved making choices in lifeboat or trolley scenarios, then the way of life that we have developed might not be adequate, in the sense that it might not give us any intelligible way to proceed. It is a mistake to think that ethics can give you answers for all possible creatures in all possible worlds.

ALEX VOORHOEVE: *Well, this seems to be what Kant thought, at least insofar as all possible rational creatures are concerned. Kant claims, for example, that it is part of our everyday thinking about moral laws like 'Thou shalt not lie' that they apply to all rational beings, independently of their empirical circumstances.*

DAVID VELLEMAN: What kind of rational creatures does he have in mind?

ALEX VOORHOEVE: *I am not sure . . . Angels maybe?*

DAVID VELLEMAN: [*laughs*] Angels. *Please.* What world do they live in? We have no conception of angels, where they live, what kind of problems they are dealing with. In my view, ethics is an empirical discipline. It is the discipline of figuring out how to live, which we carry out in practice by trial and error. Of course, this is a respect in which my view is very un-Kantian, as you point out. But I think that Kant's view of what morality tells us can be combined with an un-Kantian view of how we arrive at it and learn to apply it. And, in my view, the moral law is for dealing with the problems we face.

∽

Among these problems, are, of course, the puzzles about love outlined at the start. How can the aforementioned elements of Kant's ethics help resolve them?

As we've seen, for Kant, respecting a person involves an arresting awareness of her value as an end. What is arrested is a whole set of motives and aims that we could have if we saw her merely as a potential obstacle in the pursuit of our ends, or merely as someone we could use. When we respect a person, we realize that we should treat her in ways that she could rationally agree to being treated; in other words, we treat her as morality demands.

For Velleman, love is, like respect, an arresting awareness of a person's value as an end. However, he believes that love goes beyond respect by arresting our tendencies towards emotional self-protection from a person. We naturally have tendencies to close ourselves off from others. Love, Velleman claims, 'disarms these emotional defences; it makes us vulnerable to the other'. As a consequence, love can unleash a host of positive emotional responses, like sympathy, fascination, and attraction.

But love also renders us vulnerable to feelings of hurt, indignation, and resentment.

What so disarms us, Velleman claims, is our recognition in others of a capacity for rational self-governance. We see that they are capable of responding to us with respect and that they aspire to respond to us in this way; we may also see that they are capable of responding to us with love. This recognition of the person's potential for good is what makes our emotional defences against them feel unnecessary.

Though this is a startling thesis, there is something familiar in this idea of love as vulnerability to another person created by an arresting awareness of that person's potential for good. Consider again *The Crying Game*, for example. Because Dil has come to see Fergus's essentially good character, her love for the ex-IRA operative survives her discovery of his involvement in the kidnapping and death of the soldier she once loved. (The film portrays Fergus as a good man who had become involved in a role that does not befit his nature.) Velleman's conception of love also seems to fit the love of Sister Helen Prejean for the murderer and rapist Matthew Poncelet in the film *Dead Man Walking*, which is based on Sister Prejean's awareness of the potential for good hidden under Poncelet's brash, aggressive persona. But, equally, there are love stories which don't appear to fit this account. Did Eva Braun's love for Hitler, for example, really spring from her recognition of the good in him?

ॐ

DAVID VELLEMAN: Well, the word 'love' has many different meanings. I am not taking about romantic love — the feeling of 'being in love'. I am also not talking about attachment. And then there is a kind of benevolent affection that we have, not only for people, but also for pets, for flower gardens, for stamp collections even, which we display when we act towards them with a kind of loving care. I am not talking about that either.

About Eva Braun and Hitler . . . Recently, I have been reading a lot about Hitler, the Holocaust, and evil. I think Hitler had in him the capacity to be good. That is what makes what he did as bad as it is. Had he been evil incarnate, he wouldn't have had the capacity to be good and he wouldn't have put this capacity to evil uses.

ALEX VOORHOEVE: *So Eva Braun's love for him might actually fit your model of love?*

DAVID VELLEMAN: It might. I would say one further thing, though. Love has a perceptual component. We respect the other person when we *know* that they are a person. But in order to love this person, we have to *see* the person in him — really look at, take in, and become vulnerable to him. The idea is that on the surface, the human organism doesn't necessarily reveal the person. And so there have to be characteristics in which we can see the person. That's what people mean when they say they love someone for the way he looks, or acts, or talks, or walks: these are what enable them to see the person within, making him lovable. They love him *through* these characteristics, but it is the person they love. Now, I think that any person who fully understood what Hitler was up to would have a very hard time seeing the person within. (The goodness in Hitler was not just under a bushel, as I put it before; it was buried under a mountain of hatred and cruelty.) So, in my view, there is nothing loveable about him. Nonetheless, I think it is intelligible that people loved him. Someone who had the whole man in view would find it difficult to love him, but partly because of the way he managed information, and partly because of his followers' self-deception, it was possible for them to love him.

ALEX VOORHOEVE: *Your view that love is a response to something we accurately perceive in someone seems to be at odds with what we commonly think of as love's blindness . . .*

DAVID VELLEMAN: Well, that is the problem with being *in* love. Being in love involves misperception, what Freud called transference, valuing in the person not the characteristics of that person, but (possibly imagined) characteristics of people from your past, such as your mother or father. As a teacher, for example, you may be the object of a student's transference love. This student may have some fantasy of the wise man or the powerful woman, or whatever it is. He doesn't love you — he has a crush on you.

All this is not the kind of love I am talking about. I think Iris Murdoch really got it right. Murdoch says that love is a capacity to *really see* another. There is a kind of love that is not overvaluing, and not fantasy, that depends on unclouding the eye, *actually seeing* the other. The way to see the appeal of Murdoch's view is to think about it from the perspective of how we want to be loved. Do we want to be overvalued? Do we want to be the object of another person's fantasies? Do we want the other person to project onto us the images of others, including her parents, whom she idealized in the past? I don't think so. We want the other to see us for who we are. When I want you to love me, I want you to see *me*. To feel *me*. To peel away the fantasies, peel away the overvaluation, and just see me for what I am.

ALEX VOORHOEVE: *Is this because being loved for characteristics you don't really possess is uncomfortable, because it exposes you to the risk that your lover would abandon you if she were to see you for what you are?*

DAVID VELLEMAN: That type of discomfort is not the real issue. After all, for some people, it may be deeply uncomfortable to be loved for who they are. Stanley Cavell, for example, has an interpretation of *King Lear* according to which what drives the story is the pain of being truly seen by those who love you.

ALEX VOORHOEVE: *What, then, is the attraction of being loved in the way you describe?*

DAVID VELLEMAN: Well, as I said, going back to Kant, I think that, as persons, we have at our core something that is potentially a force for good. And I think that whatever ambivalence we have towards ourselves — and even if we hate ourselves — we are aware that, deep down, there is something good in us. I also believe that we want other people to see the good in us and that we think of that as our true self. My true self is my better self — this force for good that makes me a person. And we want *that* to be acknowledged and valued.

Now, if you thought that you were not worthy of love for who you truly are, then the forms of love we discussed before — that involve being loved for the wrong reasons — would be the most you could hope for. And then, uncomfortable as it is, you would think, 'Well, this is as good as it gets.' But often, when someone loves you for who you are not, you want to disabuse him of his view, because you think: 'There are other, perfectly good reasons for loving me, because in me there is something that really is worthy of love, something that one can see without resorting to fantasy.'

ALEX VOORHOEVE: *How does your view resolve the puzzles that arise from the thought that we are loved for being uniquely valuable to the person who loves us?*

DAVID VELLEMAN: I believe that uniqueness is not what we really want — or at least, that we can be satisfied with something different: being loved just for being a person, which involves being valued as an end and having the other really pay attention to us without consideration of alternatives. It is one of those situations in which you think that you want one thing, you get something else, and then you realize that what you got is what you wanted all along. At first, you think that to be valued as special you need to be considered unique, but then you realize that you want to be valued in a non-comparative way. To return to the case of sibling rivalry: you come to realize that you don't really want to be appreciated as *different from* or *better than* your siblings. You just want to be appreciated for yourself, without the others being held up to you for comparison. So I solved my problem! [*laughs*]

And, you know, I think that what *creates* the problem is something I mentioned previously when we discussed incommensurability, namely that people have a wrong conception of value, one in which all value allows for comparative assessment. It is because people have this wrong idea about value that they are messed up in a certain way. They are overly competitive. And they try to get you attached to them in ways that you are not attached to other people, because they think that your love for them is based on the characteristics that make them special to you, like your shared history. So they try to have things in common with you that you don't have in common with other people, and they become jealous when you have things in common with other people. They are confused.

ALEX VOORHOEVE: *Are they really confused? If we love someone for what we have shared with him alone, then no one could have the properties we value in him. A shared history can therefore make him uniquely valuable to us in a way that would, after all, vindicate the characteristics-based model of love. It would explain, for example, why, as lovers, we are typically not concerned with 'trading up', since no one else could have what we value most in the object of our love. This is, for example, the theory of love proposed in the children's book* The Little Prince. *The Little Prince loves and cares for a lone rose that grows near his home, because he believes her to be the single most beautiful flower in the universe. Upon leaving his home, however, he comes across a garden with five thousand roses, all as beautiful as his rose. The realization that his rose is not uniquely beautiful comes as a great shock, and the Little Prince experiences a crisis, wondering whether his love for her makes any sense. A friendly fox manages to resolve his crisis by pointing out that his rose is 'unique in all the world' because of the time he has spent with her. As the Little Prince says to the five thousand roses upon returning to their garden after the fox's lesson:*

> To be sure, an ordinary passer-by would think that my rose looked just like you. But in herself alone she is more important than all the hundreds of you other roses: because it is she that I have watered; because it is she that I have put under the glass globe; because it is she that I have sheltered behind the

screen; because it is for her that I have killed the caterpillars; because it is she that I have listened to, when she grumbled, or boasted, or even sometimes when she said nothing. Because she is *my* rose.

DAVID VELLEMAN: Well, I have not been focusing on the Little Prince's crisis — I have been approaching matters from the *rose's* perspective. I mean, she is thinking: 'I know perfectly well there is a whole garden of roses out there just like me. How can he love me in the way that I want to be loved? I am no better than any other rose!' I think the Little Prince's answer to this question is based on a very egocentric conception of love, one which says to the beloved: 'What makes you worthy of my love is what you are *to me*; what you have been *to me*; the role you have played in *my* life; the investment that *I* have made.' A better answer is: 'As a rose, you merit a kind of appreciation which simply pays attention to *you*, and doesn't compare you to other roses.'

ALEX VOORHOEVE: *If one's relationships of care aren't the basis of love, what are the connections between love and such relationships?*

DAVID VELLEMAN: In my view, love is an emotion that usually goes along with care and attachment, but that is distinct from them. It is true, though, that one way to see the person in the way that I am talking about is to be in a caring relationship with him. In such a relationship, you see his vulnerability; you see his personality. The love that I am talking about can often arise only in a caring relationship. There are also times when an established relationship would rupture without the kind of love I am talking about. So love and attachment go together, and sometimes they need each other. But I don't think wanting to have a caring relationship is essential to love.

You know, there are people in my life that I have known for a long time, but with whom I don't really have a relationship. One of these people is a colleague of my wife, whose child went to school with one of my children. We don't have a very substantive relationship. But I *really* love her. When people hear this, they say: 'Are you *crazy*? You love someone whom you know merely as your wife's colleague and as a parent of a child that went to school with one of your children??' I think people react in this way because they see as essential to love something that I believe is merely sometimes connected to it, which is a desire to be with and care for the person you love. Love, in my view, doesn't essentially consist in having such desires. Instead, as I've tried to describe the phenomenology of the attitude, it is like wonder and awe. It is a kind of suspension and a kind of openness. What happens to this person affects me deeply: I am vulnerable to emotions like sympathy for her, and I imagine that she might be able to make me angrier than others — because I am disarmed by this person. I really care *about* this person without caring *for* her or wanting to take care *of* her. There are many cases in which one can love someone without feeling a desire to be with or do something for them. For example, if some of your students genuinely love you (rather than just have a crush on you), this doesn't involve on their part a desire to be with or care for you.

When I present this work and people find out what I think about love, they think that I am incredibly promiscuous about love. Because I love *all kinds of people*. But once you see what love really is, I think this isn't incredible, although there comes a point of emotional exhaustion, of course. You can't love everyone.

ALEX VOORHOEVE: *If what is loved in a person — just his person-hood — remains constant, how can your view explain the disappearance of love?*

DAVID VELLEMAN: This has to do with the difficulty of seeing the person in the way required to love him. There are certain things we say we love a person for. As I said, those are *not* the things that we value in a person; we love him *through* those things. Now, although what people really value in you does not change, the things in which people see that value *can* change. So people can stop loving you. And that is because your self-presentation no longer makes palpable to them what they value in you.

ALEX VOORHOEVE: *That is not the way someone who falls out of love might describe it. She might say of the person she used to love that he's become a different person. You would have to say to her: 'You're really saying that the characteristics through which you saw the person you loved, through which you became open to him, have changed. But what you valued in him has not.' But I think she could respond: 'Not at all. I see him perfectly well. I just don't love what I see anymore.'*

DAVID VELLEMAN: Well, part of what you are describing is not the disappearance of the love I am talking about. It may be the end of attachment or the end of a relationship. And a person might stop wanting to be with or care for a person even though she still loves him. But really seeing a person, being open to him, is hard, and what enabled one to do so can change.

ALEX VOORHOEVE: *In closing, I'd like to turn to our second puzzle about love, concerning its relation to morality. Many have thought that Kantian morality requires us to take a purely impartial view of all others and that this stands in the way of loving some people wholeheartedly. Why do you think this perspective on Kant's thought is mistaken?*

DAVID VELLEMAN: As we discussed, I think both love and respect involve an awareness of the same value, the response to which is to treat each person as an end, and to appreciate each person for who he or she is, without comparison to others. So at the level of attitudes, the respect you have for everyone does not threaten your love of particular people, and loving particular people does not threaten the moral attitude of respect that you ought to have for everyone.

Take Bernard Williams's example of the man who can save only one of several people and who chooses to save his wife. Most people think that the man should save his wife out of love for her. I agree, if 'love' in this context means attachment, mutual care, a shared history, and all of the other things that I have been distinguishing from the emotion that interests me. But if we are talking about that emotion — the love that consists in awe or wonder at really seeing another person for what he or she is — then I think that love isn't a basis for preference. Suppose that the Little Prince's rose discovered that he was utterly indifferent to the fate of those thousands of other roses. She would say, 'If you really loved me, you would see me and value me for what I am, and *I am a rose*. So how can you be indifferent to roses?'

This brings us back to sibling rivalry, too. The lesson of family life is that my parents' love for my brothers confirms rather than competes with their love for me. If my parents preferred me to my brothers, I would have to wonder, 'Could they really love me for what I am, for my true self?' The goodness in me is the goodness of a thinking, feeling *self* — goodness that I can see in my brothers, too. If my parents didn't see it in them, I would have to wonder what they saw in me. I don't want them to prefer me (as Yeats said) 'for my yellow hair', which is brighter than my brothers', since all of us will soon go grey.

So love and moral respect for people are actually supportive of one another. The experience of love is an experience that develops the moral sensibility. And if you have a view of love in which it is inimical to morality, then this becomes a complete mystery: how can it be that people who are deprived of loving families are the ones who end up being morally deficient, and the people who grow up in loving families tend to be the ones who have a strong moral core? Love is a moral education. You need a view that explains this, and that needs to be a view in which these two attitudes are mutually supportive, not mutually undermining.

ALEX VOORHOEVE: *Can you say more about how love is a moral education?*

DAVID VELLEMAN: When parents love a child, they show the child what it is to take another as an end, because they take the child as their end, and the child sees all the ways in which this blocks them from taking into consideration certain things in their deliberations about the child. It makes certain things unthinkable for them. And the child thinks: 'Wow, a person is the sort of thing that makes these kinds of things unthinkable.' So he learns about the value of persons by being loved.

But something else happens as well: through loving and admiring his parents, the child comes to admire their will, which takes him as an end in himself, as it does other persons. And in admiring their will for being constrained in this way by his and other people's value, he admires and internalizes an ideal that is equivalent to the moral law, which commands us to be constrained by the value of persons — that is, to treat them always as ends.

This is one of the things that I think Freud got right. And I think that Freud's views on this topic offer a way of understanding Kant. In Kant, there is a tension between seeing the moral law, on the one hand, as an external constraint and, on the other hand, as a law that you give to yourself. And the question is: how are we going to understand that *you*, autonomously, put yourself under something that is also an external constraint? If you want to figure out how morality works, you have to figure out how you get this strange combination of externality and internality of the moral will.

Now, Freud's answer is that it comes through the introjection of an external authority figure.[1] I think there is a lot of truth to this. When I think to myself, 'You can't do that!', I hear my father's voice — I can't help it! I say it to myself, and yet I am saying it to myself in the voice of my father. So I am giving myself an external constraint, after all.

---

[1] In psychoanalysis, 'introjection' is the internalization of the parent figures and their values, which leads to the formation of conscience.

The moment that we become a moral agent is the moment that the voice of conscience doesn't represent itself to us any more as a *purely* external voice—the father, the rabbi, and so on—but as our autonomous application of their words, adopted as our own out of admiration for the ideal represented by the original speakers. This is the voice of conscience. And the voice of conscience becomes our own because we take it to represent an ideal, a way of thinking and acting we admire. We love in our parents their capacity to take us as an end, and through loving this in them, we come to aspire to it, we come to regard as an ideal this capacity to take persons as an end. And taking others as an end is what morality demands. So it is through being loved and loving in return that we become moral agents.

References and further reading

David Velleman's *Self to Self* was published by Cambridge University Press in 2006. He is also the author of *Practical Reflection* (Princeton: Princeton University Press, 1989), *The Possibility of Practical Reason* (Oxford: Oxford University Press, 2000), and *How We Get Along* (Cambridge: Cambridge University Press, forthcoming).

My characterization of love's puzzling nature and its representation in film draws on Luc Bovens, 'Love's Constancy and Neil Jordan's *The Crying Game*' (unpub. ms, 2008). The 'one thought too many' comment is from Bernard Williams, 'Persons, Character and Morality', in *Moral Luck* (Cambridge: Cambridge University Press, 1981): 1–19. All of the references to Kant's moral theory are to *Grounding for the Metaphysics of Morals*, trans. J. W. Ellington (Indianapolis: Hackett, 1994). Velleman also refers to Elizabeth Anderson, *Value in Ethics and Economics* (Cambridge, Mass.: Harvard University Press, 1995), Stanley Cavell, 'The Avoidance of Love: A Reading of *King Lear*', in his *Must We Mean What We Say?* (Cambridge: Cambridge University Press, 2nd edn 2002): 267–356, and Iris Murdoch, *The Sovereignty of Good* (New York: Routledge, 1970).

For the Little Prince's adventures, see Antoine de Saint-Exupéry, *The Little Prince*, trans. T. V. F. Cuffe (London: Penguin, 1995). For a philosophical account of love not unlike the Little Prince's, see Robert Nozick, 'Love's Bond', in his *The Examined Life: Philosophical Meditations* (New York: Simon and Schuster, 1989): 68 – 86.

INDEX